Section 1
Assignments

GEORGIA MATHEMATICS 1
Second Edition

Assignments and Skills Practice

Carnegie Learning®
THE COGNITIVE TUTOR® COMPANY

Carnegie Learning®
THE COGNITIVE TUTOR® COMPANY

Pittsburgh, PA
Phone 888.851.7094
Fax 412.690.2444

www.carnegielearning.com

Acknowledgements

We would like to thank those listed below who helped to prepare the Cognitive Tutor®
Georgia Mathematics 1 Assignments and Skills Practice.

William S. Hadley
Jaclyn Snyder
Jan Sinopoli
The Carnegie Learning Development Team

Mathematics was used in a variety of ways to create the building on the front cover. Architects designed the front of the building with curves that were structurally sound and pleasing to the eye. Interior designers created windows and rooms which optimized the use of ambient light while minimizing heating and cooling costs. As you work through the Cognitive Tutor® *Georgia Mathematics 1* text and software, you will see additional opportunities for using mathematics in your everyday activities.

ISBN 978-1-934800-30-0
Assignments and Skills Practice

Printed in the United States of America
1-4/2008 HPS
2-4/2009 HPS

Assignment

Name _____   Date _____

Human Growth
Multiple Representations of Relations and Functions

The table shows the average foot size recorded in a survey for given age groups of children.

Age (years)	Average Foot Size (in.)
1	6
2	6.5
3	7
4	7.5
5	8
6	8
7	8.5
8	8.5
9	9
10	9
11	9.5
12	10.5

1. Create a scatter plot of the relation between age and average foot size on the grid shown.

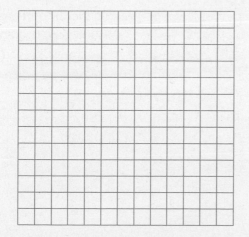

2. Does it make sense to connect the points of the scatter plot? Why or why not? If so, connect the points.

3. Describe the shape of the graph.

4. What are the domain and range of the relation?

5. Is the relation a function? Explain.

6. The relation only includes ages up to 12 years.

a. Using the graph, what would you predict as the increase in average foot size from the ages of 13 to 18 years?

b. Using this prediction, what would you predict as the foot size of an 18 year old?

c. Does this prediction make sense? Why or why not?

Name _____ Date _____

A shoe store uses a formula to calculate the size of a shoe according to the shoe's "last." A last is a template that is used to make the shoe. To determine the size of a child's shoe, the matching last is found, and the last length is multiplied by three. Then 12 is subtracted from the product. The lasts are measured in inches in multiples of one third.

7. What size is the shoe that fits a child's foot whose matching last is

   a. 7 inches long?

   b. 5 inches long?

   c. 6 inches long?

8. What is the last length matching a shoe of

   a. size 12?

   b. size 0?

9. Explain how to calculate the last length for a given shoe size.

10. Enter the values you determined in Questions 7 and 8 in the table.

Last Length (in.)	Shoe Size (children's)

11. Create a scatter plot of the relation between the last lengths and the shoe sizes in your table.

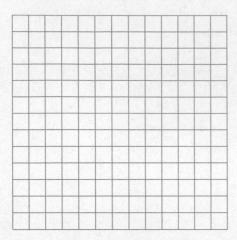

12. Does it make sense to connect the points of the scatter plot? Explain.

13. What are the domain and range of the relation?

14. Is the relation a function? Explain.

15. What are the variable quantities in this situation? Define a variable to represent each quantity.

16. Which variable represents the independent quantity? Which represents the dependent quantity? What are the constant quantities in this situation?

17. Use the variables from Question 15 to write an algebraic equation for converting from last length to children's shoe size.

1

© 2009 Carnegie Learning, Inc.

Assignment

Name _____   Date

Down and Up
Linear and Absolute Value Functions

In Elsie's house, the heating is controlled by a thermostat. When the temperature in the house is below 60°F, the heat turns on. It increases the temperature by 2 degrees per hour, until it reaches 70°F. Then the heat shuts off. The house cools at a rate of 2 degrees per hour.

1. Suppose that the heat has just turned off, and the temperature is now 70°F. Elsie starts her stopwatch at zero. What will the temperature be after

   a. 30 minutes?

   b. 45 minutes?

   c. 2 hours 15 minutes?

2. How long after the heat turns off will it take for the temperature to be

   a. 64°F?

   b. 61.5°F?

   c. 60°F?

3. Once the temperature reaches 60°F, the heat turns on again. Elsie is still counting time on her stopwatch. What will the temperature be after

   a. 6 hours?

   b. 7 hours 30 minutes?

4. How much time will have passed on the stopwatch when the temperature once again reaches

    a. 66°F?

    b. 69.5°F?

5. What are the variable quantities in this situation? Which is the independent quantity? Which is the dependent quantity?

6. Use the values from Questions 1 through 4 to complete the following table.

Independent Quantity	Dependent Quantity

Name _____ Date _____

7. Create a scatter plot of the relation between time and temperature in Elsie's house over a 10-hour period.

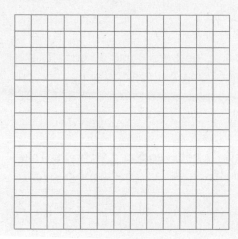

8. Connect the points of the scatter plot. Why does it make sense in this situation to connect the points?

9. Describe the shape of the graph.

10. What are the domain and range of this relation?

11. Is the relation a function? Explain.

12. Does the graph have a maximum point or points? If so, which point or points? Explain.

13. Does the graph have a minimum point or points? If so, which point or points? Explain.

14. Look at the part of the graph where the domain is between 0 and 5 hours. This portion of the graph resembles a linear function. What is the slope of this portion of the function?

15. Look at the part of the graph where the domain is between 5 and 10 hours. This portion of the graph also resembles a linear function. What is the slope of this portion of the function?

16. Use a graphing calculator to graph the equation $y = 60 + |-2x + 10|$ for $0 \leq x \leq 10$. Sketch the graph on the grid.

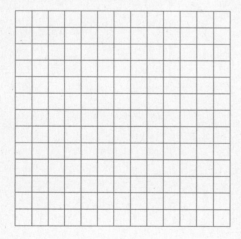

17. How does the graph in Question 16 compare to the graph in Question 7?

18. The equation $y = 60 + |-2x + 10|$ is an absolute value function that models the temperature function in Elsie's house within the domain $0 \leq x \leq 10$. Write the equation of the line of symmetry for this function.

Assignment

Name _____ Date _____

Let's Take a Little Trip!
Every Graph Tells a Story

The graph shows the relation between time in minutes and Bobby's speed in miles per hour as he rides his bicycle to run errands. Use the graph to answer the questions.

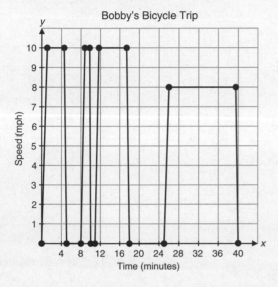

Bobby's Bicycle Trip

1. Is the relation between Bobby's time and his speed a function? Explain.

2. Identify any extrema on the graph. What do these points represent in the situation?

3. What are the domain and range of the relation?

4. How fast was Bobby moving after

   a. 2 minutes?

   b. 8.5 minutes?

   c. 30 minutes?

5. During which times was Bobby moving

   a. 5 mph?

   b. 8 mph?

6. Write a paragraph about Bobby's bicycle trip. Include and explain any intervals of increase and intervals of decrease you see on the graph.

Name _____ Date _____

Hazel throws a beanbag straight up. An equation that can be used to model the height of the beanbag over time is $y = -16x^2 + 60x + 4$, where x represents the time after she throws the beanbag in seconds, and y represents the height of the beanbag in feet.

7. Complete the table of values using the equation modeling the beanbag.

Time (seconds)	Height (feet)
0	
0.25	
0.5	
0.75	
1	
1.25	
1.5	
1.75	
2	
2.25	
2.5	
2.75	
3	
3.25	
3.5	
3.75	

8. Use the table to create a graph showing the relation between time and the height of the beanbag.

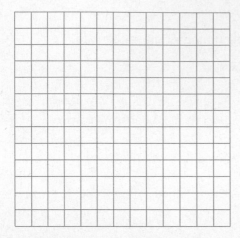

9. Describe the shape of the graph. Does the graph's shape describe the path of the beanbag? Explain.

10. What was the beanbag's average speed and direction

   a. during the first 0.25 second?

   b. between 0.25 and 0.5 second?

   c. between 0.5 and 0.75 second?

   d. between 1.5 and 1.75 seconds?

e. between 1.75 and 2 seconds?

f. between 2 and 2.25 seconds?

11. What do you notice about the average speed and direction of the beanbag over time? Based on your experience, does this situation make sense? Explain.

12. Identify the domain, range, extreme points, intervals of increase and decrease, and line of symmetry for the function modeling Hazel's beanbag.

Domain:

Range:

Extreme point:

Interval of increase:

Interval of decrease:

Line of symmetry:

1

Assignment

Name _____ Date _____

Building a Better Box
Cubic and Indirect Variation Functions

Carol has a stack of construction paper that she plans to make into craft boxes. Each piece of paper measures 9 inches by 12 inches. To make the boxes, Carol will cut out squares at each corner and fold up the sides into an open box shape. She will tape the sides of the box together and use the remaining paper to make tops to match the open boxes.

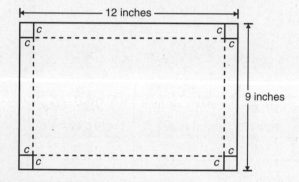

1. What height, length, and width of a craft box result if the length of each side of a corner square is

   a. 1 inch?

   b. 2 inches?

   c. 3 inches?

   d. 4 inches?

2. What is the largest size of corner square that Carol can cut out to make a box?

3. Write a formula for the volume of a craft box.

4. What is the volume of the box that results if Carol cuts corner squares with side lengths of

   a. 1 inch?

   b. 2 inches?

   c. 3 inches?

   d. 4 inches?

5. Use your answers from Questions 1 through 4 to complete the table. Fill in the new values as well.

Side Length of Square (inches)	Height of Box (inches)	Length of Box (inches)	Width of Box (inches)	Volume of Box (cubic inches)
0				
0.5				
1				
1.5				
2				
2.5				
3				
3.5				
4				
4.5				

6. Use the table to create a scatter plot for the relation between the side length of the corner squares and the volume of the craft box.

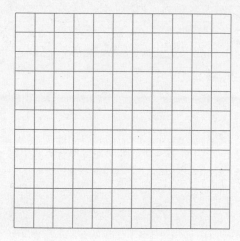

7. Draw a smooth curve connecting the points. Why does it make sense to connect the points?

8. Is the relation a function? Explain.

9. Use the graph to estimate the maximum volume of a craft box. What is the length of each side of a corner square that Carol would need to cut to get a craft box with the largest volume?

10. What are the domain and range of the function?

11. If Carol cuts a square with a side length of c inches, what are the resulting height, length, and width of the craft box?

12. If Carol cuts a square with a side length of c inches, what is the resulting volume of the craft box?

13. Write a cubic equation to describe the volume of one of Carol's craft boxes, v, in cubic inches, in terms of the side length of a corner square, c, in inches.

In Sonia's class, the teacher plans to hand out an equal number of colored pencils to each student. The teacher has 300 pencils.

14. How many colored pencils will each student receive if there are

   a. 5 students?

   b. 10 students?

   c. 20 students?

   d. 50 students?

15. Does the question make sense if there are more than 300 students? Explain.

16. Complete the following table using your answers from Question 14. Fill in the new values as well.

Number of Students	Number of Pencils per Student
1	
5	
6	
10	
15	
20	
30	
50	
60	
300	

17. Use the table to create a scatter plot of the relation between the number of students and the number of colored pencils per student.

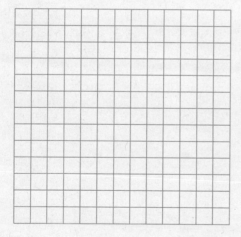

18. Does it make sense to connect these points in a smooth curve? Explain.

19. Is the relation a function? Explain. If so, what type of function describes this situation?

20. Define variables for the number of students and the number of pencils per student. Use the variables to write an equation to describe the situation.

Assignment

Name _____ Date _____

How Far Can You See?
How Many Ancestors?
Square Root and Exponential Functions

Nate is making a pedestal in the shape of a rectangular prism for the base of a table. Its height will be 3 feet. Its width and length will be equal, so that the pedestal's top and bottom faces are squares. He is trying to decide on a side length for the square faces. The table shows some of the possible volumes for the pedestal, and the corresponding dimensions.

Volume of Pedestal (cubic feet)	Length and Width of Pedestal (feet)
0.75	0.5
3	1
6.75	1.5
12	2
18.75	2.5
27	3

1. Create a scatter plot of the relation between the volume of the pedestal and its length and width. Use the volume as the independent quantity and the length and width as the dependent quantity.

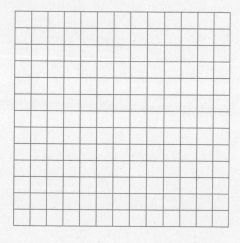

2. Connect the points on the graph with a smooth curve. Why does it make sense to connect the points?

3. Describe the shape of the graph.

4. Can you use the graph to predict the length and width of a pedestal with a volume of 48 cubic feet? Explain.

5. Can you use the graph to predict the length and width of a pedestal with a volume of 300 cubic feet? Explain.

6. Is this relation a function? Explain. If so, what type of function?

7. The equation that models this function is $s = \sqrt{\frac{1}{3}v}$, where s represents the length and width of the pedestal in feet, and v represents the volume in cubic feet. Use the equation to answer Questions 4 and 5.

8. What are the domain and range of the function $s = \sqrt{\frac{1}{3}v}$?

Name _____   Date _____

9. How would you describe a sensible domain and range for the situation?

On a certain island, there were no rabbits until 1981, when they were introduced by tourists (three pet rabbits escaped and began the island's wild rabbit population). Naturalists watching the island's rabbit population in the years since have concluded that each year there are approximately 3 times as many rabbits as there were the previous year (this approximation takes into account both birth and death rates).

10. Use the naturalists' approximation to complete the table.

Time since the Introduction of Rabbits (years)	Number of Rabbits on the Island
1	
2	
3	
4	
5	

11. Use the information in the table to make a scatter plot of the relation between time in years and number of rabbits on the island. Connect the points on the graph with a smooth curve.

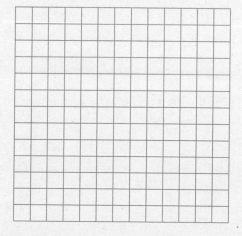

12. Describe the shape of the graph.

13. Can you use the graph to predict the number of rabbits in the sixth year?

14. Can you use the graph to predict the number of rabbits in the 20th year?

15. Is the relation between years and number of rabbits a function? If so, what kind?

16. The equation that models the naturalists' approximation is $y = 3^x$, where x represents the number of years and y represents the number of rabbits. Use the equation to answer Questions 13 and 14.

17. What are the domain and range of the function $y = 3^x$?

18. What would be a sensible domain and range for the situation involving numbers of rabbits? Explain.

Assignment

Name _____ Date _____

Functional Function: *F* of *x* it is!
Functional Notation

The function $f(x) = \frac{9}{5}c + 32$ represents the temperature in degrees Fahrenheit that is equivalent to a temperature of *c* degrees Celsius.

1. What are the domain and range of this function?

2. Use the equation $f(x) = \frac{9}{5}c + 32$ to evaluate the function at each value of *c*. Explain what each means in terms of temperature, and how each of the given expressions would be read.

   a. $f(-70) =$

   b. $f(0) =$

   c. $f(10) =$

   d. $f(30) =$

   e. $f(100) =$

3. Create a graph of the relation between temperature in degrees Celsius and temperature in degrees Fahrenheit.

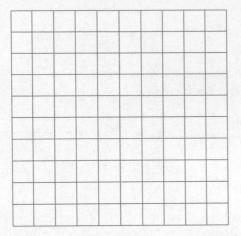

4. Calculate the value of c that makes each equation true. Explain what it means in terms of temperature.

    a. $f(c) = -13$

    b. $f(c) = 0$

c. $f(c) = 68$

d. $f(c) = 100$

2

5. Complete the table to show equivalent Celsius and Fahrenheit temperatures, using all of the values you calculated in Questions 2 and 3.

Temperature (°C)	Temperature (°F)

Ali travels from Cleveland, Ohio to Houston, Texas and back by bus. She keeps track of the distance she has traveled and the time it takes along the way. The function $d(t)$ represents Ali's total distance traveled, in miles, at a given time t, in hours.

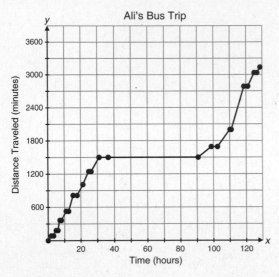

6. Use the graph to evaluate the function at each value. Explain what each means in terms of Ali's bus trip.

   a. $d(10) \approx$

   b. $d(20) \approx$

   c. $d(30) \approx$

   d. $d(40) \approx$

   e. $d(50) \approx$

7. Use the graph to find the value or values that makes each equation true. Explain what each means in terms of Ali's bus trip. Where do you think Ali was at each time?

   a. $d(t) = 1500$

   b. $d(t) = 1750$

© 2009 Carnegie Learning, Inc.

c. $d(t) = 2200$

d. $d(t) = 2750$

e. $d(t) = 3100$

2

8. Complete the table, using the values you calculated in Questions 6 and 7.

Time (hours)	Approximate Distance Traveled (miles)
10	
20	
30	
40	
60	
70	
80	
90	
100	
110	
120	
130	

Assignment

Name _____   Date _____

Numbers in a Row!
Introduction to Sequences

Use the given pattern to answer the questions.

1. The figures in the pattern have been made from toothpicks. Use the pattern to answer the following questions.

Each figure is made from toothpicks.

  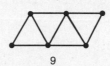

Number
of toothpicks: 3   5   7   9

a. Describe the pattern in terms of the numbers of toothpicks. Then sketch the next two terms of the pattern and the tenth term of the pattern.

b. Complete the table. Use the table to write an explicit formula that can be used to calculate the number of toothpicks in the *n*th term of the pattern.

Term Number	Value of Term (number of toothpicks)
1	
2	
4	
6	
10	
n	

c. Use the formula from part (b) to calculate a_{50}.

d. Write a recursive formula for the sequence represented by the pattern.

2. Use the pattern to answer the following questions.

Each figure is made up of squares.

Number
of squares: 1   4   9   16

a. Describe the pattern in terms of the blocks. Then sketch the next two terms of
the pattern and the tenth term of the pattern.

b. Complete the table. Use the table to write an explicit formula that can be used to
calculate the number of blocks in the nth term of the pattern.

Term Number	Value of Term (number of squares)
1	
2	
4	
6	
10	
n	

c. Use the formula from part (b) to calculate a_{25}.

d. Write a recursive formula for the sequence represented by the pattern.

3. Use the pattern of numbers to answer the following questions.
   3, 8, 13, 18, . . .

   a. Describe the pattern. Then write the next two terms of the pattern and the tenth term of the pattern.

   b. Complete the table. Use the table to write an explicit formula that can be used to calculate the nth term of the pattern.

Term Number	Value of Term
1	
2	
4	
5	
10	
n	

   c. Use the formula from part (b) to calculate a_{100}.

   d. Write a recursive formula for the sequence represented by the pattern.

4. Use the pattern of numbers to answer the following questions.
   3, 9, 27, 81, . . .

   a. Describe the pattern. Then write the next two terms of the pattern and the tenth term of the pattern.

   b. Complete the table. Use the table to write an explicit formula that can be used to calculate the nth term of the pattern.

Term Number	Value of Term
1	
2	
3	
5	
10	
n	

   c. Use the formula from part (b) to calculate a_{16}.

   d. Write a recursive formula for the sequence represented by the pattern.

Assignment

Name _____   Date _____

Adding or Multiplying
Arithmetic and Geometric Sequences

Calculate the first four terms of each arithmetic sequence.

1. $a_n = 8n$

2. $a_1 = 5, a_n = a_{n-1} + 15$

3. $a_n = n + 3$

4. $a_1 = 0, a_n = a_{n-1} - 2$

5. $a_n = 6n - 6$

For each arithmetic sequence, identify the common difference and determine the next two terms in the sequence. Then write a recursive formula and an explicit formula for the sequence.

6. $5, 7, 9, 11, \ldots$

7. $-5, 0, 5, 10, \ldots$

8. 100, 89, 78, 67, …

9. 1, 10, 19, 28, …

10. $\dfrac{1}{2}$, 2, $\dfrac{7}{2}$, 5, …

Calculate the first four terms of each geometric sequence.

11. $g_n = 3^{n-1}$

12. $g_1 = 4, g_n = \left(\dfrac{3}{4}\right) g_{n-1}$

13. $g_n = 32 \left(\dfrac{1}{2}\right)^{n-1}$

14. $g_1 = 1, g_n = -7g_{n-1}$

15. $g_n = \dfrac{1}{4} (10)^{n-1}$

Name _____ Date _____

For each geometric sequence, identify the common ratio and determine the next two terms in the sequence. Then write a recursive formula and an explicit formula for the sequence.

16. 5, 15, 45, 135, …

17. 320, 160, 80, 40, …

18. 1, −7, 49, −343, …

19. −2, 2, −2, 2, …

20. $\frac{1}{27}, \frac{1}{9}, \frac{1}{3}, 1, \ldots$

© 2009 Carnegie Learning, Inc.

Classify each sequence as arithmetic, geometric, or neither. For each arithmetic sequence, identify the common difference. For each geometric sequence, identify the common ratio. If the sequence is neither, describe the pattern.

21. $100, 20, 4, \frac{4}{5}, \ldots$

22. $1, 13, 25, 37, \ldots$

23. $10, 20, 40, 80, \ldots$

24. $2, 4, 16, 256, \ldots$

25. $3, -21, 147, -1029, \ldots$

26. $50, 45, 40, 35, \ldots$

27. $2, 5, 9, 14, \ldots$

28. $3, \frac{8}{3}, \frac{7}{3}, 2, \ldots$

Assignment

Name _____ Date _____

Home, Home on the Domains and Ranges
Domains and Ranges of Algebraic Functions

Graph each function. Then identify the type of function and determine the domain and range of the function.

1. $a(x) = \frac{2}{3}x + 3$

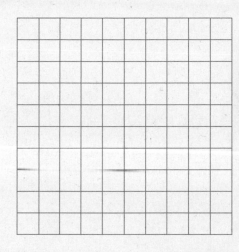

2. $b(x) = -|x - 3|$

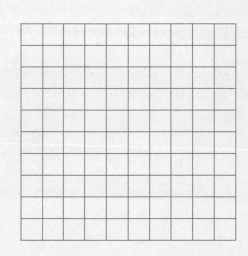

3. $c(x) = |2x| + 5$

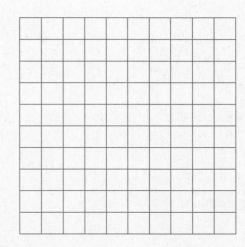

4. $d(x) = x^2 + 2x + 1$

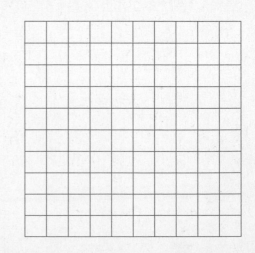

5. $f(x) = -x^3 + 2$

6. $g(x) = 4\sqrt{x + 3}$

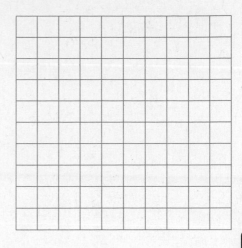

7. $h(x) = -x^2 + 10$

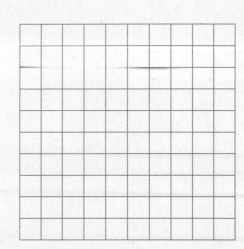

8. $j(x) = 3^x + 3$

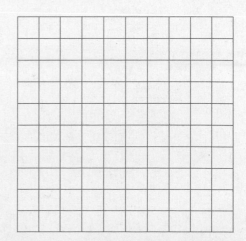

9. $k(x) = \dfrac{2}{x + 5}$

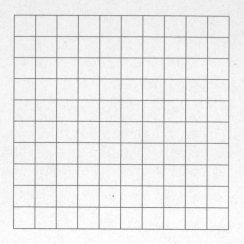

Assignment

Name _____ Date _____

Rocket Man
Extrema and Symmetry

For each function, sketch a graph and determine the domain and range. Then determine the *x*- and *y*-intercepts, any vertical or horizontal lines of symmetry, and any extreme points, and label them on the graph.

1. $l(x) = -2x$

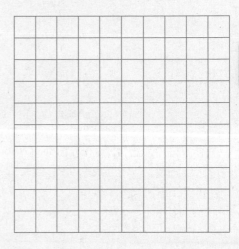

2. $m(x) = -3|x| + 2$

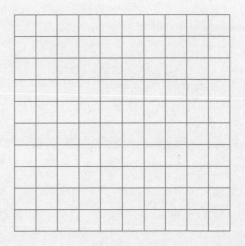

3. $n(x) = \left| \dfrac{1}{2}x - 2 \right|$

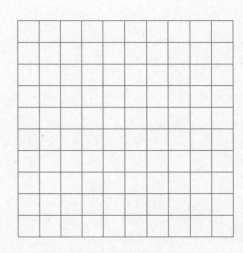

2

4. $p(x) = \dfrac{5}{x} + 3$

5. $q(x) = 2^x - 4$

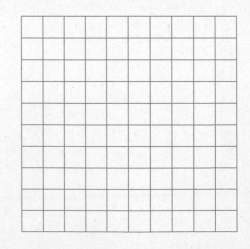

6. $r(x) = -\sqrt{2x} + 4$

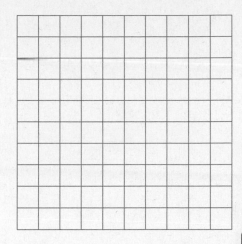

7. $s(x) = x^2 + x - 6$

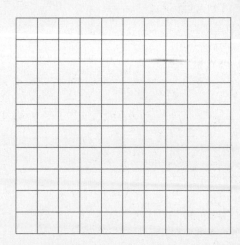

8. $t(x) = -3x^2$

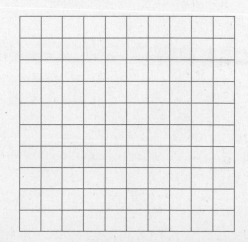

9. $u(x) = -x^3 + 4x$

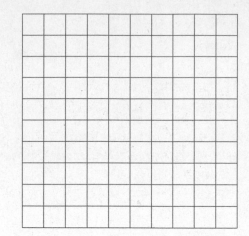

Assignment

Name _____   Date _____

Changing Change
Rates of Change of Functions

The graph of the function $v(x) = \frac{4}{x}$ is shown on the grid. The points (1, 4) and (4, 1) are labeled. Use this function and its graph to answer Questions 1 through 11.

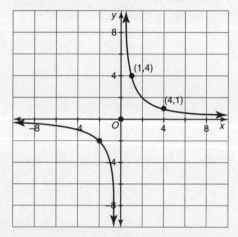

1. What type of function is $v(x)$?

2. Calculate the average rate of change between the points (1, 4) and (4, 1).

3. Draw a line between the points (1, 4) and (4, 1). What is the slope of the line?

4. How does the slope of the line compare to the average rate of change between the two points?

5. Evaluate $v(x)$ for $x = 2$. Represent the result as an ordered pair.

6. Calculate each average rate of change.

   a. Between the point from Question 5 and (1, 4)

   b. Between the point from Question 5 and (4, 1)

7. Draw a line between the point from Question 5 and (1, 4). Draw another line between the point from Question 5 and (4, 1). What is the slope of each line?

8. How does the slope of each line compare to the average rate of change between each pair of points?

9. Describe the rates of change for the portion of the graph right of the origin.

10. What do you think will be true about the average rate of change between pairs of points to the left of the origin?

11. What can you conclude about the average rates of change for inverse variation functions?

Name _____ Date _____

The graph of the function $w(x) = 4\sqrt{x}$ is shown on the grid. The points (1, 4) and (9, 12) are labeled. Use this function and its graph to answer Questions 12 through 21.

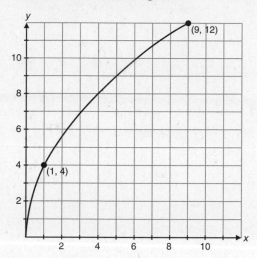

12. What type of function is $w(x)$?

13. Calculate the average rate of change between the points (1, 4) and (9, 12).

14. Draw a line between the points (1, 4) and (9, 12). What is the slope of the line?

15. How does the slope of the line compare to the average rate of change between the two points?

16. Evaluate $w(x)$ for $x = 4$. Represent the result as an ordered pair.

17. Calculate each average rate of change.

a. Between the point from Question 16 and (1, 4)

b. Between the point from Question 16 and (9, 12)

18. Draw a line between the point from Question 16 and (1, 4). Draw another line between the point from Question 16 and (9, 12). What is the slope of each line?

19. How does the slope of each line compare to the average rate of change between each pair of points?

20. Describe the rates of change for the whole graph.

21. What can you conclude about the average rates of change for square root functions?

Assignment

Name _____ Date _____

A Little Dash of Logic
Two Methods of Logical Reasoning

Joseph reads a journal article that states that yogurt with live cultures greatly helps digestion and prevents problems associated with lactose intolerance. He notices that his mother has problems with digestion and is lactose intolerant. He suggests that she try eating yogurt because he thinks it may help her feel better.

1. What is the specific information in this situation?

2. What is the general information in this situation?

3. What is the conclusion in this situation?

4. Did Joseph use inductive or deductive reasoning to make his conclusion? Explain.

5. Is Joseph's conclusion correct? Explain.

Sadie reads an article that gives statistics about American families. She learns that the average American family has 2 parents and 2.3 children. She concludes that her neighbors, who are average Americans, probably have 2.3 children.

6. What is the specific information in this situation?

7. What is the general information in this situation?

8. What is the conclusion in this situation?

9. Did Sadie use inductive or deductive reasoning to make her conclusion? Explain.

10. Is Sadie's conclusion correct? Explain.

Nick watches baseball games on television. He noticed that the last five times that the Wolverines played against the Spartans, the Spartans won. Nick concludes that the Spartans always win against the Wolverines.

11. What is the specific information in this situation?

12. What is the general information in this situation?

13. What is the conclusion in this situation?

14. Did Nick use inductive or deductive reasoning to reach his conclusion? Explain.

15. Is Nick's conclusion correct? Explain.

3

Lena has noticed that sometimes her face swells after she eats. She thinks she may be allergic to a type of food, so she takes careful notes over the next month, writing down all the ingredients of each meal and noting when her face swells. Reviewing her notes, she finds that the only common ingredient in the meals she ate previous to her face swelling was coconut. Lena concludes that she is allergic to coconut.

16. What is the specific information in this situation?

17. What is the general information in this situation?

18. What is the conclusion in this situation?

19. Did Lena use inductive or deductive reasoning to reach her conclusion? Explain.

20. Is Lena's conclusion correct? Explain.

Chaun is looking through records at a record store with her friend Ronaldo. She comes across a record she has not heard by a band she enjoys. Ronaldo knows that Chaun has five records at home by this band and that she likes all of them. He concludes that she will probably like any record made by this band. He tells Chaun so. She buys the record, saying to herself, "I will probably like this record, because I like records made by this band."

21. What conclusion did Ronaldo make? Why?

22. What type of reasoning did Ronaldo use? Explain.

23. What conclusion did Chaun make? Why?

24. What type of reasoning did Chaun use? Explain.

25. Is Ronaldo's conclusion definitely true? Is Chaun's conclusion definitely true? Explain.

The first five numbers in a sequence are 7, 21, 63, 189, and 567.

26. What is the next number in the sequence? How did you calculate the next number?

27. What type or types of reasoning did you use to find the next number? Explain the reasoning you used and the order of your conclusions.

3

3

Assignment

Name _____   Date _____

What's Your Conclusion?
Hypotheses, Conclusions, Conditional Statements, Counterexamples, Direct and Indirect Arguments

Read each pair of statements. Then write a valid conclusion.

1. Statement: If you hear thunder, there must be lightning.

   Statement: You hear thunder.

   Conclusion:

2. Statement: If Jon is hungry, he wants food.

   Statement: Jon is hungry.

   Conclusion:

3. Statement: We will not be able to go sledding if it does not snow.

   Statement: It has not snowed.

   Conclusion:

4. Statement: A number is positive if it is greater than zero.

   Statement: The number −3 is less than zero.

   Conclusion:

5. Statement: If Trisha's cat Alexander stops meowing, he must have been fed.

   Statement: Alexander has not been fed.

   Conclusion:

Read each statement and conclusion. Then write the additional statement required to reach the conclusion.

6. Statement: If Matt soundproofs his basement, he can play drums at home.

   Statement:

   Conclusion: Therefore, Matt can play drums at home.

7. Statement: If Jason leaves his dinner in the oven too long, it gets burned.

   Statement:

   Conclusion: Therefore, he did not leave it in the oven too long.

8. Statement: You are at the North Pole if walking in any direction takes you south.

   Statement:

   Conclusion: Therefore, you are at the North Pole.

9. Statement: Julie will get tired if she dances all night.

   Statement:

   Conclusion: Therefore, Julie did not dance all night.

10. Statement:

    Statement: Dutch is making yogurt.

    Conclusion: Therefore, he needs milk.

11. Statement:

    Statement: Alina got home early.

    Conclusion: Therefore, she had time to fix her bicycle.

12. Statement:

    Statement: It is not April.

    Conclusion: Therefore, Jonas and Gabriel are not the same age.

Use Questions 1 through 12 to answer the following questions.

13. In Questions 1 through 12, the first statement is a conditional statement. For each conditional statement in Questions 1 through 12, underline the hypothesis with a solid line and underline the conclusion with a dotted line.

14. List the questions that used direct argument to reach their conclusions.

15. List the questions that used proof by contrapositive to reach their conclusions.

Name _____ Date _____

Melania noticed that $3^2 = 9 > 3$, $10^2 = 100 > 10$, and $5^2 = 25 > 5$. She proposes that the square of any number is greater than the number.

16. Did Melania use inductive or deductive reasoning to reach her conclusion? Explain.

17. Is Melania correct? If she is incorrect, give a counterexample.

P.J. noticed that $(-3)^2 = 9$, $(-3)^4 = 81$, and $(-3)^0 = 1$. Thinking, "each power of -3 is positive," he concluded that $(-3)^3$ must also be positive.

18. Did P.J. use inductive reasoning, deductive reasoning, or both to reach his conclusion? Explain.

19. Is P.J. correct? Explain. What type of argument did you use to decide? Explain.

In Questions 20 through 23, write a statement or statements that fit the given criteria.

20. Write a conditional statement. Underline the hypothesis with a solid line and the conclusion with a dotted line.

21. Use your conditional statement from Question 20 to write a direct argument.

22. Use your conditional statement from Question 20 to write an indirect argument.

23. Write a false assertion. Then provide a counterexample to show that it is false.

Assignment

Name _____ Date _____

You Can't Handle the Truth (Table)
Converses, Inverses, Contrapositives, Biconditionals, Truth Tables, Postulates, and Theorems

Consider the conditional statement "If I complete my homework, then I receive extra credit in class." Use this statement to answer Questions 1 through 10.

1. What is the hypothesis, p? What is the conclusion, q?

   Hypothesis, p:

   Conclusion, q:

2. Assume that p is true and q is true. What does that mean?

3. Could this statement be true? What is the truth value of the conditional statement when p is true and q is true?

4. Assume that p is true and q is false. What does that mean?

5. Could this statement be true? What is the truth value of the conditional statement when p is true and q is false?

6. Assume that p is false and q is true. What does that mean?

7. Could this statement be true? What is the truth value of the conditional statement when p is false and q is true?

8. Assume that p is false and q is false. What does that mean?

9. Could this statement be true? What is the truth value of the conditional statement when p is false and q is false?

10. Summarize the information from Questions 1 through 9 by completing the truth table.

p	q	$p \mapsto q$

For each conditional statement, (a) identify the hypothesis, (b) identify the conclusion, (c) determine whether the conditional statement is true, (d) write the converse of the conditional statement, and (e) determine whether the converse is true.

11. If an organism can perform photosynthesis, then the organism is a plant.

   a. Hypothesis, p:

   b. Conclusion, q:

   c. Is the conditional statement true? Explain.

   d. Converse:

   e. Is the converse true? Explain.

12. If Agioso is in his room, then he is in his house.

   a. Hypothesis, p:

   b. Conclusion, q:

   c. Is the conditional statement true? Explain.

   d. Converse:

   e. Is the converse true? Explain.

13. If the Sun is down, then it is daytime.

    a. Hypothesis, p:

    b. Conclusion, q:

    c. Is the conditional statement true? Explain.

    d. Converse:

    e. Is the converse true? Explain.

14. If Molly is a teenager, she is 13 years old.

    a. Hypothesis, p:

    b. Conclusion, q:

    c. Is the conditional statement true? Explain.

    d. Converse:

    e. Is the converse true? Explain.

3

For each conditional statement, (a) determine whether the conditional statement is true, (b) identify the negation of the hypothesis, (c) identify the negation of the conclusion, (d) write the inverse of the conditional statement, and (e) determine whether the inverse is true.

15. If an organism can perform photosynthesis, then the organism is a plant.

    a. Is the conditional statement true?

    b. Not p:

    c. Not q:

    d. Inverse:

    e. Is the inverse true? Explain.

16. If Agioso is in his room, then he is in his house.

    a. Is the conditional statement true?

    b. Not p:

    c. Not q:

    d. Inverse:

    e. Is the inverse true? Explain.

17. If the Sun is down, then it is daytime.

    a. Is the conditional statement true?

    b. Not p:

    c. Not q:

    d. Inverse:

    e. Is the inverse true? Explain.

18. If Molly is a teenager, she is 13 years old.

    a. Is the conditional statement true?

    b. Not p:

    c. Not q:

    d. Inverse:

    e. Is the inverse true? Explain.

For each conditional statement, (a) determine whether the conditional statement is true, (b) write the contrapositive of the conditional statement, and (c) determine whether the contrapositive is true.

19. If an organism can perform photosynthesis, then the organism is a plant.

    a. Is the conditional statement true?

    b. Contrapositive:

    c. Is the contrapositive true? Explain.

20. If Agioso is in his room, then he is in his house.

    a. Is the conditional statement true?

    b. Contrapositive:

    c. Is the contrapositive true? Explain.

21. If the Sun is down, then it is daytime.

    a. Is the conditional statement true?

    b. Contrapositive:

    c. Is the contrapositive true? Explain.

22. If Molly is a teenager, she is 13 years old.

    a. Is the conditional statement true?

    b. Contrapositive:

    c. Is the contrapositive true? Explain.

23. Summarize the information from Questions 11 through 22 by completing the sentences.

    a. If a conditional statement is true, then its converse

    b. If a conditional statement is false, then its converse

    c. If a conditional statement is true, then its inverse

    d. If a conditional statement is false, then its inverse

    e. If a conditional statement is true, then its contrapositive

    f. If a conditional statement is false, then its contrapositive

    g. A conditional statement and its _____ are logically equivalent.

3

24. Which conditional statement from Questions 11 through 22 can be rewritten as a true biconditional statement? Rewrite it as a biconditional statement.

a. Conditional statement:

b. Biconditional statement:

25. Describe what a *postulate* is and what a *theorem* is.

Assignment

Name _____ Date _____

Proofs Aren't Just for Geometry
Introduction to Direct and Indirect Proof with the Properties of Numbers

For each conditional statement in Questions 1 through 4, determine whether the statement is true or false. If it is true, write a direct and an indirect proof of the statement. For each proof, write the steps in one column and the reasons in another. If the statement is false, prove it is false by counterexample.

1. Conditional statement: If $ab + ac = b + c$, then $a = 1$.

2. Conditional statement: If a and b are real numbers, then $10a + b = 10(a + b)$.

3

3. Conditional statement: If a and b are real numbers, then $\dfrac{3(2a + 2b)}{6} = a + b$.

4. Conditional statement: If $ab + ac = \dfrac{b + c}{\frac{1}{a}}$, then $b + c = 0$.

5. Identify the error in the proof. Correct the statement if possible.

If $2a + 2b = 4a$, then $b = 2$.

Steps	Reasons
$2(a + b) = 4a$	Distributive law
$\dfrac{2(a + b)}{2} = \dfrac{4a}{2}$	Algebraic equations remain true if you perform the same operation on both sides.
$a + b = 2a$	Multiplicative inverse
$a - a + b = 2a - a$	Algebraic equations remain true if you perform the same operation on both sides.
$b = 2$	Additive inverse

3

Assignment

Name _____ Date _____

Squares and More
Using Patterns to Generate Algebraic Functions

Use the following pattern to answer Questions 1 through 5.

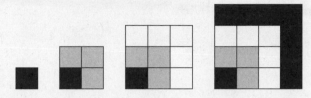

...

1. Sketch the design that continues the pattern.

2. Complete the table to summarize the numbers and colors of the squares used in each step of the pattern.

Squares in Design	1	2	3	4	5
Black squares					
Gray squares					
White squares					
New squares					
Total squares					

3. Continue the table for the following numbers.

Squares in Design	6	8	10
Black squares			
Gray squares			
White squares			
New squares			
Total squares			

4. Write an expression for the number of new squares that are added to create the *n*th design of the series from the *n* − 1th design.

5. Write an expression for the total number of squares in the *n*th design of the series.

Use the following pattern to answer Questions 6 through 15.

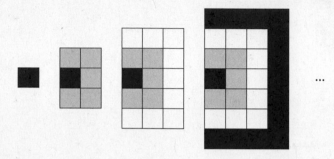

...

6. Sketch the design that continues the pattern.

7. Complete the table to summarize the numbers and colors of the squares used in each step of the pattern.

Squares in Design	1	2	3	4	5
Black squares					
Gray squares					
White squares					
Horizontal squares in each row					
Vertical squares in each column					
New squares					
Total squares					

8. Continue the table for the following numbers.

Squares in Design	6	8	10
Black squares			
Gray squares			
White squares			
Horizontal squares in each row			
Vertical squares in each column			
New squares			
Total squares			

9. Write an expression for the number of horizontal squares in each row of the nth design of the series.

10. Write an expression for the number of vertical squares in each column of the nth design of the series.

11. Write an expression for the total number of squares in the nth design of the series.

12. Bobby says that to obtain the number of new squares in the *n*th design of the series, you have to multiply the number of vertical squares in each row of that design by two and then subtract 1 from the result. Write an expression that represents Bobby's pattern.

13. Channell says that to obtain the number of new squares in the *n*th design of the series, first you have to subtract *n* from 3, and then you have to subtract that result from three times *n*. Write an expression that represents Channell's pattern.

14. Show whether Bobby's and Channell's expressions are the same.

15. Determine whose expression for the number of new squares is correct: Bobby, Channell, both, or neither. Explain your answer.

Assignment

Name _____ Date _____

Areas and Areas
Using Multiple Representations of Algebraic Functions

Lauren is dividing a community garden into square plots, where members will grow their plants. Each square plot will be x feet on a side, with a 1-foot-wide divider along one of its sides, and a 3-foot-wide walkway along the front, as shown below.

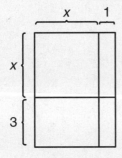

1. What is the area of each square plot? Label the diagram.

2. What is the area of each divider? Label the diagram.

3. What is the area of each walkway? Label the diagram.

4. Use area composition to write an expression for the total area of the square plot, the divider, and the walkway.

5. What is the length of the square plot, divider, and walkway?

6. What is the width of the square plot, divider, and walkway?

7. Use the length and width from Questions 5 and 6 to write an expression for the total area of the square plot, divider, and the walkway.

8. You wrote the total area in two different ways in Questions 4 and 7. Show how the two expressions are equivalent.

9. Complete the table.

Width of Square Plot	Total Width of Plot	Total Length of Plot	Area of Square Plot	Area of Divider	Area of Walkway	Total Area
5						
6						
8						
10						
x						

10. Write a function $A(x)$ to represent the total area of the plot, divider, and walkway for a lot with side length x.

11. What are the domain and range of $A(x)$ in terms of the problem situation?

4

Name _____ Date _____

12. Graph $A(x)$.

Each square plot of a community garden is _x_ feet on a side. Within each plot, the members of the community must plant a 2-foot wide section with flowers to attract bees. The members will plant vegetables In the remainder of the plot, as shown.

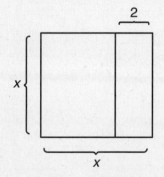

13. What is the area of each square plot?

14. What is the area of each section with flowers? Label the diagram.

15. What is the area of each section with vegetables? Label the diagram.

16. What is the length of each section with vegetables?

17. What is the width of each section with vegetables?

18. Use the length and width from Questions 16 and 17 to write an expression for the total area of each section with vegetables.

19. You wrote the total area in two different ways in Questions 15 and 18. Show how these expressions are equivalent.

20. Complete the table.

Width of Square Plot	Length of Section with Vegetables	Area of Plot	Area of Section with Flowers	Area of Section with Vegetables
5				
6				
8				
10				
x				

21. Write a function $A(x)$ to represent the total area of the section with vegetables.

22. What are the domain and range of $A(x)$ in terms of the problem situation?

23. Graph $A(x)$.

Assignment

Name _____ Date _____

Models for Polynomials
Operations with Polynomials

For each sum or difference, sketch the resulting model. Then calculate the sum or difference.

1. $(4x + 1) + (2x + 2) =$

2. $(3x + 2) - (2x + 1) =$

3. $(2x^2 + 5) - (x^2 + 2) =$

4. $(x^2 + 2x + 3) + (x^2 + 5x) =$

For each sum or difference, sketch the resulting model. Then calculate the sum or difference.

5. $(3x^2 + x + 1) + (-x^2 - 5x + 2) =$

6. $(x^2 - 5x - 3) + (-2x^2 + 6x + 7) =$

7. $(3x^2 + 2x - 2) - (2x^2 - x + 1) =$

Calculate each sum or difference without sketching a model.

8. $(7x^2 - 8) + (-3x^2 - 4x) =$

9. $(-2x^2 + 10x - 5) + (14x^2 - 4x) =$

10. $(-x^2 + 3) - (8x^2 - 4) =$

11. $(-5x^2 - 5x) - (-7x^2 + 6x - 13) =$

12. $(x^2 - 3x - 7) - (x^2 + 11x - 7) =$

For each product, sketch the resulting model. Then calculate the product.

13. $(x + 5)(x + 3) =$ 　　　　　　　　　　**14.** $(x - 3)(x + 2) =$

4

15. $(x - 4)(x - 1) =$

16. $(x + 3)(x - 3) =$

Assignment

Name _____ Date _____

Another Factor
Dividing and Factoring Quadratic Trinomials

Perform each multiplication using the method specified.

1. Use a multiplication table to multiply $(x + 8)(x - 4)$.

2. Use the distributive property to multiply $(x - 6)(x - 10)$.

3. Use a multiplication table to multiply $(2x + 3)(3x - 2)$.

4. Use the distributive property to multiply $(x - 5)(x + 5)$.

Perform each division using an area model.

5. $(x^2 + 7x + 12) \div (x + 4) =$

6. $(x^2 - 4x - 12) \div (x - 6) =$

7. $(x^2 - 4) \div (x - 2) =$

4

Perform each division using a multiplication table.

8. $(x^2 + 13x - 30) \div (x - 2) =$

9. $(x^2 - 14x + 49) \div (x - 7) =$

10. $(x^2 - x - 42) \div (x + 6) =$

11. $(x^2 - 121) \div (x - 11) =$

Perform each division using long division.

12. $(x^2 + 10x + 16) \div (x + 2) =$

13. $(x^2 + 5x + 6) \div (x + 3) =$

14. $(x^2 - 12x - 13) \div (x + 1) =$

15. $(x^2 - 12x + 27) \div (x - 3) =$

Factor each trinomial using an area model.

16. $(x^2 + 9x + 18) =$

17. $(x^2 - x - 6) =$

18. $(x^2 - 3x + 2) =$

4

Assignment

Name _____ Date _____

More Factoring
Factoring Quadratic Trinomials

Factor the trinomials by using the method of factor pairs and sums.

1. $x^2 + 14x + 45$

2. $x^2 - 9x + 20$

3. $x^2 - 50x + 49$

4. $x^2 + 7x - 30$

5. $x^2 + 18x - 40$

6. $x^2 + 27x + 50$

7. $x^2 - 51x + 98$

8. $x^2 + 15x + 44$

9. $x^2 - 17x - 60$

4

10. $x^2 - 16x + 39$

11. $x^2 - 16x - 36$

12. $x^2 - 11 - 80$

13. $x^2 - 16x + 63$

14. $x^2 - 99 - 100$

4

Assignment

Name _____ Date _____

Radically Speaking!
Operations with Square Roots

Calculate the missing side of each right triangle.

1. $a = 5, b = 12, c = ?$

2. $a = 3, b = ?, c = 5$

3. $a = ?, b = 7, c = 10$

4. $a = 10, b = 30, c = ?$

Calculate each product.

5. $\sqrt{5} \cdot \sqrt{5}$

6. $\sqrt{2} \cdot \sqrt{3}$

7. $\sqrt{7} \cdot \sqrt{7}$

8. $\sqrt{18} \cdot \sqrt{2}$

9. $\sqrt{12} \cdot \sqrt{3}$

10. $\sqrt{12} \cdot \sqrt{12}$

11. $\sqrt{4} \cdot \sqrt{25}$ **12.** $\sqrt{36} \cdot \sqrt{9}$

Simplify each radical completely.

13. $\sqrt{84}$ **14.** $\sqrt{48}$

15. $\sqrt{28}$ **16.** $\sqrt{108}$

17. $\sqrt{288}$ **18.** $\sqrt{125}$

19. $\sqrt{150}$ **20.** $\sqrt{300}$

Calculate each product and simplify completely.

21. $\sqrt{7} \cdot \sqrt{14}$

22. $\sqrt{54} \cdot \sqrt{3}$

23. $\sqrt{12} \cdot \sqrt{27}$

24. $\sqrt{75} \cdot \sqrt{6}$

25. $\sqrt{10} \cdot \sqrt{70}$

26. $\sqrt{10} \cdot \sqrt{80}$

27. $\sqrt{10} \cdot \sqrt{90}$

28. $\sqrt{21} \cdot \sqrt{77}$

29. $\sqrt{2} \left(\sqrt{14} + \sqrt{10} \right)$

30. $\sqrt{8} \left(\sqrt{6} + \sqrt{10} \right)$

4

4

Assignment

Name _____ Date _____

Working with Radicals
Adding, Subtracting, Dividing, and Rationalizing Radicals

Calculate the sum or difference.

1. $5\sqrt{6} + 2\sqrt{6}$

2. $17\sqrt{2} - 6\sqrt{2}$

3. $\sqrt{3} + \sqrt{27}$

4. $2\sqrt{7} - 9\sqrt{7} + 7\sqrt{2}$

5. $-\sqrt{8} + 5\sqrt{2} + 2\sqrt{3}$

4

Calculate the quotient and simplify.

6. $15\sqrt{5} \div 3\sqrt{5}$

7. $\sqrt{75} \div 6\sqrt{3}$

8. $14\sqrt{2} \div \sqrt{8}$

9. $\dfrac{\sqrt{2}}{\sqrt{8}} \div \dfrac{\sqrt{2}}{\sqrt{40}}$

10. $\dfrac{\sqrt{2}}{\sqrt{18}} \div \dfrac{\sqrt{2}}{\sqrt{6}}$

Simplify the expression by rationalizing the denominator.

11. $\dfrac{5}{\sqrt{2}}$

12. $\dfrac{3}{\sqrt{3}}$

13. $\dfrac{6}{\sqrt{10}}$

14. $\dfrac{4}{\sqrt{6}}$

15. $\dfrac{21}{\sqrt{7}}$

16. $\dfrac{3}{\sqrt{15}}$

17. $\dfrac{8}{\sqrt{26}}$

18. $\dfrac{3}{\sqrt{34}}$

Simplify the expression completely.

19. $\dfrac{2\sqrt{45}}{3} + \dfrac{7\sqrt{5}}{3}$

20. $\dfrac{\sqrt{98}}{5} + \dfrac{8\sqrt{2}}{5}$

21. $\dfrac{\sqrt{8}}{4} - \dfrac{\sqrt{18}}{6}$

22. $\dfrac{\sqrt{512}}{\sqrt{9}} - \dfrac{2}{3\sqrt{2}}$

23. $\dfrac{\sqrt{12}}{\sqrt{33}} \div \dfrac{6}{\sqrt{22}}$

24. $\dfrac{\sqrt{6}}{\sqrt{7}} \div \dfrac{\sqrt{39}\sqrt{10}}{\sqrt{91}}$

4

Assignment

Name _____   Date _____

Rain Gutters
Modeling with Functions

Lily is having a party. She has $30 and wants to buy brownies for $0.75 each and sandwiches for $3 each for her guests. How many of each can she buy?

1. Complete the table to show the number of sandwiches and brownies that Lily can afford.

Number of Sandwiches	Dollars Spent on Sandwiches	Dollars Left for Brownies	Number of Brownies
10			
9			
8			
7			
6			
5			
4			
3			
2			
1			
0			

2. Based on the table, describe the relationship between the number of sandwiches and the number of brownies.

3. As the number of sandwiches decreases by 1, how does the number of brownies change?

4. As the number of sandwiches decreases by 2, how does the number of brownies change?

5. As the number of sandwiches increases by 1, how does the number of brownies change?

6. Describe how to calculate the number of brownies for any number of sandwiches.

7. Define a function $b(s)$ for the number of brownies, b, for a number of sandwiches s.

4

8. Graph the function $b(s)$.

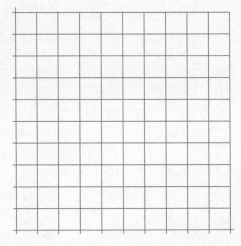

9. What are the domain and range of $b(s)$?

10. What type of function is $b(s)$?

Brenda is digging a garden in her backyard. The garden will be a square that is x feet on a side. Within the square garden area, Brenda divides a 2-foot-wide section along a side in which she will plant cantaloupe. The rest of the garden will be for vegetables.

11. Calculate the area of the vegetable section if the garden is 5 feet on its side.

12. Calculate the area of the vegetable section if the garden is 3.5 feet on its side.

13. Complete the table.

Side Length of the Garden	Length of the Vegetable Section	Width of the Vegetable Section	Area of the Vegetable Section
2			
3			
4			
5			
6			
7			
8			
9			
10			

14. Define a function $V(x)$ for the area of the vegetable section, V, for a garden with a side length of x.

15. Graph the function $V(x)$.

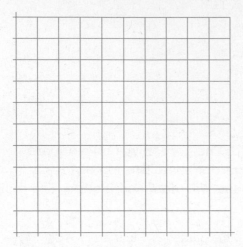

16. What type of function is $V(x)$?

17. Set the function $V(x)$ equal to 0 and calculate the values of x.

18. What are the intercepts of $V(x)$? What does each mean in terms of the problem? Is there any intercept that doesn't make sense in terms of the problem?

19. What is the vertex of $V(x)$? What does it mean in terms of the problem?

20. What is the equation of the axis of symmetry?

21. What are the domain and range of $V(x)$?

4

4

© 2009 Carnegie Learning, Inc.

Assignment

Name _____ Date _____

More Areas
More Modeling with Functions

Maria is planning to build a house. The base of the house will be a square that is x feet on each side. A 4-foot walkway will surround the house on all four sides. To one side, along the entire walkway, there will be a 12-foot-wide garden. Use this information to answer Questions 1 through 10.

1. Draw a diagram of the plot that includes the house, walkway, and garden. Label all dimensions in the diagram.

2. What is the area of the base of the house?

3. What is the area of the walkway? Write the area as a simplified expression.

4. What is the area of the garden? Write the area as a simplified expression.

5. What is the total area of the plot? Write the area as a simplified expression.

6. What is the total length of the plot?

7. What is the total width of the plot?

8. Use the length and width from Questions 6 and 7 to write an expression for the total area of the plot.

9. You wrote the area of the plot in two different ways in Questions 5 and 8. Show how these expressions are equivalent.

10. Suppose that the square base of the house is 40 feet on each side. Calculate each area.

   a. Area of the base of the house

   b. Area of the walkway

   c. Area of the garden

   d. Total area of the plot

4

Marjane is designing a house. On a square lot that is _x_ feet on each side, she wants to have a 12-foot-wide garden along all four sides of the house. On one side of the house, there will be a 5-foot-wide walkway that will cut through the middle of the garden from one edge of the lot to the front of the house.

11. Draw a diagram of the plot that includes the house, walkway, and garden. Label all dimensions in the diagram.

12. What is the area of the square lot?

13. What is the area of the walkway?

14. What is the area of the garden? Write the area as a simplified expression.

15. What is the area of the base of the house? Write the area as a simplified expression.

16. What is the side length of the base of the house?

17. Using the side length of the base of the house, write an expression for the total area of the base of the house.

18. You wrote the area of the base of the house in two different ways in Questions 15 and 17. Show how these expressions are equivalent.

19. Suppose that the square plot is 100 feet on each side. Calculate each area.

    a. Area of the square plot

    b. Area of the garden

    c. Area of the walkway

    d. Area of the base of the house

Assignment

Name _____ Date _____

Properties of Triangles
Angle Relationships in a Triangle

The measure of ∠A in △ABC is 36°. Use this information to answer Questions 1 through 3.

1. **a.** Give three examples of possible angle measures for ∠B and ∠C that make △ABC an acute triangle.

   b. Draw △ABC with $m\angle A = 36°$, $m\angle B = 80°$, and $m\angle C = 64°$.

   c. Name the angles of △ABC from smallest to largest.

   d. Name the sides of △ABC from shortest to longest.

2. a. Give three examples of possible angle measures for $\angle B$ and $\angle C$ that make $\triangle ABC$ an obtuse triangle.

b. Draw $\triangle ABC$ with $m\angle A = 36°$, $m\angle B = 120°$, and $m\angle C = 24°$.

c. Name the angles of $\triangle ABC$ from smallest to largest.

d. Name the sides of $\triangle ABC$ from shortest to longest.

5

3. a. Can $\triangle ABC$ be a right triangle? If yes, how many unique triangles can be formed? Explain.

b. Draw $\triangle ABC$ with $m\angle C = 90°$.

c. Name the angles of $\triangle ABC$ from smallest to largest.

d. Name the sides of $\triangle ABC$ from shortest to longest.

Use the diagram to answer Questions 4 through 6.

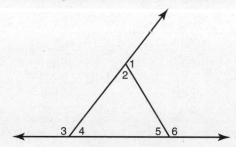

4. a. Name the interior angles of the triangle.

b. Name the labeled exterior angles of the triangle.

5. a. With respect to $\angle 1$, which angles are remote interior angles?

b. With respect to $\angle 3$, which angles are remote interior angles?

c. With respect to $\angle 6$, which angles are remote interior angles?

6. Is the equation $m\angle 3 = m\angle 2 + m\angle 5$ true? Explain.

Determine the measures of $\angle 1$ and $\angle 2$.

7.

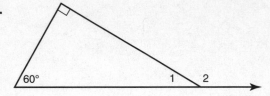

8.

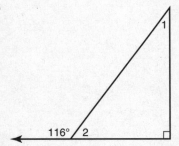

Solve for x in each triangle in Questions 9 through 11.

9.

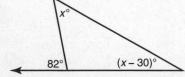

10.

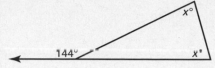

11.

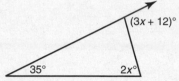

12. Use the diagram to write an inequality that states the Exterior Angles Inequality Theorem.

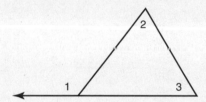

13. Use the diagram and the Exterior Angles Inequality Theorem to answer parts (a) and (b).

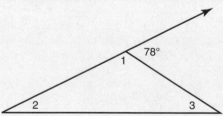

a. Write an inequality for $m\angle 3$.

b. Write an inequality for $m\angle 2$.

5

Assignment

Name _____ Date _____

Properties of Triangles
Side Relationships in a Triangle

List the interior angles of each triangle in order from smallest to largest.

1.
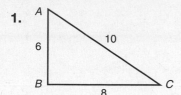

2.
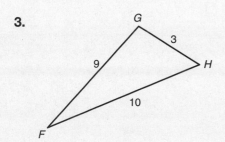

3.

4.

Determine whether the set of segment lengths given will form a triangle. If they will, classify the triangle as scalene, isosceles or equilateral. Explain your answer.

   5. 3 cm, 4 cm, 5 cm

   6. 6 cm, 6 cm, 10 cm

   7. 65 in., 30 in., 12 in.

5

   8. 20 in., 20 in., 20 in.

Name _____ Date _____

Answer the following questions about triangles.

9. A triangle has side lengths of 16 feet and 7 feet. What length(s) can be used for the third side to form an isosceles triangle? Explain.

10. How can you determine the smallest and largest interior angle of a triangle using only the side lengths?

Use the Triangle Inequality Theorem to write an inequality for x in Questions 11 through 16.

11.

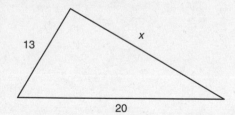

12.

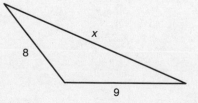

13.

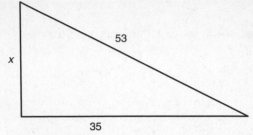

14. A triangle with side lengths 2, 6, and *x*

15. A triangle with side lengths *x*, 100, and 86

16. A triangle with side lengths *x*, 9, and 12

Assignment

Name _____   Date _____

Properties of Triangles
Points of Concurrency

In Questions 1 through 3, perform each of the following constructions using a compass and a straight edge.

1. Construct the angle bisector of ∠*BAC*.

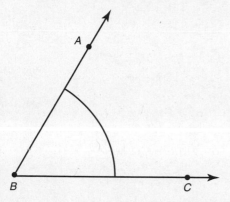

2. Construct the perpendicular bisector of $\overline{AB}$.

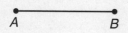

3. Construct a segment perpendicular to $\overline{AB}$ that passes through point C.

4. Construct the incenter of $\triangle DEF$.

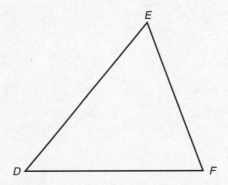

5. Construct the circumcenter of $\triangle ABC$.

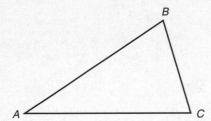

6. Construct the circumcenter of △*DEF*.

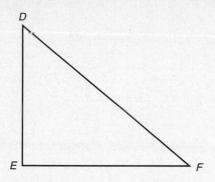

7. Construct the circumcenter of △*GHI*.

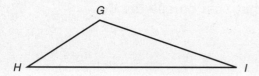

8. Construct the centroid of △*ABC*.

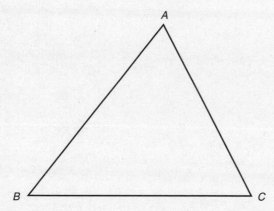

5

9. Construct the orthocenter of ΔJKL.

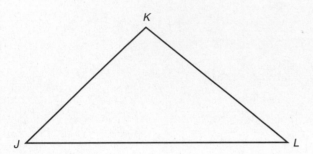

In Questions 10 through 14, write the term that best completes the statement.

10. The incenter of a triangle is the point of concurrency of the _____ of a triangle.

11. The circumcenter of a triangle is the point of concurrency of the _____ of a triangle.

12. The centroid of a triangle is the point of concurrency of the _____ of a triangle.

13. The orthocenter of a triangle is the point of concurrency of the _____ of a triangle.

5

Answer the following questions about triangles.

14. For an acute triangle, where is the circumcenter located?

15. For a right triangle, where is the circumcenter located?

16. For an obtuse triangle, where is the circumcenter located?

17. Suppose that the length of a median of a triangle is 6 inches. What is the distance along the median from the vertex to the centroid? What is the distance from the centroid to the midpoint opposite the vertex?

5

5

Assignment

Name _____ Date _____

Properties of Triangles
Direct and Indirect Proof

Complete each proof.

1. The Triangle Exterior Angle Theorem states:

   The measure of the exterior angle of a triangle is equal to the sum of the measures of the two remote interior angles of the triangle.

   Prove the Triangle Exterior Angle Theorem using a two-column proof by contradiction.

   The reasons for the proof are provided. Write each step of the proof.

   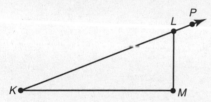

   Given: Triangle *KLM* with exterior ∠*PLM*

   Prove: $m\angle K + m\angle M = m\angle PLM$

Statements	Reasons
	1. Given
	2. Negation of conclusion
	3. Addition Property of Inequality
	4. Triangle Sum Theorem
	5. Linear Pair Postulate
	6. Definition of a Linear Pair
	7. Substitution using equations from steps 3, 4, and 6.

5

2. Complete the direct proof. The reasons for the proof are provided. Write each step of the proof.

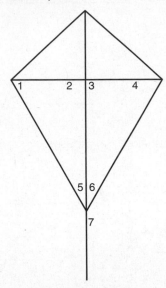

Given: $m\angle 1 = m\angle 4$, $m\angle 2 = m\angle 3$

Prove: $m\angle 5 = m\angle 6$

Statements	Reasons
	1. Given
	2. Given
	3. Triangle Sum Theorem
	4. Triangle Sum Theorem
	5. Substitution using equations from steps 3 and 4
	6. Substitution using equations from steps 1, 2, and 5
	7. Subtraction Property of Equality

3. Complete the indirect proof. The steps for the proof are provided. Write a reason for each step.

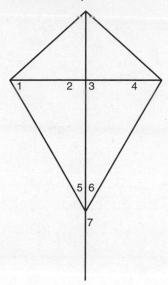

Given: $m\angle 1 = m\angle 4$, $m\angle 2 = m\angle 3$

Prove: $m\angle 7 = m\angle 1 + m\angle 3$

Statements	Reasons
1. $m\angle 1 = m\angle 4$	
2. $m\angle 2 = m\angle 3$	
3. $m\angle 7 \neq m\angle 1 + m\angle 3$	
4. $m\angle 7 = m\angle 3 + m\angle 4$	
5. $m\angle 7 = m\angle 3 + m\angle 1$	
6. $m\angle 7 \neq m\angle 7$	

4. Complete the direct proof. The steps for the proof are provided. Write a reason for each step.

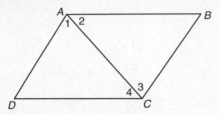

Given: $m\angle 1 = m\angle 3$

Prove: $m\angle DAB + m\angle ABC = 180°$

Statements	Reasons
1. $m\angle 1 = m\angle 3$	
2. $m\angle 2 + m\angle ABC + m\angle 3 = 180°$	
3. $m\angle 2 + m\angle ABC + m\angle 1 = 180°$	
4. $(m\angle 1 + m\angle 2) + m\angle ABC = 180°$	
5. $m\angle 1 + m\angle 2 = m\angle DAB$	
6. $m\angle DAB + m\angle ABC = 180°$	

Assignment

Name _____ Date _____

Quilting and Tessellations
Introduction to Quadrilaterals

List all of the types of quadrilaterals that have the given characteristics.

1. four right angles

2. four congruent sides

3. one pair of opposite sides parallel

4. two pairs of opposite sides parallel

5. opposite angles congruent

6. two pairs of congruent adjacent sides

7. sum of interior angles is 360°

8. four sides

6

6

Assignment

Name _____   Date _____

When Trapezoids Are Kites
Kites and Trapezoids

Quadrilateral *ABDC* is a kite.

1. Draw $\overline{CB}$.

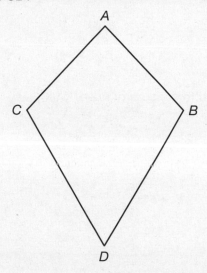

2. Name the triangles formed in the kite by $\overline{CB}$.

3. Are the two triangles congruent? Explain your reasoning.

4. Classify each triangle by its side length. Explain your reasoning.

5. What do you know about $\angle ACB$ and $\angle ABC$? Explain your reasoning.

6

6. What do you know about $\angle DCB$ and $\angle DBC$? Explain your reasoning.

7. How are $\angle ACD$ and $\angle ABD$ related? Explain your reasoning.

8. How is the sum of $m\angle ACB$ and $m\angle DCB$ related to the sum of $m\angle ABC$ and $m\angle DBC$? Explain your reasoning.

6

Assignment

Name _____ Date _____

Binocular Stand Design
Parallelograms and Rhombi

In parallelogram *GRAM*, $\overline{GR} \parallel \overline{MA}$ and $\overline{GM} \parallel \overline{RA}$. Use the figure to complete Questions 1 through 3.

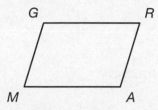

1. Suppose that $m\angle G = 107°$. What is $m\angle A$? Explain your reasoning.

2. Suppose that $m\angle R = 77°$. What is $m\angle G$? Explain your reasoning.

3. Suppose that $GR = 14$ yards. What is the length of $\overline{MA}$? Explain your reasoning.

4. Suppose that the measure of one angle of a parallelogram is 57°. Calculate the measures of the other angles of the parallelogram.

5. The measures of two consecutive angles of a parallelogram are given by the expressions (m + 46°) and ($3m$ − 90°). Calculate the measure of each angle of the parallelogram in degrees. Show all your work.

In rhombus *MBUS*, $\overline{MB} \parallel \overline{SU}$ and $\overline{MS} \parallel \overline{BU}$. Use the figure to complete Questions 6 through 8.

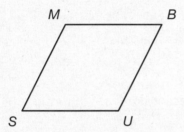

6. Suppose that $m\angle B = 33°$. What is $m\angle U$? Explain your reasoning.

7. Suppose that $m\angle U = 117°$. What is $m\angle M$? Explain your reasoning.

8. Suppose that MS = 121 millimeters. What is the length of $\overline{US}$? Explain your reasoning.

6

In rhombus *MBUS*, $\overline{MB} \parallel \overline{SU}$, $\overline{MS} \parallel \overline{BU}$, and diagonals $\overline{MU}$ and $\overline{BS}$ intersect at point *O*. Use the figure to complete Questions 9 through 11.

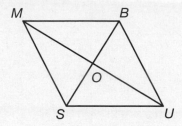

9. Suppose that *MU* = 55 millimeters. What other segment measures do you know in the diagram? Explain your reasoning.

10. Suppose that *BO* = 28 millimeters. What other segment measures do you know in this diagram? Explain your reasoning.

11. What is $m\angle SOU$? Explain your reasoning.

6

6

Assignment

Name _____ Date _____

Positive Reinforcement
Rectangles and Squares

In rectangle *RECT*, $\overline{RE} \parallel \overline{TC}$, $\overline{RT} \parallel \overline{EC}$, $\overline{RC}$ and $\overline{ET}$ are diagonals, and point *A* is the intersection of the diagonals. Use the figure to complete Questions 1 though 4.

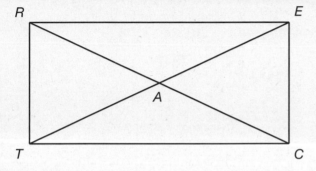

1. Is △*REC* congruent to △*TCE*? Explain your reasoning.

2. Is ∠*ERC* congruent to ∠*TCR*? Explain your reasoning.

3. Is ∠*ECR* congruent to ∠*TRC*? Explain your reasoning.

4. Is $\overline{RC}$ congruent to $\overline{TE}$? Explain your reasoning.

5. Segment *SU* and segment *QR* bisect each other, are perpendicular, and are congruent to each other. Must quadrilateral *SQUR* be a square? Justify your conclusion.

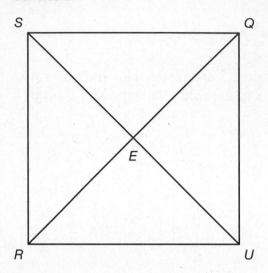

Assignment

Name _____ Date _____

Stained Glass
Sum of the Interior Angle Measures in a Polygon

1. Calculate the sum of the interior angles in a nonagon. Show all your work.

2. Suppose that the nonagon from Question 1 is a regular nonagon. Calculate the measure of each interior angle in the nonagon. Show all your work.

3. Calculate the sum of the interior angles of a 50-gon. Show all your work.

4. Calculate the measure of each interior angle in a regular pentagon. Show all your work.

6

5. Calculate the measure of each interior angle in an equiangular hexagon. Show all your work.

6. In your own words, explain how to calculate the sum of the interior angles in any polygon.

7. In your own words, explain how to calculate the measure of each interior angle in a regular polygon.

8. Given a regular polygon with *n* sides, write a formula to determine the measure of each interior angle.

Assignment

Name _____ Date _____

Pinwheels
Sum of the Exterior Angle Measures in a Polygon

Use the following triangle to complete Questions 1 through 6.

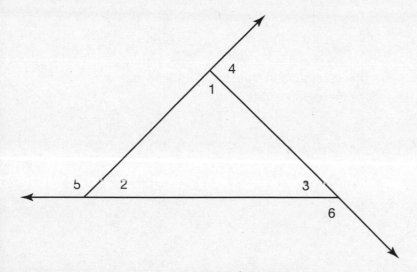

1. Calculate $m\angle 1 + m\angle 4$. Explain how you found your answer.

2. Calculate $m\angle 2 + m\angle 5$. Explain how you found your answer.

3. Calculate $m\angle 3 + m\angle 6$. Explain how you found your answer.

4. What is the sum of the measures of the angles 1, 2, 3, 4, 5, and 6? Explain how you found your answer.

5. Find $m\angle 1 + m\angle 2 + m\angle 3$. Explain how you found your answer.

6. What is the difference of the sum that you found in Question 4 and the sum that you found in Question 5? What does this demonstrate?

Assignment

Name _____ Date _____

Rolling, Flipping, and Pulling
Probability and Sample Spaces

List all of the possible outcomes to show the sample space for the event. Then determine the probability of the event.

1. rolling a 3 on a six-sided number cube

2. flipping a coin three times and getting tails all three times

3. choosing a red tile from a bag of 4 red tiles and 6 blue tiles

4. drawing a number less than 8 from a stack of nine cards numbered 2 through 10

5. flipping a coin twice and getting at least one tail

7

6. choosing a blue tile from a bag of 3 yellow tiles, 4 red tiles, and 5 green tiles

7. drawing the number 6 from a standard deck of playing cards

8. rolling two number cubes and getting a sum that is an even number

7

Name _____   Date _____

Suppose that you roll a six-sided number cube and then you spin the spinner shown.

9. Make a table to show the sample space of the events.

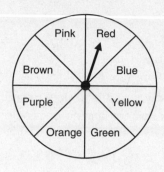

10. What are the total number of possible outcomes?

11. Are the events dependent or independent?

12. Use your table to determine the probability of rolling a 1 and the spinner landing on green.

7

13. Use your table to determine the probability of rolling an odd number and the spinner landing on red.

14. Use your table to determine the probability of rolling a number greater than 2 and the spinner landing on a color that begins with the letter B.

15. Use your table to determine the probability of rolling a number less than 7 and the spinner landing on yellow.

16. Use your table to determine the probability of rolling an even number and the spinner landing on gray.

Assignment

Name _____ Date _____

Multiple Trials
Compound and Conditional Probability

1. The following table shows the sample space for first flipping a coin and then rolling a number cube.

	Heads	Tails
1	H,1	T,1
2	H,2	T,2
3	H,3	T,3
4	H,4	T,4
5	H,5	T,5
6	H,6	T,6

a. What is the probability of getting a head *and* then rolling a 4? Explain your answer.

b. What is the probability of getting a tail *and* then rolling a number less than 5? Explain your answer.

2. **a.** You draw a card from a standard deck. You then replace the card, shuffle the deck, and draw a card again. What is the probability of getting a club twice in a row?

   b. You draw a card from a standard deck. You then draw another card from a second standard deck. What is the probability of getting two clubs?

   c. Are your answers to (a) and (b) the same? Explain why or why not.

3. The school's chess club has 18 members. The club needs to choose three members to travel to meet at another school.

   a. Calculate the probability that club members Julia, Felix, and Marc will be chosen.

   b. Calculate the probability that either Julia, Felix, or Marc will be chosen.

4. Suppose you draw two cards out of a standard deck.

   a. If the first card is a 7 of clubs, what is the probability that both cards have numbers on them that add up to 16? Explain your answer.

   b. If the first card is a 6 of diamonds, what is the probability that both cards have numbers on them that add up to less than 10? Explain your answer.

7

Name _____ Date _____

5. A brook trout fisherman catches a fish two casts in a row 16% of the time. He has a 40% chance of catching a fish on each cast. If he catches a fish on his first cast, what is the probability that he will catch a fish on the second cast?

7

7

Assignment

Name _____ Date _____

Counting
Permutations and Combinations

1. Use any eight letters of the alphabet and the formula for permutations to answer the questions. Show your work.

    a. How many three-letter strings can there be without repetition?

    b. How many five-letter strings can there be without repetition?

2. Calculate the number of four-letter strings that can be formed from the letters in the word BOOK.

3. Calculate the number of seven-letter strings that can be formed from the letters in the word GEORGIA.

4. There are four tire positions on a car—left front (LF), left rear (LR), right front (RF), and right rear (RR).

   a. List the arrangements that are equivalent to LR, LF, RF, RR.

   b. How many different possible tire position arrangements are there?

   c. Suppose the spare tire is added to the list of positions. How many different possible arrangements are there now?

5. Five friends—Abe (A), Bea (B), Charlie (C), Daisy (D), and Edgar (E)—are eating lunch together at a round table.

   a. List the seating arrangements that are equivalent to C, E, B, A, D.

   b. How many different possible table arrangements are there for the group?

c. Suppose two more friends join the group. How many different possible table arrangements are there for the new, larger, group?

6. State whether permutations or combinations should be used to answer the questions. Then calculate the answer.

   a. A CD player in a car holds six CDs. In how many different orders can they be loaded?

   b. If you have nine CDs, how many six-CD sets could be chosen from your CD collection?

   c. How many different 4-player practice teams could be chosen from a 9-player soccer team?

   d. A soccer team plays with nine different positions on the field. The goalie always stays in goal, but the remaining players can play any position. In how many different ways can the players fill these positions?

7. Using a standard deck of playing cards, what is the probability of drawing four aces in a row?

8. Suppose you pick any three digits at random from the number 4732. What is the probability of making a three-digit number whose value is less than 400?

7

Assignment

Name _____ Date _____

Trials
Independent Trials

1. You have a color cube with one brown face and five orange faces. You roll the cube twice. Calculate the probability of each outcome. Show your work.

   a. What is the probability of rolling two browns?

   b. What is the probability of rolling one brown and one orange?

   c. What is the probability of rolling two oranges?

   d. Are the probabilities in (a), (b), and (c) the same? Why or why not?

2. What is the eighth row of Pascal's Triangle?

3. You have a bag of fruit containing two apples and four oranges. Calculate the probability of each outcome.

   a. Suppose that you close your eyes, reach into the bag, and choose a piece of fruit at random. What is the probability of choosing an apple?

   b. Suppose that you close your eyes, reach into the bag, and choose a piece of fruit at random. What is the probability of choosing an orange?

   c. Suppose that you close your eyes, reach into the bag, and choose a piece of fruit at random. You do this four times. What is the probability of choosing one apple and three oranges? Show your work, including use of combinations.

   d. Suppose that you close your eyes, reach into the bag, and choose a piece of fruit at random. You do this five times. What is the probability of choosing two apples and three oranges? Show your work, including use of combinations.

4. You have a color cube with two yellow faces and four green faces. Calculate the probability of each outcome. Show your work.

   a. Use Pascal's Triangle to calculate the probability of rolling two greens and four yellows when the color cube is rolled six times.

b. Use Pascal's Triangle to calculate the probability of rolling six greens and one yellow when the color cube is rolled seven times?

5. You have a regular octahedron with five sides painted green and three sides painted yellow. Calculate the probability of each outcome.

a. What is the probability of rolling a green?

b. What is the probability of rolling a yellow?

c. What is the probability of rolling three yellows and three greens in six rolls? Show your work.

d. What is the probability of rolling two yellows and five greens in seven rolls? Show your work.

7

Assignment

Name _____   Date _____

To Spin or Not to Spin
Expected Value

You are on a game show where you throw a bean bag at a group of 9 targets. Each target has different amounts of money marked on it: $200, $400, $100, $200, $500, $300, $600, $400, and $300. Use this information to answer Questions 1 and 2.

1. What amount could you expect to win from a random throw that hits a target? Show your work and explain each step. (Round all amounts to the nearest dollar.)

7

2. Suppose the game show host offers you $350 cash to keep instead of throwing a bean bag at the targets. Should you keep the $350 or throw a bean bag? Explain your answer.

3. Suppose the game show host offers you $270 cash to keep instead of throwing a bean bag at the targets. Should you keep the $270 or throw a bean bag? Explain your answer.

7

Name _____ Date _____

You are playing a game where you draw a card from a deck that contains cards numbered from 2 to 9 for each of 4 suits. You win $1 times the number on the card drawn. Use this information to answer Questions 4 through 6.

4. What is the expected value you could expect to win from a random draw? Show your work and explain each step. (Round all amounts to the nearest cent.)

7

5. Suppose you are offered $7 cash to keep instead of drawing a card. Should you keep the $7 or draw a card? Explain your answer.

6. Suppose you are offered $5 cash to keep instead of drawing a card. Should you keep the $5 or draw a card? Explain your answer.

7. Suppose you get a $50 parking ticket. You can choose to either pay the ticket or go to court and try to get it overturned. Assume that there is a 50% chance that you'll win, and have to pay $0, and a 50% chance that you'll lose and have to pay the ticket plus court fees, for a total of $125. What should you do, pay the ticket or take it to court? Explain your answer.

Name _____   Date _____

8. A lottery ticket costs $3. There is a single $6 million jackpot for the drawing. It is expected that 2.5 million tickets will be sold. Does it make sense to buy a ticket for this drawing? Explain your answer.

7

Assignment

Name _____ Date _____

8

Taking the PSAT
Measures of Central Tendency

Define each term in your own words.

1. mean

2. median

3. mode

The following data show the test scores for a ninth grade Algebra class. Jessica received a score of 71% on the test. She wants to analyze the data to see how her score compares to the scores of the rest of the students in the class.

Ninth grade Algebra test scores: 61, 55, 71, 84, 58, 93, 82, 91, 47, 88, 84, 65, 46, 61, 84, 55, 69, 67, 73, 63, 37, 67, 72, 75, 73, 74, 95, 82, 73, 71

4. Create a stem-and-leaf plot of the data.

3		7 | 1 = _____
4		
5		
6		
7		
8		
9		

5. What information about the data set can easily be seen after creating the stem-and-leaf plot? Use complete sentences in your answer.

6. Describe the distribution of the data. Use a complete sentence in your answer

7. Analyze the data by finding the mean, median, and mode of the test scores. Use complete sentences in your answer.

8. Describe how Jessica's score compares to the scores of the rest of the students in the class. Use a complete sentence in your answer.

9. Describe a real-life data set for which the median is a much better representation of the data set than the mean. Use complete sentences in your answer.

Assignment

Name _____ Date _____

How Many People?
Population Data and Samples

The following table shows the populations of the 50 states in the U.S. in 2008.

State	Population (est., 2008)	State	Population (est., 2008)
California	36,756,666	Kentucky	4,269,245
Texas	24,326,974	Oregon	3,790,060
New York	19,490,297	Oklahoma	3,642,361
Florida	18,328,340	Connecticut	3,501,252
Illinois	12,901,563	Iowa	3,002,555
Pennsylvania	12,448,279	Mississippi	2,938,618
Ohio	11,485,910	Arkansas	2,855,390
Michigan	10,003,422	Kansas	2,802,134
Georgia	9,685,744	Utah	2,736,424
North Carolina	9,222,414	Nevada	2,600,167
New Jersey	8,682,661	New Mexico	1,984,356
Virginia	7,769,089	West Virginia	1,814,468
Washington	6,549,224	Nebraska	1,783,432
Arizona	6,500,180	Idaho	1,523,816
Massachusetts	6,497,967	Maine	1,316,456
Indiana	6,376,792	New Hampshire	1,315,809
Tennessee	6,214,888	Hawaii	1,288,198
Missouri	5,911,605	Rhode Island	1,050,788
Maryland	5,633,597	Montana	967,440
Wisconsin	5,627,967	Delaware	873,092
Minnesota	5,220,393	South Dakota	804,194
Colorado	4,939,456	Alaska	686,293
Alabama	4,661,900	North Dakota	641,481
South Carolina	4,479,800	Vermont	621,270
Louisiana	4,410,796	Wyoming	532,668

Use the sample to answer Questions 1 through 6.

State	Population	Absolute Deviation from Mean	Absolute Deviation from Median
Texas	24,326,974		
Pennsylvania	12,448,279		
New Jersey	8,682,661		
Indiana	6,376,792		
Minnesota	5,220,393		
Kentucky	4,269,245		
Mississippi	2,938,618		
New Mexico	1,984,356		
New Hampshire	1,315,809		
South Dakota	804,194		

1. Which state in the sample has the largest population? The smallest population?

2. How many states in the sample have populations over 3,000,000? Under 2,000,000?

3. Calculate each measure of central tendency for the sample. Show your work.

   a. Mean

   b. Median

   c. Mode

4. Determine each quartile for the sample.

    a. First quartile

    b. Third quartile

5. Graph a box-and-whisker plot for the sample.

6. For each data value in the sample, calculate the absolute deviation from the mean. Enter the results in the third column of the previous table.

7. What is the average absolute deviation from the mean?

8. For each data value in the sample, calculate the absolute deviation from the median. Enter the results in the fourth column of the previous table.

9. What is the average absolute deviation from the median?

10. Based on your calculations, what can you conclude about the population of the states in the United States?

11. Decide on a criterion for choosing a sample of states. Then choose 10 different states using the criterion. List the states and their populations in the table. Explain the criterion that you used.

State	Population

12. Calculate each measure of central tendency for your sample. Show your work.

a. Mean

b. Median

c. Mode (If there is no mode, explain why not.)

13. Determine each quartile for your sample.

a. First quartile

b. Third quartile

14. Graph a box-and-whisker plot for your sample.

8

15. Compare the box-and-whisker plots from Questions 5 and 14. What are the similarities? What are the differences?

Assignment

Name _____ Date _____

Let's Compare!
Population and Sample Means

The following table shows the 25 cities in Georgia with the highest elevations.

City	Elevation (in feet)
Sky Valley	3410
Hartwell	3280
Mountain City	2168
Dillard	2144
Hiawassee	1980
Tiger	1963
Young Harris	1020
Clayton	1925
Blairsville	1893
Morganton	1807
Blue Ridge	1722
Lookout Mountain	1700
Cleveland	1570
Mount Airy	1560
Baldwin	1540
Tallulah Falls	1520
Cornelia	1500
McCaysville	1487
Jasper	1480
Dahlonega	1454
Helen	1440
Clarkesville	1430
Bremen	1424
Raoul	1420
Clermont	1410

© 2009 Carnegie Learning, Inc.

The following table shows a sample of six of the cities from the previous table. Use the sample to answer Questions 1 through 4.

City	Elevation (in feet)
Sky Valley	3410
Hartwell	3280
Mountain City	2168
Dillard	2144
Hiawassee	1980
Tiger	1963

1. Do you think that the six cities in the sample are a random sample of the 25 cities in Georgia with the highest elevations? Explain your answer.

2. Calculate the mean of the sample. Show your work.

3. The mean of the entire data set is approximately 1806.24. How does the mean of the sample compare to the mean of the entire data set? Why do you think this is?

4. Suppose you want to choose a random sample from the table of the 25 cities in Georgia with the highest elevations.

   a. What is the probability of choosing each city?

Name _____ Date _____

b. Describe two ways you could pick a random sample of cities.

5. Use the random number generator function on your calculator to complete the following table for a random sample of six cities from the original data set.

Sample Number	Mean	Sample Number	Mean

The following table shows a sample of six of the cities from the original table of 25 cities. Use the information in the table to answer Questions 6 through 8.

City	Elevation (in feet)
Sky Valley	3410
Hiawassee	1980
Blairsville	1893
Cleveland	1570
Cornelia	1500
Helen	1440

6. Do you think that the six cities in the sample are representative of the 25 cities in Georgia with the highest elevations? Explain your answer.

7. Calculate the mean of the sample. Show your work.

8. Compare the mean of the entire data set, 1806.24, to the mean of this sample. How would you explain any difference between the two values?

Assignment

Name _____ Date _____

An Experiment of Your Own
Collecting and Analyzing Sample Data

1. Suppose that you collected the following data. The data show the numbers of pets owned by ten randomly selected students from your school.

Sample Number	1	2	3	4	5	6	7	8	9	10
Number of Pets	0	3	2	0	2	5	1	2	0	5

   a. Calculate the mean of your sample data.

   b. Based on your sample and your sample mean, what can you predict about the population from which the sample was taken?

2. One of your friends collected her own data by randomly selecting ten students from your school. Your sample and her sample are shown in the following table to form a small group sample.

Sample Number	Number of Pets	Sample Number	Number of Pets
1	0	11	4
2	3	12	2
3	2	13	0
4	0	14	1
5	2	15	4
6	5	16	1
7	1	17	2
8	2	18	1
9	0	19	3
10	5	20	0

a. Calculate the mean of the small group sample.

b. Based on this small group sample and the small group sample mean, what can you predict about the population from which the sample was taken?

c. Compare your sample mean in Question 1 with the small group sample mean.

Name _____   Date _____

3. Two more of your friends collected their own data by each randomly selecting ten students from your school. All four samples are shown in the following table to form a large group sample.

Sample Number	Number of Pets	Sample Number	Number of Pets	Sample Number	Number of Pets	Sample Number	Number of Pets
1	0	11	4	21	2	31	3
2	3	12	2	22	1	32	2
3	2	13	0	23	3	33	0
4	0	14	1	24	2	34	4
5	2	15	4	25	0	35	1
6	5	16	1	26	4	36	0
7	1	17	2	27	0	37	2
8	2	18	1	28	1	38	1
9	0	19	3	29	2	39	4
10	5	20	0	30	0	40	0

a. Calculate the mean of the large group sample.

b. Based on the large group sample and the large group sample mean, what can you predict about the population from which the sample was taken?

c. Compare your sample mean in Question 1 with the large group sample mean.

4. Create a random sample of size ten from the large group sample. Enter this random sample in the following table.

Sample Number	1	2	3	4	5	6	7	8	9	10
Number of Pets										

a. Calculate the mean of the random sample.

b. Based on the random sample and the random sample mean, what can you predict about the population from which the sample was taken?

c. Compare your sample mean and the random sample mean.

d. Compare the large group sample mean and the random sample mean.

© 2009 Carnegie Learning, Inc.

5. Of the four samples—your sample, the small group sample, the larger group sample, and the random sample—which do you think would provide the best information about the population? Which do you think would provide the worst information about the population? Explain.

6. Suppose the actual mean of the entire population is 1.73. Compare all of your sample means to the population mean. How well does each sample mean represent the population? Why?

8

Assignment

Name _____ Date _____

Shifting Away
Vertical and Horizontal Translations

1. Graph each cubic function on the grid.

   a. $y = x^3$

   b. $y = x^3 + 3$

   c. $y = x^3 - 3$

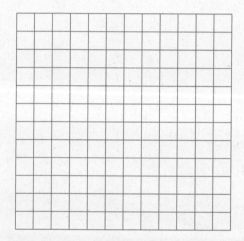

2. Graph each square root function on the grid.

   a. $y = \sqrt{x}$

   b. $y = \sqrt{x} + 3$

   c. $y = \sqrt{x} - 3$

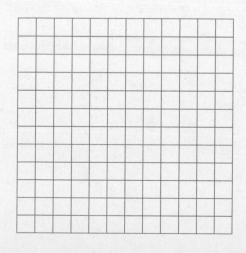

3. Graph each linear function on the grid.

a. $y = -x$

b. $y = -x + 3$

c. $y = -x - 3$

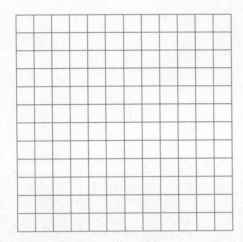

4. In Questions 1 through 3, part (a) is a basic function.

a. Describe how adding 3 changed each graph in part (b).

b. Describe how subtracting 3 changed each graph in part (c).

5. The graph of a function $j(x)$ is shown. Sketch the graph of

a. $j(x) + 4$

b. $j(x) - 2$

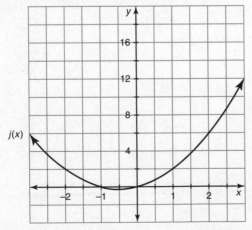

Name _____ Date _____

6. The graph of the function $k(x)$ is shown. Write a function in terms of $k(x)$ for each vertical translation shown.

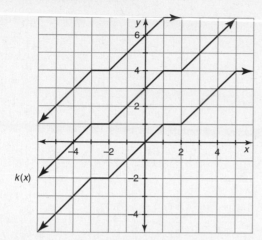

7. Graph each indirect variation function on the grid.

a. $y = \dfrac{1}{x}$

b. $y = \dfrac{1}{x + 3}$

c. $y = \dfrac{1}{x - 3}$

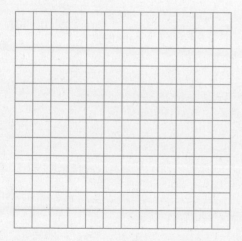

8. Graph each linear function on the grid.

   a. $y = -x$

   b. $y = -(x + 3)$

   c. $y = -(x - 3)$

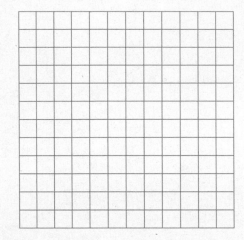

9. Graph each cubic function on the grid.

   a. $y = x^3$

   b. $y = (x + 3)^3$

   c. $y = (x - 3)^3$

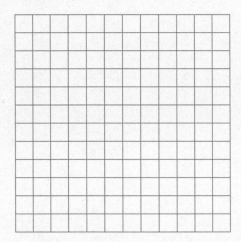

Name _____   Date _____

10. In Questions 7 through 9, part (a) is a basic function.

   a. Describe how adding 3 within the parentheses changed each graph in part (b).

   b. Describe how subtracting 3 within the parentheses changed each graph in part (c).

11. Compare Question 3 to Question 8. What is the difference between the equations in each part of Question 3 and those in the corresponding parts of Question 8? What is the difference between the graphs? Explain.

12. The graph of a function $l(x)$ is shown. Sketch the graph of

   a. $l(x + 4)$

   b. $l(x - 3)$

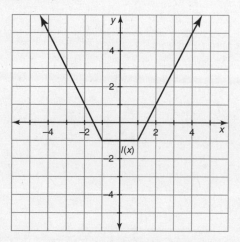

13. The graph of the function $m(x)$ is shown. Write a function in terms of $m(x)$ for each horizontal translation shown.

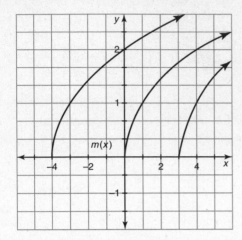

Assignment

Name _____   Date _____

Expanding, Contracting, and Mirroring Dilations and Reflections

9

1. Graph each quadratic function on the grid.

   a. $n(x) = -x^2$

   b. $p(x) = -2x^2$

   c. $q(x) = -\frac{1}{2}x^2$

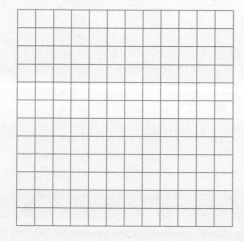

2. Complete the table to calculate the rate of change from $x = 0$ to $x = 1$ for each function in Question 1.

Function	Value at $x = 0$	Value at $x = 1$	Rate of Change
$n(x) = -x^2$	$n(0) =$	$n(1) =$	$\dfrac{\Delta n(x)}{\Delta x} =$
$p(x) = -2x^2$	$p(0) =$	$p(1) =$	$\dfrac{\Delta p(x)}{\Delta x} =$
$q(x) = -\dfrac{1}{2}x^2$	$q(0) =$	$q(1) =$	$\dfrac{\Delta q(x)}{\Delta x} =$

3. Graph each cubic function on the grid.

a. $r(x) = x^3$

b. $s(x) = 2x^3$

c. $t(x) = \frac{1}{2}x^3$

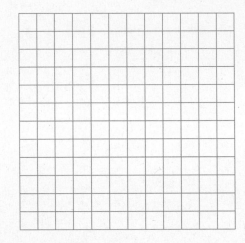

4. Complete the table to calculate the rate of change from $x = 0$ to $x = 1$ for each function in Question 3.

Function	Value at $x = 0$	Value at $x = 1$	Rate of Change
$r(x) = x^3$	$r(0) =$	$r(1) =$	$\frac{\Delta r(x)}{\Delta x} =$
$s(x) = 2x^3$	$s(0) =$	$s(1) =$	$\frac{\Delta s(x)}{\Delta x} =$
$t(x) = \frac{1}{2}x^3$	$t(0) =$	$t(1) =$	$\frac{\Delta t(x)}{\Delta x} =$

5. In Questions 1 and 3, part (a) is a basic function.

a. Describe how multiplying by 2 changed each graph in part (b).

b. Describe how multiplying by $\frac{1}{2}$ changed each graph in part (c).

Name _____ Date _____

6. For Questions 2 and 4

    a. Describe how multiplying the original function by 2 changed each rate of change.

    b. Describe how multiplying the original function by $\frac{1}{2}$ changed each rate of change.

7. Graph each function on the grid shown.

    a. $u(x) = x + 2$

    b. $v(x) = -x + 2$

    c. $w(x) = 2^x$

    d. $y(x) = 2^{-x}$

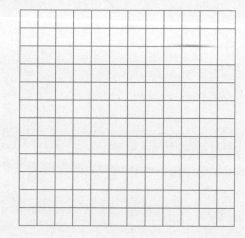

8. For Question 7,

    a. write $v(x)$ in terms of $u(x)$.

    b. write $y(x)$ in terms of $w(x)$.

9. What is the line of reflection for the graphs in Question 7?

10. Graph each function on the grid shown.

a. $e(x) = x + 2$

b. $f(x) = -(x + 2)$

c. $g(x) = x^2$

d. $h(x) = -x^2$

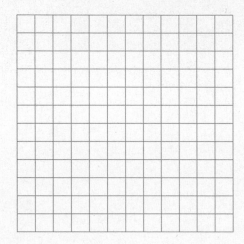

11. For Question 10,

a. write $f(x)$ in terms of $e(x)$.

b. write $h(x)$ in terms of $g(x)$.

12. What is the line of reflection for the graphs in Question 10?

Name _____ Date _____

13. Graph each function on the grid shown.

a. $j(x) = 2^x$

b. $k(x) = -2^{-x}$

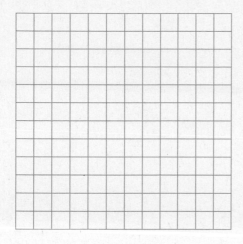

14. In Question 13, write $k(x)$ in terms of $j(x)$.

15. The graph of $m(x)$ is shown. Sketch the graph of

a. $n(x) = m(-x)$

b. $p(x) = -m(x)$

c. $q(x) = -m(-x)$

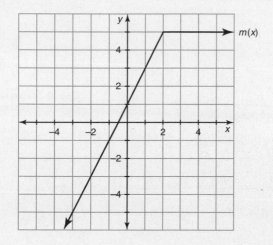

Assignment

Name _____ Date _____

Mirroring!
Symmetry and Odd/Even

1. Graph each quadratic function on the grid.

   a. $a(x) = -x^2$

   b. $b(x) = -x^2 + x + 6$

   c. $c(x) = -x^2 - x + 6$

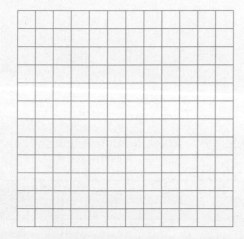

2. For each function in Question 1, identify the vertex, y-intercept, x-intercept(s), and line of symmetry.

Function	Vertex	y-intercept	x-intercept(s)	Line of Symmetry
$a(x) = -x^2$				
$b(x) = -x^2 + x + 6$				
$c(x) = -x^2 - x + 6$				

3. Graph each absolute value function on the grid.

   a. $d(x) = |x|$

   b. $e(x) = |x + 2| - 1$

   c. $f(x) = |x - 2| + 1$

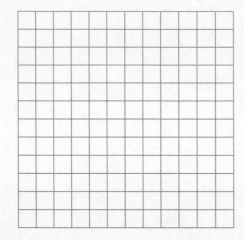

4. For each function in Question 3, identify the vertex, *y*-intercept, *x*-intercept(s), and line of symmetry.

Function	Vertex	y-intercept	x-intercept(s)	Line of Symmetry
$d(x) = |x|$				
$e(x) = |x + 2| - 1$				
$f(x) = |x - 2| + 1$				

5. Identify the equation of the line of symmetry, if it exists, for each graph shown.

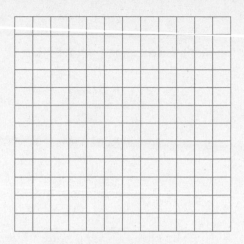

a. Line of symmetry of $g(x)$:

b. Line of symmetry of $h(x)$:

c. Line of symmetry of $j(x)$:

6. Graph each function on the grid shown.

a. $k(x) = x^2 + 2$

b. $l(x) = x^3 + 2x$

c. $m(x) = x^4 - 2x^2$

d. $n(x) = x^5 - 2x^3$

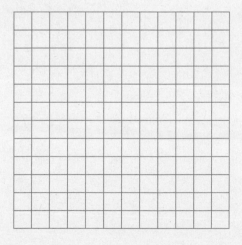

7. In Question 6, which functions are even?

8. Describe the result of reflecting the graphs of the functions in Question 7 about the *y*-axis.

9. In Question 6, which functions are odd?

10. Describe the result of reflecting the graphs of the functions in Question 9 about the *y*-axis and then about the *x*-axis.

11. The portion of the graph of *p*(*x*) to the right of the *y*-axis is shown. Sketch the portion of the graph to the left of the *y*-axis if

a. the function is an even function.

b. the function is an odd function.

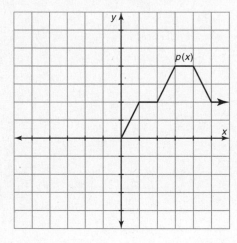

Assignment

Name _____ Date _____

Machine Parts
Solving Equations Graphically

Dave bakes cranberry muffins in batches. He starts the first batch after preparing the batter, which takes him 50 minutes. After that, each batch takes 30 minutes to bake. In comparison to Dave, Stefannie uses a different recipe to make cranberry muffins. Preparing the batter takes her 30 minutes, and each batch takes her 40 minutes. Use this information to answer Questions 1 through 11.

1. Define variables for the independent and dependent quantities. Then write equations for the total time it takes Dave and Stefannie each to bake a given number of batches of cranberry muffins.

2. Graph the equations in Question 1 on the grid shown.

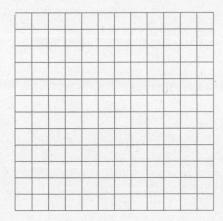

3. Does it make sense to connect the points of each graph? Explain.

4. Identify the slope and *y*-intercept for each function. What do the slope and *y*-intercepts mean in terms of the situation?

5. If Dave and Stefannie each bake 2 batches of muffins, calculate the time it takes each of them. Who takes less time? Explain.

6. If Dave and Stefannie each bake fewer than 2 batches, who takes less time?

7. If Dave and Stefannie each bake more than 2 batches, who takes less time?

8. Complete the table.

Number of Batches of Muffins (batches)	Time it takes Dave (minutes)	Time it takes Stefannie (minutes)
x		
1		
2		
3		
4		
5		
6		
7		

9. Use the table of values to determine the point(s) of intersection. How did you find the point(s) of intersection in the table?

10. Use the graph in Question 2 to determine the point(s) of intersection. How did you find the point(s) of intersection on the graph?

11. Use the equations to solve for the point(s) of intersection algebraically.

Use the equation $x^3 = 7x^2 - 10x$ to answer Questions 12 through 14.

12. To solve the equation $x^3 = 7x^2 - 10x$ graphically, define the function $a(x)$ to equal the left side of the equation, and the function $b(x)$ to equal the right side of the equation.

Name _____ Date _____

13. Use a table of values to determine the point(s) of intersection of $a(x)$ and $b(x)$. What is the solution(s) to the equation $x^3 = 7x^2 - 10x$?

x		
0		
1		
2		
3		
4		
5		
6		
7		
8		

14. Use a graph to determine the points of intersection of $a(x)$ and $b(x)$. What is the solution(s) to the equation $x^3 = 7x^2 - 10x$?

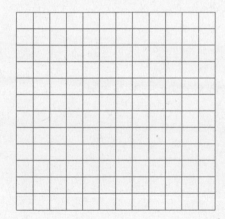

9

15. Consider the equation $x^2 = 4x - 3$.

a. Define the function $c(x)$ equal to the left side of the equation and the function $d(x)$ equal to the right side of the equation.

b. Graph the functions $c(x)$ and $d(x)$ from part (a).

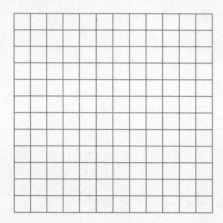

c. Are the functions $c(x)$ and $d(x)$ consistent or inconsistent?

d. If possible, determine the solution(s) to the equation $x^2 = 4x - 3$.

Assignment

Name _____ Date _____

Roots and Zeros
Calculating Roots of Quadratic Equations and Zeros of Quadratic Functions

Factor and solve each quadratic equation, if possible. Check your answers.

1. $x^2 + 5x - 24 = 0$

2. $x^2 - 6x + 9 = 0$

3. $x^2 + 13x + 30 = 0$

4. $x^2 - 15x + 36 = 0$

Calculate the root(s) of each quadratic equation. Check your answers.

5. $x^2 - 144 = 0$

6. $x^2 - 7x + 12 = 0$

10

7. Use the quadratic function $f(x) = x^2 - 6x + 5$ to answer parts (a) through (c).

a. Graph the quadratic function on the grid below.

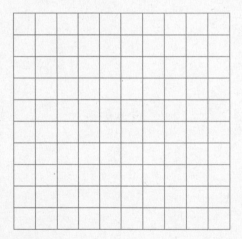

b. Identify the vertex, x- and y-intercepts, and line of symmetry. Label each on the graph.

Vertex:

y-intercept:

x-intercept(s):

Line of symmetry:

c. What are the zeros of $f(x) = x^2 - 6x + 5$?

Name _____ Date _____

Calculate the zeros of each quadratic function, if possible. Check your answers.

8. $f(x) = x^2 - 11x + 28$

9. $f(x) = x^2 + 4x - 45$

10. $f(x) = x^2 - 6x + 14$

11. $f(x) = x^2 + 18x + 81$

12. $f(x) = x^2 - 10x + 24$

Assignment

Name _____ Date _____

Poly High
Factoring Polynomials

The graph of the polynomial function $f(x) = \frac{1}{2}x^3 + 4$ is shown. Use this function and its graph to answer Questions 1 and 2.

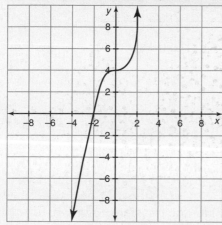

10

1. Identify the zero(s), *y*-intercept, and line of symmetry for *f*(*x*). Label each on the graph.

    a. zero(s):

    b. *y*-intercept:

    c. line of symmetry:

2. Sketch the graph of each transformed function on the same graph as *f*(*x*).

    a. *f*(*x*) − 4

    b. *f*(*x* + 3)

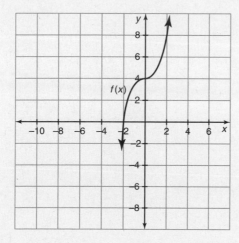

3. Describe how each graph is formed from the graph of $f(x)$.

a. Six is subtracted from x: $f(x - 6)$.

b. Four is added to $f(x)$: $f(x) + 4$.

4. Write a function in terms of $f(x)$ for each of the following.

a. The graph of $f(x)$ is shifted up 3 units.

b. The graph of $f(x)$ is shifted left 10 units.

c. The graph of $f(x)$ is shifted right 2 units and down 5 units.

5. The graph of $f(x)$ is shown. Write a function in terms of $f(x)$ for the transformed graph.

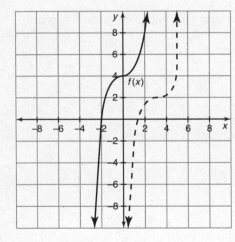

Factor and solve each polynomial equation.

6. $x^2 + 2x - 8 = 0$

7. $x^2 - 12x + 27 = 0$

© 2009 Carnegie Learning, Inc.

8. $x^4 + 5x^2 + 6 = 0$

9. $x^4 - 13x^2 + 36 = 0$

10. $9x^3 + 72x^2 - 81x = 0$

11. $3x^4 - 24x^3 + 45x^2 = 0$

10

12. $x^2 - x - 2x + 2 = 0$

13. $3x^4 - 9x^3 - 12x^2 + 36x = 0$

Assignment

Name _____ Date _____

Rational Thinking
Rational Equations and Functions

1. Consider the rational function $y = \frac{1}{x}$.

a. Complete the following table.

x	y
−4	
−2	
−1	
1	
2	
4	

b. Graph the function.

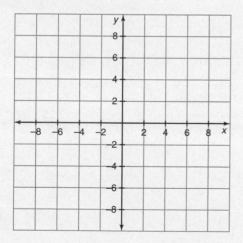

c. Identify the domain, range, x- and y-intercepts, and asymptotes.

Domain:

Range:

x-intercept(s):

y-intercept(s):

Asymptotes:

Solve each of the following rational equations.

2. $\dfrac{-4}{x} = -2$

3. $\dfrac{8}{x} - 3 = 17$

4. $\dfrac{18}{x} - 6 = \dfrac{3}{x}$

5. $\dfrac{4}{x} = 3 - \dfrac{4}{x}$

6. $\dfrac{20}{x+3} = 5$

7. $\dfrac{8}{x+5} = \dfrac{10}{x+9}$

10

8. $\dfrac{x+4}{x-6} = 6$

9. $\dfrac{x+5}{x+8} = \dfrac{1}{2}$

10. $\dfrac{4}{x-3} + \dfrac{2x}{x^2-9} = \dfrac{1}{x+3}$

11. $\dfrac{1}{x+3} + \dfrac{1}{x-3} = \dfrac{1}{x^2-9}$

Name _____ Date _____

12. $\dfrac{5(x-4)}{x^2-16} + \dfrac{3x}{x+4} = 1$

10

10

Assignment

Name _____ Date _____

Work, Mixture, and More
Applications of Rational Equations and Functions

1. Two teams of construction workers have been contracted to build an addition for your school library. If Team A works alone, they can complete the job in 32 days. If Team B works alone, they can complete the job in 20 days.

   a. How much of the job can Team A complete in x days? How much of the job can Team B complete in x days? Which team can complete more of the job in the same number of days?

   b. Suppose that Team A and Team B work together for x days. How much of the job can they complete in x days?

   c. Write and solve an equation to calculate the number of days it would take both teams working together to complete the job.

2. A 250-milliliter acid solution contains 35% acid.

   a. What would be the acid concentration if you added 30 milliliters of water to the solution? What would be the acid concentration if you added 100 milliliters of water to the solution?

   b. Write a function to represent the fractional concentration $C(x)$ of the solution when x milliliters of water is added to the solution.

   c. How much water should you add to the solution if you want a 10% acid solution?

3. You buy a new fish tank for $800. It is estimated to cost about $125 each year to own including cleaning supplies, electricity, food, etc.

    a. Assuming that these estimates are reliable, what is the average annual cost if you have the fish tank for 5 years? 10 years? 20 years?

    b. Write a function that shows the average annual cost $C(x)$ of the fish tank over x years.

    c. How many years did you have the fish tank if the average annual cost was $225?

10

4. Graph the function. Determine the domain, range, asymptotes, discontinuities, and end behavior of the function.

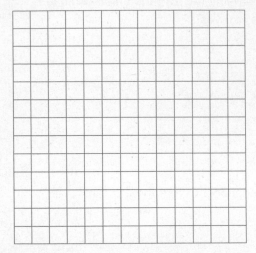

Domain:

Range:

Asymptotes:

Discontinuities:

End behavior:

Assignment

Name _____ Date _____

Rad Man!
Radical Equations and Functions

The graph of the basic radical function $f(x) = \sqrt[3]{x}$ is shown. Use this function and its graph to answer Questions 1 and 2.

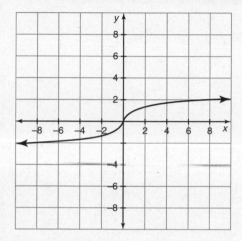

1. Identify the zero(s) and y-intercept of $f(x) = \sqrt[3]{x}$. Label each point on the graph.

   a. zero(s):

   b. y-intercept:

2. Sketch the graph of each transformed function on the same graph as $f(x)$.

   a. $f(x) - 3$

   b. $f(x + 4)$

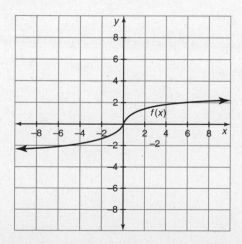

3. Describe how each graph is formed from the graph of $f(x)$.

    a. Five is subtracted from x: $f(x - 5)$.

    b. Seven is added to $f(x)$: $f(x) + 7$.

4. Write a function in terms of $f(x)$ for each of the following.

    a. The graph of $f(x)$ is shifted up 4 units.

    b. The graph of $f(x)$ is shifted left 8 units.

    c. The graph of $f(x)$ is shifted right 3 units and down 2 units.

Solve each equation for the unknown.

5. $\sqrt{x} = 8$ **6.** $\sqrt{3x} = 12$

7. $\sqrt{x + 2} = 3$ **8.** $\sqrt{x + 3} = 1$

9. $4\sqrt{x + 3} = 36$

10. $\frac{1}{2}\sqrt{x - 6} = 4$

11. $\sqrt[3]{x + 3} = 2$

12. $2\sqrt[3]{2x + 1} = 6$

10

Solve each of the following equations. Check for extraneous solutions or roots.

13. $x - 2 = \sqrt{2x + 11}$

14. $x + \sqrt{x} = 6$

15. $\sqrt[3]{x^3 + x^2 - 4x + 5} = x + 1$

Assignment

Name _____ Date _____

Connections
Algebraic and Graphical Connections

The graph of the basic absolute value function $f(x) = |x|$ and a transformed absolute value function $g(x)$ are shown on the grid. Use the functions and their graphs to answer Questions 1 through 4.

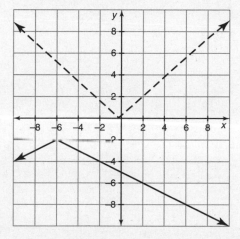

1. Identify each of the following characteristics for $f(x)$.

    a. x-intercept(s):

    b. y-intercept(s):

    c. Vertex:

    d. Line of symmetry:

2. Identify each of the following characteristics for $g(x)$.

    a. x-intercept(s):

    b. y-intercept(s):

    c. Vertex:

    d. Line of symmetry:

3. Describe how the graph of $g(x)$ is formed from the graph of $f(x)$ using four transformations.

4. a. Write a function for $g(x)$ in terms of $f(x)$.

b. Write a function for $g(x)$ using absolute value.

Solve each equation algebraically. Check your answers.

5. $2|x| - 4 = 0$

6. $\sqrt{x + 3} = 2$

7. $4^x = 4$

8. $x^2 + x - 6 = 0$

Name _____   Date _____

Solve the equation graphically.

9. $|x + 2| = x^2$

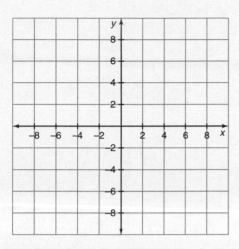

Assignment

Name _____   Date _____

Meeting Friends
The Distance Formula

**Ben is playing soccer with his friends Abby and Clay. Use the graph to answer
Questions 1 through 4.**

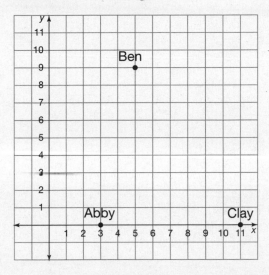

1. What is the location on the grid of each player?

2. How far does Abby have to kick the ball to Clay if each interval is measured in
   meters?

3. How far does Ben have to kick the ball to Abby?

4. How far does Ben have to kick the ball to Clay?

5. Use the grid to graph and connect each given pair of points. Beside each pair of points, write the distance between them.

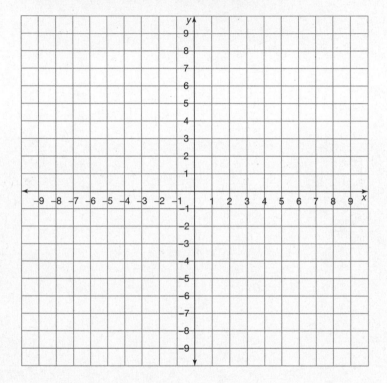

    a. (−8, 3) and (−8, 9) Distance: _____

    b. (−6, 8) and (−1, 8) Distance: _____

    c. (8, −7) and (−4, −7) Distance: _____

    d. (8, 8) and (8, −2) Distance: _____

6. Describe the method that you used to determine the distance between each pair of points in Question 5.

11

7. In Question 5, suppose that you were only given the coordinates of the points and did not graph them. Describe the method that you would use to calculate the distance between each pair of points.

8. Use the grid to graph and connect the given set of three points. Then, calculate the distances between the points.

   a. (4, 1), (2, 1), and (4, 4)

   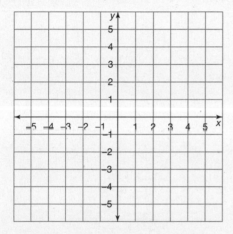

   b. (1, −4), (1, 1), and (−2, −4)

   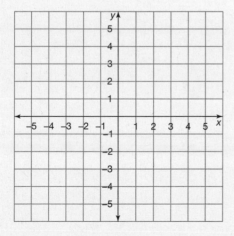

9. Describe the method that you used to calculate the distances between the points.

10. Calculate the distance between each pair of points.

    a. $(-37, -100)$ and $(14, 0)$

    Distance:

    b. $(3, 9)$ and $(4, 10)$

    Distance:

    c. $(-10, -7)$ and $(13, 17)$

    Distance:

11

Assignment

Name _____ Date _____

Treasure Hunt
The Midpoint Formula

While playing in the sandbox, you see your friend at the water fountain. Use the graph to answer Questions 1 through 3.

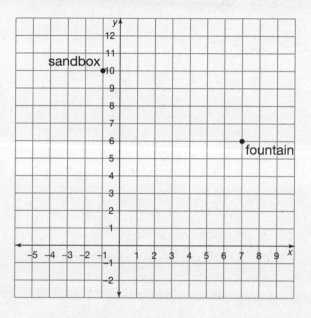

1. What are the coordinates of the sandbox and fountain?

2. Calculate the distance between the point representing the sandbox and the point representing the fountain. Each grid square represents a square that is one meter long and 1 meter wide.

3. You decide to meet your friend halfway between the fountain and sandbox. Calculate the midpoint of the line segment that passes through the point representing the sandbox and the point representing the fountain.

Use the Midpoint Formula to calculate the midpoint of each line segment with the given endpoints.

4. $(-2, 5)$ and $(4, 1)$

5. $(4, 3)$ and $(-2, -5)$

6. $(-3, -4)$ and $(3, -6)$

7. If you know the midpoint of a line segment is $(2, 1)$, and one endpoint is $(3, -2)$, how can you calculate the other endpoint?

8. Calculate the midpoint of the line segment with endpoints $(-3, 8)$ and $(4, 1)$.

9. Explain how you can prove that your answer in Question 8 is the midpoint.

11

Assignment

Name _____ Date _____

Parking Lot Design
Parallel and Perpendicular Lines in the Coordinate Plane

The graphs of three lines are shown on the grid. Use this information to answer Questions 1 through 4.

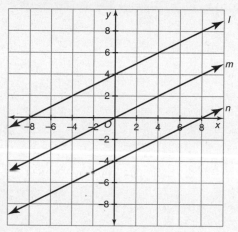

1. What is the slope of each line?

   a. Line *l*:

   b. Line *m*:

   c. Line *n*:

2. What is the *y*-intercept of each line?

   a. Line *l*:

   b. Line *m*:

   c. Line *n*:

3. Write the equation of each line in slope-intercept form.

   a. Line *l*:

   b. Line *m*:

   c. Line *n*:

4. Explain what the slopes and *y*-intercepts of lines *l*, *m*, and *n* tell you about the relationship between the lines.

5. Write an equation in slope-intercept form for a line that is parallel to the line given by $y = 2x - 6$ and that has each of the following characteristics.

   a. 2 units above the given line

   b. 8 units below the given line

   c. passes through the point (0, 8)

   d. passes through the point (6, 0)

6. Without graphing the lines, determine whether each pair of lines given by the equations are parallel. Show all your work.

   a. $3x - y = 4$ and $2y - 6x = 12$

b. $2y = -8x + 10$ and $4x - y = -5$

The graphs of three lines are shown on the grid. Use this information to answer Questions 7 through 10.

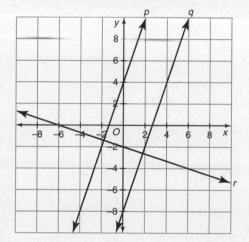

7. What is the slope of each line?

   a. Line p:

   b. Line q:

   c. Line r:

8. What is the y-intercept of each line?

   a. Line p:

   b. Line q:

   c. Line r:

9. Write the equation of each line in slope-intercept form.

   a. Line p:

   b. Line q:

   c. Line r:

10. Explain what the slopes and y-intercepts of lines p, q, and r tell you about the relationship between the lines.

11. Write an equation in slope-intercept form for the line that is perpendicular to the line given by each equation and that passes through the given point.

    a. $y = 2x + 4$; point $(2, 0)$

    b. $y = -x - 6$; point $(3, 3)$

12. Write equations for a horizontal line and a vertical line that pass through the point $(-3, 5)$.

13. Write an equation for the line that is perpendicular to the line given by $y = -2$ and that passes through the point $(3, 4)$.

14. Write an equation for the line that is perpendicular to the line given by $x = 20$ and that passes through the point $(3, 4)$.

15. The equation of line *l* on the grid below is $y = -2x - 4$. Point *D* is at (4, 3).

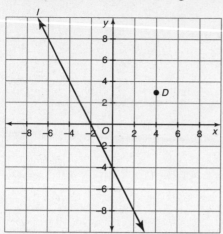

a. Draw the shortest line segment possible between point *D* and line *l* on the grid. Label the point where the segment and line *l* intersect point *C*.

b. Write an equation for the line that contains $\overline{CD}$.

c. Calculate the point of intersection of $\overline{CD}$ and line *l*.

d. Calculate the distance from point *D* to line *l*.

Assignment

Name _____   Date _____

Building a Hedge
Triangles in the Coordinate Plane

Triangle *FGH* has vertices at *F*(−4, 2), *G*(4, 2), and *H*(4, −2). Triangle *FGH* is
inscribed in circle *O*.

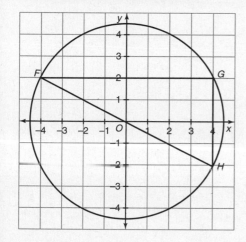

1. Calculate the slope of each side of triangle *FGH*.

   a. Slope of $\overline{FG}$:

   b. Slope of $\overline{GH}$:

   c. Slope of $\overline{FH}$:

2. Classify triangle *FGH* by its angles.

Triangle *ABC* has vertices at *A*(−2, 8), *B*(−8, −6), and *C*(4, −6).

3. Graph triangle *ABC* on the grid.

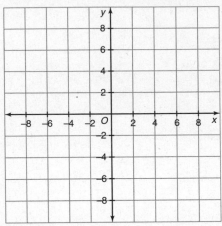

4. **a.** Classify triangle *ABC* by its side lengths.

b. Verify the classification algebraically.

Triangle *PQR* has vertices at *P*(−1, 1), *Q*(4, −2), and *R*(−4, −2).

5. Graph triangle *PQR* on the grid below.

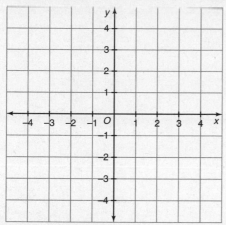

6. **a.** Classify triangle *PQR* by its side lengths.

b. Verify the classification algebraically.

11

7. Use algebra to locate the centroid of triangle *FGH* from Question 1.

Name _____ Date _____

8. Use algebra to locate the circumcenter of triangle *FGH* from Question 1.

11

Assignment

Name _____ Date _____

Planning a Subdivision
Quadrilaterals in the Coordinate Plane

1. Quadrilateral *ABCD* has vertices *A*(−1, 6), *B*(3, 2), *C*(−1, −2), and *D*(−5, 2).

   a. Graph quadrilateral *ABCD*.

   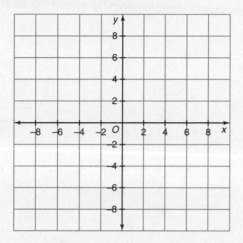

   b. Classify quadrilateral *ABCD* in as many ways as possible.

c. Prove your classification using algebra.

2. Quadrilateral *EFGH* has vertices $E(-2, -1)$, $F(-1, 2)$, $G(5, 0)$, and $H(4, -3)$.

a. Graph quadrilateral *EFGH*.

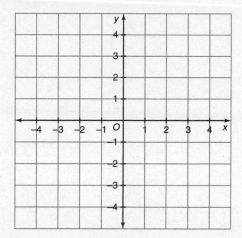

b. Classify quadrilateral *EFGH* in as many ways as possible.

c. Prove your classification using algebra.

3. Triangle *ABC* has vertices *A*(−1, 4), *B*(3, 0), and *C*(−3, −4), as shown on the grid.

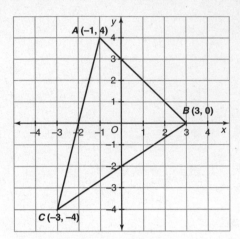

a. Determine and label point *D*, the midpoint of $\overline{AB}$:

b. Determine and label point *E*, the midpoint of $\overline{BC}$:

c. Determine and label point *F*, the midpoint of $\overline{AC}$:

d. Draw the midsegments of triangle *ABC*. Calculate the length of each side and midsegment of triangle *ABC*.

e. Classify quadrilateral *DECF,* formed by midsegments and segments of the triangles sides, in as many ways as possible.

f. Prove your classification using algebra.

g. Classify quadrilaterals *ADEF* and *DBEF*. Explain your classification.

4. Calculate the area of quadrilateral *DECF* from Question 3.

Section 2

Skills Practice

Skills Practice

Name _____ Date _____

Human Growth
Multiple Representations of Relations and Functions

Vocabulary

Discuss the similarities and differences between each set of terms.

1. relation and function

2. domain and range

Problem Set

Create a scatter plot of the relation defined by each table. Then determine if each relation is a function.

3.

Day	Inches of Rain
1	2
2	0
3	0
4	0.5
5	1
6	0.5
7	1
8	0

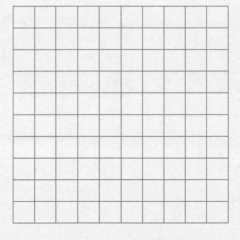

4.

Day	Average Temperature
1	60
2	64
3	72
4	70
5	72
6	68
7	66
8	62

5.

Day	Average Humidity
1	90%
2	40%
3	50%
4	80%
5	90%
6	80%
7	90%
8	40%

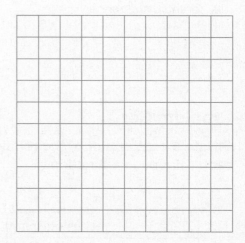

6.

Day	Average Pressure
1	29.5
2	30
3	30.3
4	29.7
5	29.6
6	29.8
7	29.6
8	30.2

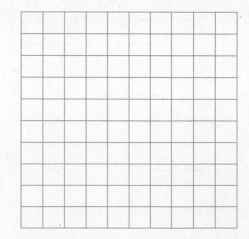

Name _____ Date _____

Determine the domain and range of each relation. Then use the scatter plot to make the prediction.

7. The scatter plot shows the relation between the ages of trees in years and their heights in feet. Predict the average height of a tree that is 6 years old.

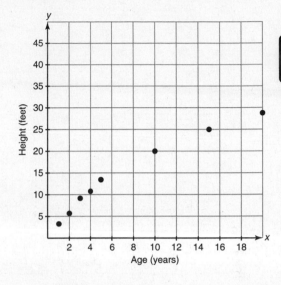

8. The scatter plot shows the relation between the ages of trees in years and the diameters of their trunks in inches. Predict the average diameter of a tree that is 13 years old.

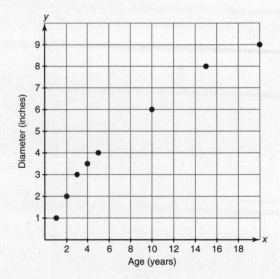

9. The scatter plot shows the weekly accumulated snowfall, in inches, for the 20 weeks of the ski season. Predict the accumulated snowfall after 11 weeks.

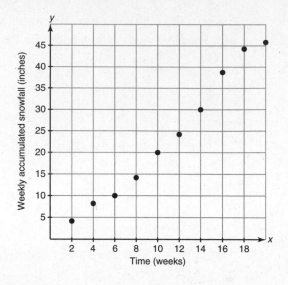

10. The scatter plot shows the water level in a reservoir given a number of days after the beginning of the year. Predict the water level at day 135.

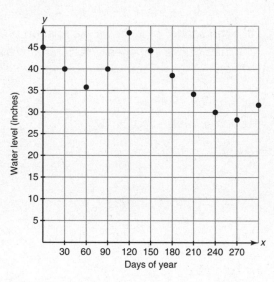

Name _____ Date _____

11. The scatter plot shows the relation between the number of people working in a restaurant and the customers' average wait time in minutes for a table. Predict the number of people working in the restaurant if a customer's average wait time for a table is 30 minutes.

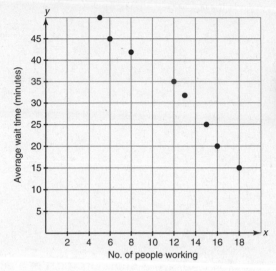

12. The scatter plot shows the relation between the diameter of a tomato in inches and its weight in pounds. Predict the diameter of a 1 pound tomato.

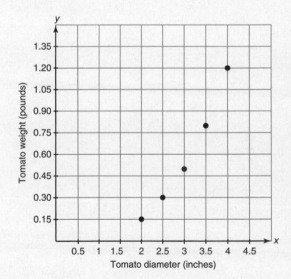

13. The scatter plot shows the cost of heating swimming pools of different sizes in gallons. Predict the size of the pool if it costs $300 to heat it.

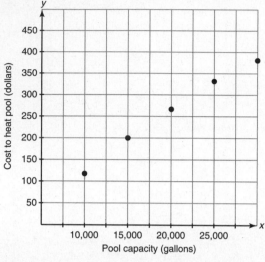

14. The scatter plot shows the cost of heating a swimming pool for different values of the average air temperature. Predict the average temperature if the pool costs $300 to heat.

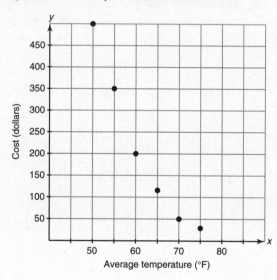

Name _____ Date _____

Write an algebraic equation to model each situation. Define the variables used in the equation.

15. Marissa has just been offered a new job. If she accepts the offer, she will receive a $150 signing bonus, plus a salary of $500 per week.

16. To lease a new car, it will cost an initial payment of $2,000 plus $225 per month.

17. Eric has 100 tickets at the beginning of his time at the amusement park. Every time he rides on one of the attractions, it will cost him 5 tickets.

18. Willa is going to knit a sweater. It cost her $10 for the pattern for the sweater, and it costs $6 for each ball of yarn she uses to knit the sweater.

Use the given information to complete each table.

19. Prints 4 U is a printing company that can print a company's name or logo on various office supplies, such as pens, mugs, and mousepads. Your boss would like to order mugs with the company's logo. Prints 4 U charges a one-time printing fee of $45 plus $3.50 per mug ordered. Use this information to complete the table.

Number of Mugs Ordered	Total Cost (dollars)
16	
25	
40	
80	

20. DVDs R Us charges a $20 membership fee and then sells DVDs for $9 each. Use the information to complete the table.

Number of DVDs Ordered	Total Cost (dollars)
15	
25	
50	
100	

21. After spending 5 hours to set up his lathe and other woodworking equipment, it takes Mario 5 minutes to create a wooden candlestick. Use this information to complete the table.

Number of Hours Working	Number of Candlesticks
5	
10	
12	
20	

22. Darren has a $600 credit at the clothing store. Each shirt costs $24. Use this information to complete the table.

Number of Shirts Bought	Remaining Credit (dollars)
5	
10	
20	
25	

Skills Practice

Name _____ Date _____

Down and Up
Linear and Absolute Value Functions

Vocabulary

Match each term with its corresponding definition.

1. linear function

    a. the unit rate of change of a linear function

2. slope

    b. the sort of symmetry that exists when a graph has two parts that are mirror images of each other

3. extreme points

    c. any function that contains an absolute value expression, such as $y = |x + 1|$

4. absolute value function

    d. a function whose graph is a line

5. line symmetry

    e. in a graph that has line symmetry, this is the line that divides the graph into two mirror images

6. line of symmetry

    f. the maximum and minimum points of a function

Problem Set

Write a linear function to model each problem situation. Define the variables used in the function.

7. A swimming pool that can hold 20,000 gallons of water is empty. It will be filled continuously at a rate of 1000 gallons per hour until it is full.

8. A helium-filled balloon has a volume of 1000 cubic inches. It gradually loses its helium at a rate of 50 cubic inches per hour until all of the helium is gone.

9. An elevator starts at the 30th floor, 300 feet above ground level, and goes down at a rate of 20 feet per second.

10. The temperature of a room is 50 degrees Fahrenheit when a heater is turned on and heats the room at a rate of 5 degrees per hour.

Write an absolute value function to model each problem situation. Define the variables used in the function.

11. A 50-gallon fish tank is emptied at a rate of 10 gallons per hour and then filled back up at the same rate until it is full.

12. An elevator starts at the 40th floor, 400 feet above the ground, and it goes down at a rate of 20 feet per second until it reaches the ground, at which point it heads back up at a rate of 20 feet per second.

1

13. The temperature in a room is 40 degrees Fahrenheit when a heater is turned on that warms the room at a rate of 4 degrees per hour until the room is 72 degrees. At that point the heater is turned off and the temperature drops at 4 degrees per hour.

14. A swimming pool that holds 30,000 gallons of water begins full and loses water at the rate of 3000 gallons per hour until it is half full, at which point water is added back into the pool at a rate of 3000 gallons per hour.

Identify the constants in each function. Then determine what each constant means in terms of the problem situation.

15. A swimming pool is full and is ready to be drained. The function $y = 18,000 - 2000x$ represents the amount of water in gallons in the swimming pool after it has been draining for x hours.

16. A room is being heated. The function $T = 50 + 5t$ represents the temperature of the room in degrees Fahrenheit after it has been heated for t hours.

17. A hot-air balloon is being filled. The function $V = 500t$ represents the volume in cubic feet of hot air in the balloon after t minutes of being filled.

18. A plane is descending for a landing. The function $A = 10{,}000 - 800t$ represents the altitude of the plane in feet after it has been descending for t minutes.

Use the given information to complete each table.

19. A silo holds 50,000 bushels of grain. When the silo is full, a conveyer is turned on, and the grain is emptied out of the silo by the conveyor at a rate of 750 bushels per hour.

Time (hours)	Amount of Grain Left in Silo (bushels)
0	
5	
24	
36	
60	
66	

20. A stadium is at its full capacity of 60,000 people. At the end of the game, the crowd exits the stadium at a rate of 2400 people per minute.

Time (minutes)	Number of People
0	
2	
5	
8	
15	
25	

Name _____   Date _____

21. A plane flying at 10,000 feet begins to ascend at a rate of 400 feet per minute until it reaches 30,000 feet.

Time (minutes)	Altitude (feet)
0	
10	
15	
25	
40	
50	

22. James has $500 in his savings account, and he decides to deposit $25 each week into the account.

Time (weeks)	Balance (dollars)
0	
3	
8	
15	
25	
50	

Graph each function. Determine the domain, range, and extrema of each function.

23. $y = x + 2$

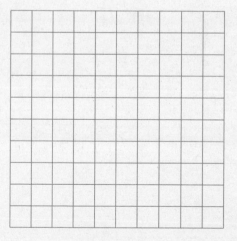

24. $y = 2x - 1$

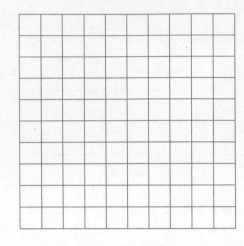

25. $y = -x + 3$

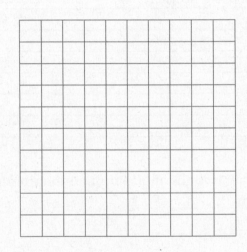

26. $y = -\dfrac{1}{2}x + 2$

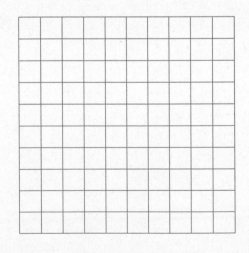

27. $y = |x + 2|$

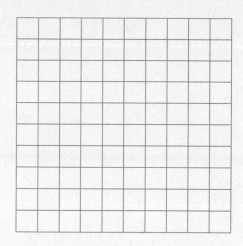

28. $y = |2x - 1|$

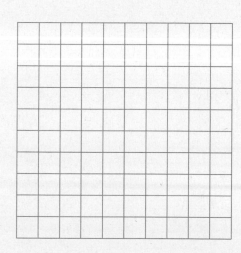

29. $y = |-x + 3|$

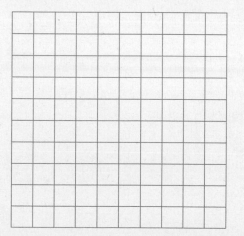

30. $y = \left| -\dfrac{1}{2}x + 2 \right|$

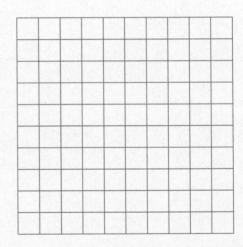

31. $y = 2 + |5x|$

32. $y = 1 - |x + 3|$

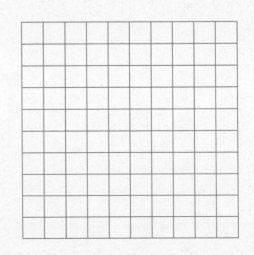

Skills Practice

Name _____ Date _____

Let's Take a Little Trip with Me!
Every Graph Tells a Story

Vocabulary

Define each term in your own words.

1. interval of increase

2. interval of decrease

3. vertical motion

4. quadratic function

Problem Set

Each graph represents the distance in miles a person is from home versus the amount of time in hours they have traveled. Describe the function in words, being sure to include the domain and range and how the distance changed from hour to hour.

5. John sets out for a walk along the beach early in the morning and returns seven hours later.

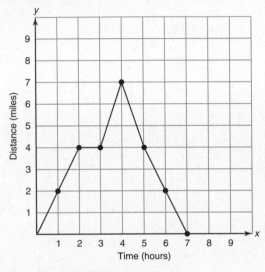

6. Peyton takes her dog for a long walk on Saturday, stopping at different places along the way.

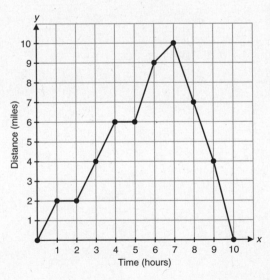

Name _____   Date _____

7. Tonya decides to walk to her friend Alexandra's house, which is 9 miles away, stay awhile, and come back home.

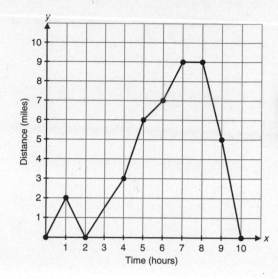

8. Tim decides to walk to his friend Ryan's house, which is 10 miles away, spend some time there, and come back home.

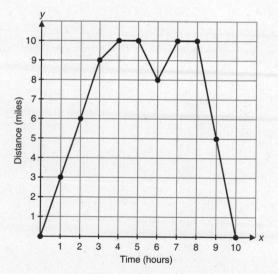

Sketch the graph of each function.

9. $y = x^2 + 1$

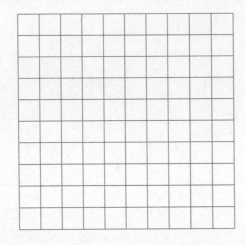

10. $y = x^2 - 1$

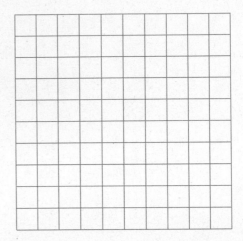

11. $y = 2x^2$

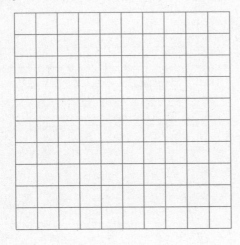

12. $y = -3x^2$

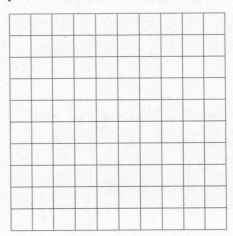

Name _____   Date _____

Determine the intervals of decrease and increase for each function.

13.

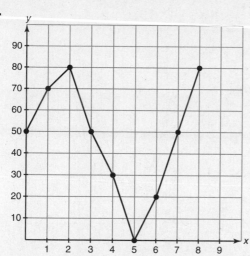

14.

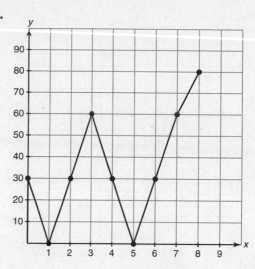

15. $y = x^2 + 3$

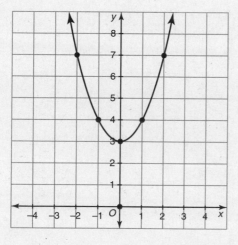

16. $y = -x^2 + 1$

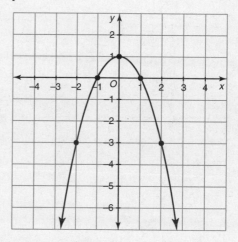

Determine the domain and range of each function shown in the graph.

17. $y = x^2 + 2x - 1$

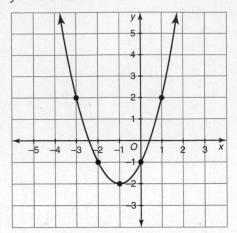

18. $y = x^2 - 4x + 5$

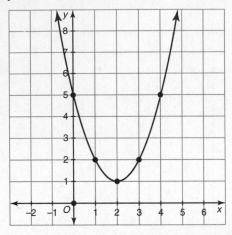

19. $y = -x^2 + 2x + 1$

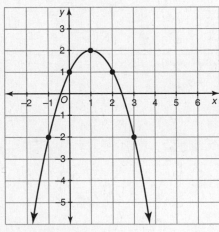

20. $y = -x^2 - 4x - 7$

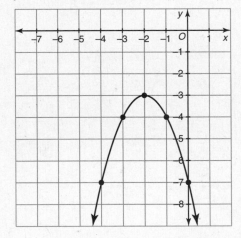

Determine the extreme point and the line of symmetry of each function shown in the graph.

21. $y = x^2 - 4x + 2$

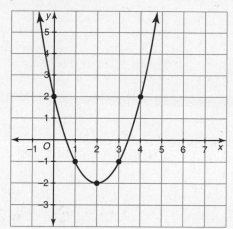

22. $y = -x^2 + 2x + 3$

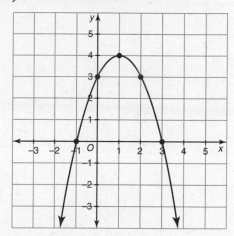

23. $y = -x^2 - 4x - 4$

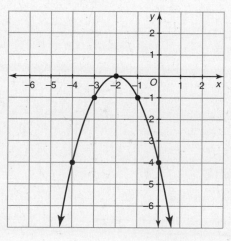

24. $y = x^2 + 2x + 3$

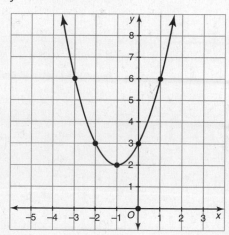

1

Skills Practice

Name _____ Date _____

Building a Better Box
Cubic and Indirect Variation Functions

Vocabulary

Provide two examples of each term.

1. cubic function

2. indirect variation function

Problem Set

Use the given information to complete each table with the appropriate measurements.

3. You are building a rectangular wading pool in your yard. You have enough materials so that the length and width of the pool, when added together, will total 20 feet. You want the depth of the pool to be half of the width of the pool. Complete the table for possible widths, lengths, depths, and volumes for the wading pool.

Width (feet)	Length (feet)	Depth (feet)	Volume (cubic feet)
0			
2			
6			
10			
16			
18			
20			

4. You are building a rectangular tool shed. You have decided that the perimeter of the tool shed will be 24 feet and that the tool shed will be twice as tall as it is wide. Complete the table for possible widths, lengths, depths, and volumes for the tool shed.

Width (feet)	Length (feet)	Height (feet)	Volume (cubic feet)
0			
3			
5			
6			
9			
10			
12			

5. You are designing a shipping crate. The perimeter must be 16 feet, and the crate must be one and a half times as tall as it is wide. Complete the table for possible widths, lengths, depths, and volumes for the shipping crate.

Width (feet)	Length (feet)	Height (feet)	Volume (cubic feet)
0			
1			
2			
4			
5			
6			
8			

6. You are building a warehouse. The length and width should add up to 100 feet, and the height should be equal to half the width. Complete the table for possible widths, lengths, depths, and volumes for the warehouse.

Width (feet)	Length (feet)	Height (feet)	Volume (cubic feet)
0			
10			
20			
50			
60			
80			
100			

Name _____ Date _____

Use the given table to create a scatter plot for the relation between the width and volume.

7. You are building a small box in the shape of a rectangular prism to hold your jewelry. You have decided that the perimeter of the base of the box will be 18 inches and that the box will be half as tall as it is wide. The table below includes some possible dimensions for the box.

Width (inches)	Length (inches)	Height (inches)	Volume (cubic inches)
0	9	0	0
1	8	0.5	4
2	7	1	14
4	5	2	40
6	3	3	54
8	1	4	32
9	0	4.5	0

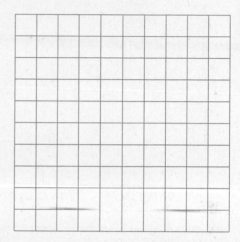

8. You are designing a large chest in the shape of a rectangular prism to store your tools. The perimeter of the base must be 20 feet, and the chest must be as tall as it is wide. The table below includes some possible dimensions for the chest.

Width (feet)	Length (feet)	Height (feet)	Volume (cubic feet)
0	10	0	0
2	8	2	32
4	6	4	96
6	4	6	144
8	2	8	128
10	0	10	0

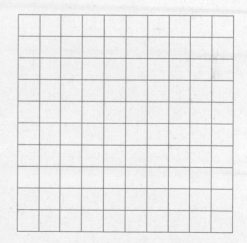

9. You are constructing a small building in the shape of a rectangular prism to house a manufacturing assembly line. The sum of the length and width should be 120 feet, and the height should be 1.2 times the width. The table below includes some possible dimensions for the building.

Width (feet)	Length (feet)	Height (feet)	Volume (cubic feet)
0	120	0	0
20	100	24	48,000
35	85	42	124,950
50	70	60	210,000
80	40	96	307,200
100	20	120	240,000
120	0	144	0

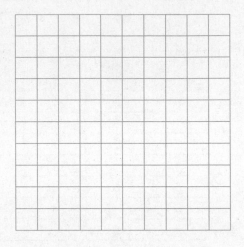

10. You are building a holding pond in the shape of a rectangular prism to hold runoff water after a storm. You have enough materials so that the length and width of the pond, when added together, will total 360 feet. You want the depth of the pond to be two-thirds the width of the pond. The table below includes some possible dimensions for the holding pond.

Width (feet)	Length (feet)	Depth (feet)	Volume (cubic feet)
0	360	0	0
30	330	20	198,000
90	270	60	1,458,000
150	210	100	3,150,000
240	120	160	4,608,000
300	60	200	3,600,000
360	0	240	0

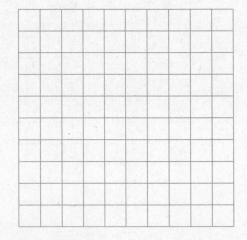

Name _____ Date _____

Use the given information to complete each table with the appropriate measurements.

11. A floor installer has 300 square feet of hardwood flooring. Complete the table with the possible lengths of a rectangular room that can be completely filled with 300 square feet of hardwood flooring.

Width (feet)	Length (feet)	Width (feet)	Length (feet)
1		20	
2		30	
3		50	
5		60	
6		100	
10		150	
15		300	

12. A wallpaper installer has 180 square feet of wallpaper to put on one rectangular wall. Complete the table with the possible widths of a rectangular wall that can be completely filled with 180 square feet of wallpaper.

Height (feet)	Width (feet)	Height (feet)	Width (feet)
1		10	
2		12	
3		15	
4		18	
5		20	
6		30	
9		60	

13. A rancher needs 480 square feet of grass to graze a single sheep. Complete the table with the possible lengths of a rectangular field that is 480 square feet.

Width (feet)	Length (feet)	Width (feet)	Length (feet)
1		16	
4		20	
6		30	
8		40	
10		60	
12		80	
15		480	

14. A gallon of paint will cover 360 square feet. Complete the table with the possible lengths of a rectangular wall that can be completely covered with a gallon of paint, assuming one coat of paint is used.

Height (feet)	Length (feet)	Height (feet)	Length (feet)
1		10	
2		12	
3		15	
4		18	
5		30	
6		60	
9		360	

Use the given information to write an equation that models the situation.

15. A box's height is two inches more than its width, and its length is two inches more than its height. Write an equation describing the box's volume in terms of its width.

16. A swimming pool's width is two feet more than half its length, and its depth is half its width. Write an equation describing the pool's volume in terms of its length.

17. A gardener has 500 square feet of sod that he wishes to set out in a rectangular area. Write an equation to represent the width of the rectangle that can be covered by 500 square feet of sod.

18. A gallon of stain covers 300 square feet of a rectangular wooden fence. What is the length of fence that can be painted with a gallon of stain in terms of its height?

1

19. The perimeter of a rectangular swimming pool is 80 feet, and its depth is one-half its width. What is an equation that describes the swimming pool's volume in terms of its width?

20. A cardboard box has a width and a length that add up to 36 inches, and its height is twice its width. What is an equation that describes the box's volume in terms of its width?

21. Charlie likes to pace in a rectangular pattern. If each of his paces is two feet long, and he takes 100 steps to pace out an entire rectangle, write an equation for the area of the rectangle that he paces in terms of the length of one of the sides.

22. Marcia is fencing off her rectangular garden. She has 80 feet of fencing. What is an equation for the area of the garden in terms of the length of one of the sides?

1

Use the given information and the graph to answer the question.

23. A rectangular water trough for horses is to be built such that the width and length add up to 6 feet and the depth is to be 1 foot more than the width. The volume of the trough is given by the formula $V = -w^3 + 5w^2 + 6w$, where w represents the width of the trough, and the graph of the function is given below. What is the largest approximate volume of the horse trough?

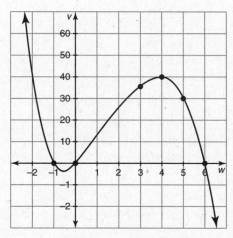

24. Jack is building a wooden chest to store his clothes. The sum of the width and length of the chest total 8 feet, while its height is the same as its width. The volume of the chest is given by the formula $V = -w^3 + 8w^2$, where w represents the width of the chest, and the graph of the function is given below. What is the largest approximate volume of the chest?

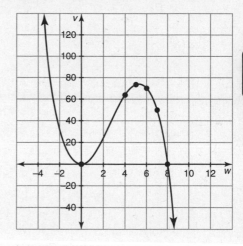

25. Suzanne has 256 square feet of flooring that she will put down in a rectangular pattern with a width w. The length of the room that can be covered with that much flooring is given by $l = \frac{256}{w}$, and the graph of the function is given below. Looking at the graph, what can you say about the maximum length of the room covered with the flooring?

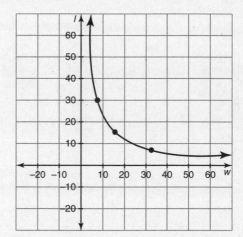

26. Federico is mapping out a garden area. It will have 400 square feet with a width of w and a length given by the formula $l = \frac{400}{w}$. The graph of the function is given below. Looking at the graph, what can you say about what happens to the length of the garden as the width gets larger?

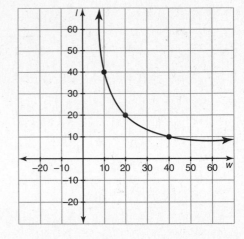

Skills Practice

Name _____ Date _____

Functional Function: *F* of *x* It Is!
Functional Notation

Vocabulary

Provide an example of each term.

1. functional notation

2. evaluate a function

Problem Set

Determine the independent and dependent variables in each situation.

3. The equation $t = 20g + 5$ represents the time, *t*, that it takes to bowl *g* games.

4. The equation $c = 12d + 8$ represents the cost, *c*, when buying *d* DVDs.

5. The equation $c = 0.44s$ represents the cost, *c*, in dollars when purchasing *s* postage stamps.

6. The equation $t = 10p + 4$ represents the time, *t*, that it takes to paint *p* fence posts.

7. The equation $g = 20m + 50$ represents the cost, *g*, in dollars of paying for *m* gym memberships.

8. The equation $m = 60h$ represents the number of revolutions, m, the minute hand of a clock makes in h hours.

Evaluate each function at the given value. Then explain what it means in terms of the problem.

9. The function $f(d) = 2d + 5$ represents the number of song downloads a person can get for d dollars. What is $f(4)$?

10. The function $f(p) = 2p + 3$ represents the amount of time in minutes it takes to wash p pots. What is $f(10)$?

11. The function $f(t) = 15t + 5$ represents the amount of time in minutes it takes to write t thank-you notes. What is $f(6)$?

12. The function $f(b) = 12b + 750$ represents the cost in dollars for printing b books with a publish-on-demand service. What is $f(100)$?

Determine the value that makes each equation true. Then explain what it means in terms of the problem.

13. The function $f(b) = 15b + 250$ represents the cost in dollars of having b books printed by a publish-on-demand book publishing company. What is the value of b such that $f(b) = 1000$?

14. The function $f(d) = d + 10$ represents the number of downloads that a person can get for d dollars. What is the value of d such that $f(d) = 50$?

15. The function $f(w) = 9w + 12$ represents the amount of time in minutes it takes a person to wash w windows. What is the value of w such that $f(w) = 75$?

2

16. The function $f(d) = \frac{9}{5}d + 32$ represents the temperature in Fahrenheit when it is d degrees in Celsius. What is the value of d such that $f(d) = 86$?

Evaluate each function for the given value.

17. If $f(x) = 3x + 5$, evaluate $f(5)$.

18. If $f(t) = 4 - 5t$, evaluate $f(2)$.

19. If $f(x) = 2x - 7$, evaluate $f(3.5)$.

20. If $f(t) = 9 - 1.5t$, evaluate $f(2.8)$.

Write a function to model each situation.

21. It takes one hour to set up a car wash and one half-hour to wash each car after everything is set up. Write a function that describes the number of hours, w, it takes to wash c cars, including setup time.

22. A movie rental club charges a one-time membership fee of $25. Movies cost $2 each to rent. Write a function that describes the cost, c in dollars, of renting m movies.

23. Lucy is 200 miles from her home and drives at a rate of 50 miles per hour towards her home. Write a function that describes the distance, d miles, she is from home after h hours of driving.

24. You go to a carnival with $100. It costs you $5 for each ride. Write a function for the amount of money you have left, m, after riding r rides.

Use each table to evaluate the function at the given value. Then explain what it means in terms of the problem.

25. The function $s(g)$ represents the number of students who received a score of g on a quiz. What is $s(80)$?

Grade on Quiz	Number of Students
0	0
10	1
20	0
30	0
40	2
50	1
60	5
70	7
80	12
90	9
100	3

26. The function $r(w)$ represents the amount of rain in inches that has fallen in the first w weeks of the year. What is $r(28)$?

Number of Weeks into the Year	Cumulative Rainfall (inches)
1	0
2	0.5
4	2
8	7
12	11
16	19
20	25.5
26	33
30	37
36	48.5
40	56.5
52	68

27. The function $h(w)$ represents the height in inches of a tomato plant w weeks after it was planted. What is $r(7)$?

Number of Weeks After Planting	Height (inches)
1	8
2	12
3	15
4	19
6	23
8	25
10	27
12	29
14	30
16	31
18	33
20	34

28. The function $s(h)$ represents the number of students in the first grade class who are h inches tall. What is $s(49)$?

Height (inches)	Number of Students
43	1
44	0
45	3
46	2
47	5
48	7
49	4
50	5
51	2
52	4
53	1

The function $r(w)$ represents the average cumulative rainfall in inches in a town after w weeks. Use the table to determine the value that makes each equation true. Then explain what it means in terms of the problem.

Number of Weeks	Cumulative Rainfall (inches)
4	2
8	6
12	11
16	17
20	24
24	30
28	36
32	41
36	45
40	51
44	55
48	57
52	60

29. $r(w) = 11$

30. $r(w) = 51$

The function $h(w)$ represents the average height in inches of a corn plant w weeks after it has been planted. Use the table to determine the value that makes each equation true. Then explain what it means in terms of the problem.

Number of Weeks After Planting	Height (inches)
1	0
2	2
3	7
4	15
5	24
6	32
7	39
8	46
9	52
10	58
11	63
12	69
13	74

31. $h(w) = 32$

32. $r(w) = 52$

Name _____   Date _____

The function *N(g)* represents the number of students in a class who received the grade *g*. Use the graph to evaluate each function. Then explain what it means in terms of the problem.

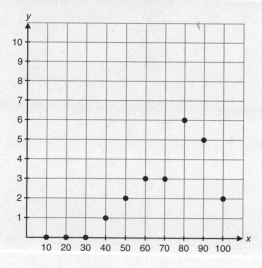

33. What is *N*(80)?

34. What is *N*(20)?

The function *T(h)* represents the temperature in degrees Fahrenheit at *h* hours past midnight. Use the graph to evaluate each function. Then explain what it means in terms of the problem.

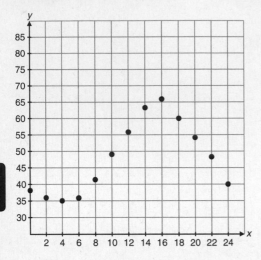

35. What is *T*(4)?

36. What is *T*(16)?

The function *T(h)* represents the temperature at *h* hours past midnight. Use the graph to determine the value that makes each equation true. Then explain what it means in terms of the problem.

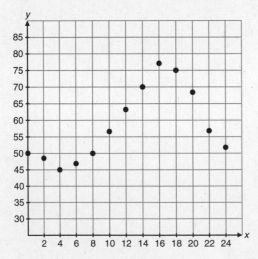

37. $T(h) = 50$

38. $T(h) = 77$

The function $S(h)$ represents the amount of merchandise in dollars that a shop sells for each hour that the shop is open during the day. Use the graph to determine the value that makes each equation true. Then explain what it means in terms of the problem.

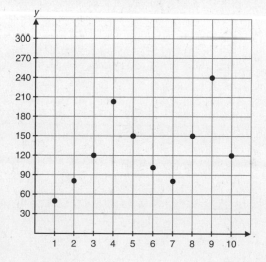

39. $S(h) = 240$

40. $S(h) = 150$

2

Name _____   Date_____

Numbers in a Row!
Introduction to Sequences

Vocabulary

Explain how each pair of terms is related by identifying similarities and differences.

1. mathematical sequence and term

2. finite sequence and infinite sequence

3. general term formula and recursive formula

Problem Set

Determine the next two terms of each sequence and describe the sequence in words.

4. 1, 3, 9, 27, …

5. $1, \frac{1}{2}, \frac{1}{4}, \frac{1}{8}, \frac{1}{16}, \ldots$

6. 3, 5, 7, 9, …

7. 16, 7, −2, −11, …

Determine the first eight terms of each sequence described.

8. The sequence of the counting numbers divided by two.

9. The sequence of the counting numbers multiplied by 3.

10. The sequence made by squaring each counting number and then subtracting the number from its square.

11. The sequence made by squaring each counting number and then adding 2.

Name _____ Date _____

Each pattern represents a sequence of numbers. Draw the next two figures in the sequence and write the terms of the sequence represented by each pattern.

12.

13.

14.

15.

Write a function whose domain is the set of counting numbers to represent each sequence.

16. 1, 4, 9, 16, 25, 36, 49, ...

17. −1, 0, 1, 2, 3, 4, 5, ...

18. 1, 3, 5, 7, 9, 11, 13, ...

19. 0, 2, 6, 12, 20, 30, 42, 56, 72, 90, ...

Use each explicit formula to write the first four terms and the tenth term of the sequence.

20. $a_n = 5n - 4$

21. $a_n = n^2 + 3$

22. $a_n = \dfrac{3}{n}$

23. $a_n = \dfrac{1}{4}(2^n)$

Write an explicit formula for each sequence.

24. 10, 15, 20, 25, …

25. 3, 9, 27, 81, …

26. 0, 3, 8, 15, 24, …

27. $\dfrac{3}{2}, \dfrac{3}{4}, \dfrac{3}{8}, \dfrac{3}{16}$

Use each recursive formula to write the first four terms of the sequence.

28. $a = \dfrac{1}{8}, a_n = 2a_{n-1}$

29. $a_1 = 5, a_n = 2a_{n-1} - 4$

30. $a_1 = 2, a_n = 3a_{n-1} + 1$

31. $a_1 = 16, a_n = \dfrac{1}{2}a_{n-1}$

Write a recursive formula for each sequence.

32. 5, 7, 9, 11, 13, 15, …

33. 5, 7, 11, 19, 35, 67, …

34. 2, 1, −1, −5, −13, −29, …

35. 2, 3, 8, 63, 3968, 15,745,023, …

2

Name _____ Date _____

Adding or Multiplying
Arithmetic and Geometric Sequences

Vocabulary

Define each term in your own words.

1. arithmetic sequence

2. geometric sequence

3. common ratio

4. common difference

Problem Set

Calculate the first four terms of each arithmetic sequence.

5. $a_n = 3n - 1$

6. $a_1 = 4, a_n = a_{n-1} + 7$

7. $a_1 = 3, a_n = a_{n-1} - 1$

8. $a_n = 4n + 5$

Determine the initial term and the common difference for each arithmetic sequence.

9. 10, 15, 20, 25, 30, …

10. 0, −2, −4, −6, −8, …

11. 31, 17, 3, −11, −25, …

12. $\frac{5}{2}$, 5, $\frac{15}{2}$, 10, $\frac{25}{2}$, …

Write a recursive formula for each arithmetic sequence.

13. 4, 12, 20, 28, 36, …

14. 10, 2, −6, −14, −22, …

15. $\frac{15}{2}$, 5, $\frac{5}{2}$, 0, $-\frac{5}{2}$, …

16. $\frac{1}{3}, 2, \frac{11}{3}, \frac{16}{3}, 7, \ldots$

Write a recursive formula and an explicit formula for each arithmetic sequence.

17. 7, 11, 15, 19, 23, ...

18. 12, 7, 2, −3, −8, ...

19. $\frac{17}{5}, 5, \frac{33}{5}, \frac{41}{5}, \frac{49}{5}, \ldots$

20. $\frac{7}{3}, 1, -\frac{1}{3}, -\frac{5}{3}, -3, \ldots$

Calculate the first four terms of each geometric sequence.

21. $a_n = 4 \cdot 3^{n-1}$

22. $a_1 = 3, a_n = 5a_{n-1}$

23. $a_1 = 5, a_n = 2a_{n-1} - 2$

24. $a_n = 5 \cdot 2^{n+1}$

Determine the initial term and the common ratio of each geometric sequence.

25. $10, 20, 40, 80, 160, \ldots$

26. $2, -4, 8, -16, 32, \ldots$

27. $3, -1, \dfrac{1}{3}, -\dfrac{1}{9}, \dfrac{1}{27}, \ldots$

28. $100, 50, 25, 12.5, 6.25, \ldots$

Write a recursive formula for each geometric sequence.

29. $4, -8, 16, -32, 64, \ldots$

30. $-\dfrac{1}{9}, -\dfrac{1}{3}, -1, -3, -9, \ldots$

31. $10, 5, \dfrac{5}{2}, \dfrac{5}{4}, \dfrac{5}{8}, \ldots$

32. $20, 4, \dfrac{4}{5}, \dfrac{4}{25}, \dfrac{4}{125}, \ldots$

Name _____ Date _____

Write a recursive formula and an explicit formula for each geometric sequence.

33. 2, −6, 18, −54, 162, …

34. $\frac{1}{16}, \frac{1}{2}, 4, 32, 256, \ldots$

35. $16, 4, 1, \frac{1}{4}, \frac{1}{16}, \ldots$

36. $30, -5, \frac{5}{6}, -\frac{5}{30}, \frac{5}{210}, \ldots$

Classify each sequence as arithmetic, geometric, or neither. If it is arithmetic or geometric, write an explicit formula for the sequence.

37. 128, 64, 32, 16, 8, …

38. 16, 27, 38, 49, 60, …

39. 4, 8, 12, 15, 18, …

40. 2, 6, 18, 54, 162, …

2

Skills Practice

Name _____   Date _____

Home, Home on the Domains and Ranges
Domains and Ranges of Algebraic Functions

Vocabulary

Provide two examples of each term. The domains and the ranges for each example should be different.

1. domain

2. range

Problem Set

Graph each function. Then determine the domain and the range of the function.

3. $y = 2x + 3$

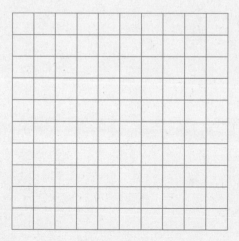

4. $y = -x - 2$

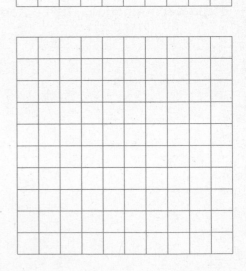

5. $y = \dfrac{1}{2}x^2$

6. $y = 1 - x^2$

7. $y = 1 + \sqrt{x}$

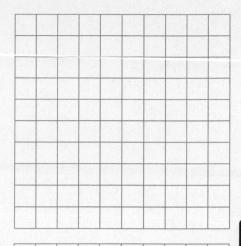

8. $y = \sqrt{-x}$

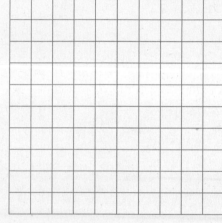

9. $y = |x + 1|$

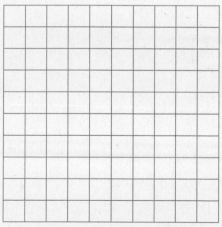

10. $y = 2 - |x|$

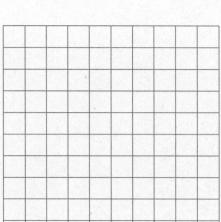

11. $y = 2$

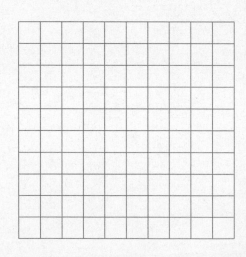

12. $y = -3$

Determine the domain and the range of each function.

13. The greatest integer function, $f(x) = \overset{\leftrightarrow}{x}$, is defined to be the greatest integer less than or equal to x. It is sometimes called the step function. Its graph is shown.

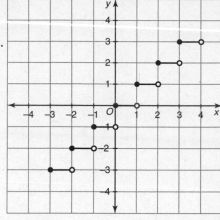

14. The graph of the function $f(x) = \sqrt{1 - x^2}$ is shown.

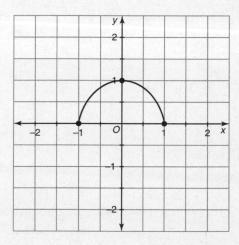

15. The graph of the function $y = x^3 - x$ is shown.

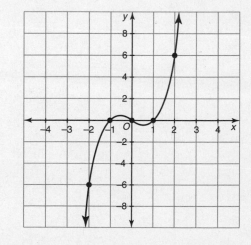

16. The graph of the function $f(x) = -\frac{1}{x}$ is shown.

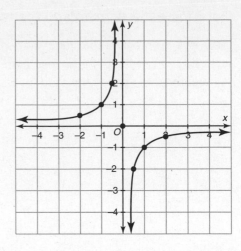

Determine the domain and range of each function. Then determine the domain and range in terms of the problem situation.

17. The commission that a car salesperson makes in dollars can be modeled by the function $f(x) = 0.05x$, where x represents his total sales in dollars.

18. A fruit market sells blueberries by the pound. The cost in dollars can be modeled by the function $f(w) = 7.75w$, where w represents the amount of blueberries in pounds.

19. A ball is tossed into the air, where it reaches a maximum height of 64 feet, and then it reaches the ground 4 seconds later. The ball's height above the ground in feet can be modeled by the function $h(t) = 64t - 16t^2$, where t is the time in seconds.

20. A single bacterium is placed in a Petri dish, and it divides to form two bacteria after one hour. Each of those bacteria divides, and so on, until after 24 hours the bacteria have used all the food in the dish, and then die. The number of bacteria can be modeled by the function $N(t) = 2^t$, where t is the time in hours.

2

2

2009 Carnegie Learning, Inc.

68   Chapter 2 ● Skills Practice

Skills Practice

Name _____ Date _____

Rocket Man
Extrema and Symmetry

Vocabulary

Write the term that best completes each statement.

1. A(n) _____ is a point where a graph crosses the x-axis.

2. A(n) _____ divides a graph in half to create two parts that are mirror images of each other.

3. A point on a graph is a(n) _____ if either all nearby points have a smaller value or all nearby points have a greater value.

4. A(n) _____ is a point where a graph crosses the y-axis.

Problem Set

Graph each function. Identify the x- and y-intercepts of the function.

5. $y = 2x + 3$

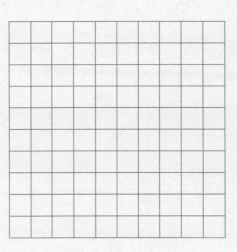

6. $y = 2 - x$

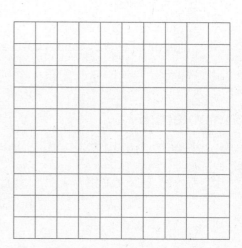

7. $y = 1 - x^2$

8. $y = x^2 - 4$

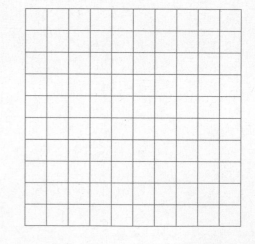

9. $y = |2x - 1|$

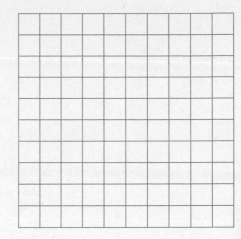

10. $y = 4 - |2x|$

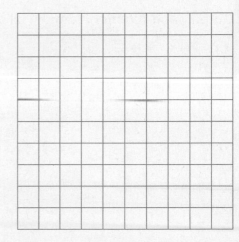

11. $y = \sqrt{x - 1}$

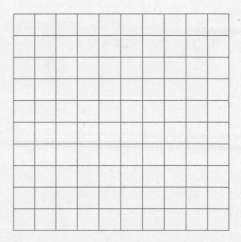

12. $y = 1 + \sqrt{x}$

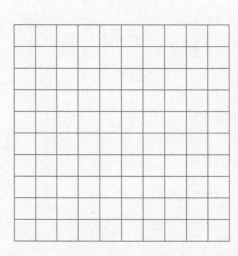

Graph each function. Identify all extreme points of the function, if any exist.

13. $y = x^2 - 2x$

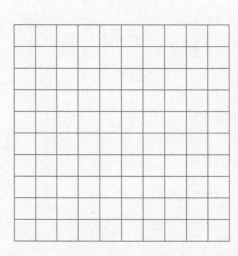

14. $y = -x^2 - 2x + 3$

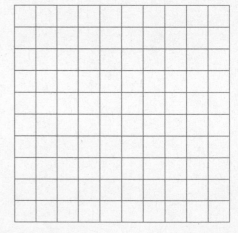

15. $y = |x - 2|$

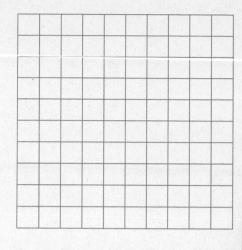

16. $y = -\frac{1}{2}|x| + 1$

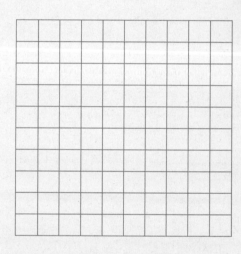

17. $y = \frac{16}{x}$

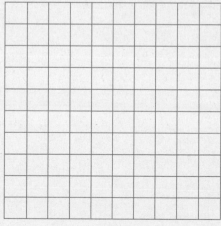

18. $y = 1 - \sqrt{x}$

2

Graph each function. Identify the line of symmetry of the function, if it exists.

19. $y = x^2 + 2x$

20. $y = -x^2 + 4x - 4$

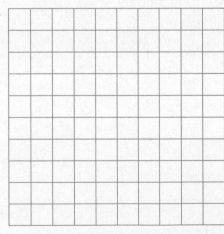

21. $y = |x + 3|$

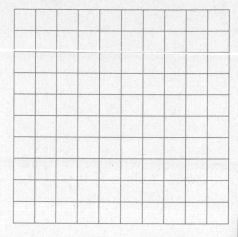

22. $y = \frac{1}{2}|x - 1| - 1$

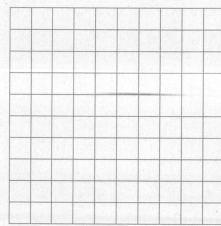

23. $y = \sqrt{x} - 2$

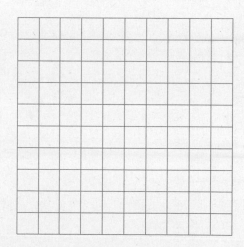

24. $y = -\dfrac{9}{x}$

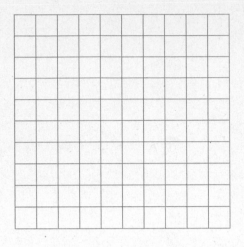

Skills Practice

Name _____   Date _____

Changing Change
Rates of Change of Functions

Vocabulary

Define each term in your own words.

1. average rate of change

2. slope

Problem Set

A function and its graph are given. Complete each table by determining the average rate of change between consecutive points. What can you say about the rates of change for each function?

3. $y = 2x - 2$

x	y	Δx	Δy	$\dfrac{\Delta y}{\Delta x}$
-4				
-1				
0				
2				
3				

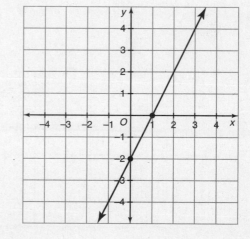

4. $y = -\dfrac{1}{2}x + 1$

x	y	Δx	Δy	$\dfrac{\Delta y}{\Delta x}$
−6				
−2				
0				
2				
4				

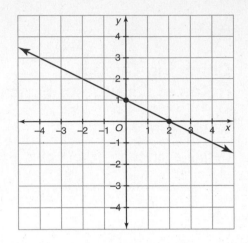

5. $f(x) = x^2 - 3$

x	y	Δx	Δy	$\dfrac{\Delta y}{\Delta x}$
−2				
−1				
0				
1				
2				

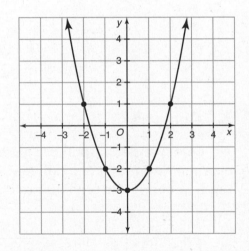

6. $g(x) = 2 - 2x - x^2$

x	y	Δx	Δy	$\dfrac{\Delta y}{\Delta x}$
−3				
−2				
−1				
0				
1				

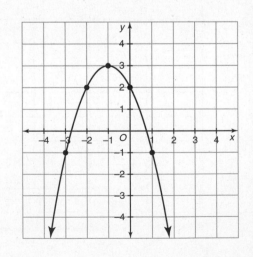

Name _____   Date _____

7. $h(x) = 2^{x-1}$

x	y	Δx	Δy	$\frac{\Delta y}{\Delta x}$
−1				
0				
1				
2				
3				

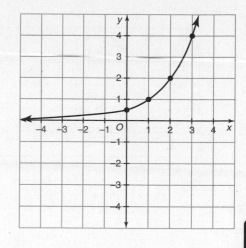

8. $h(x) = -2^{x}$

x	y	Δx	Δy	$\frac{\Delta y}{\Delta x}$
−2				
−1				
0				
1				
2				

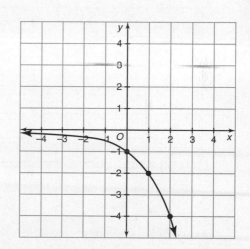

9. $g(x) = |x - 2| + 1$

x	y	Δx	Δy	$\frac{\Delta y}{\Delta x}$
0				
1				
2				
3				
4				

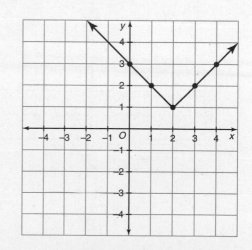

10. $y = |2x - 3|$

x	y	Δx	Δy	$\frac{\Delta y}{\Delta x}$
0				
1				
2				
3				
4				

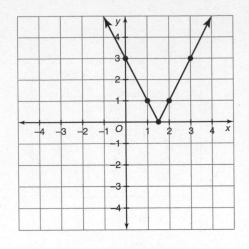

11. $h(x) = 1 - x^3$

x	y	Δx	Δy	$\frac{\Delta y}{\Delta x}$
−2				
−1				
0				
1				
2				

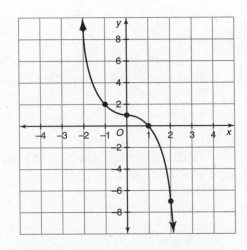

12. $p(x) = x^3 - 3x + 2$

x	y	Δx	Δy	$\frac{\Delta y}{\Delta x}$
−2				
−1				
0				
1				
2				

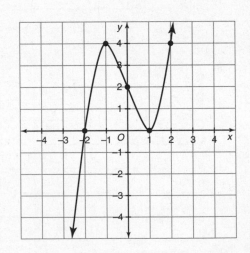

Skills Practice

Name _____ Date _____

A Little Dash of Logic
Two Methods of Logical Reasoning

Vocabulary

Define each term in your own words.

1. inductive reasoning

2. deductive reasoning

Problem Set

For each situation, identify the specific information, the general information, and the conclusion.

3. You read an article in the paper that says a high-fat diet increases a person's risk of heart disease. You know your father has a lot of fat in his diet, so you worry that he is at great risk of heart disease.

4. You hear from your teacher that spending too much time in the sun without sunblock increases the risk of skin cancer. Your friend Susan spends as much time as she can outside working on her tan without sunscreen, so you tell her that she is increasing her risk of skin cancer when she is older.

5. Janice tells you that she has been to the mall three times in the past week, and every time there were a lot of people there. "It's always crowded at the mall," she says.

6. John returns from a trip out West and reports that it was over 100 degrees every day. "It's always hot out West," he says.

3 **Determine the type of reasoning used in each situation. Then determine whether the conclusion is correct.**

7. Jason sees a line of 10 school buses and notices that each is yellow. He concludes that all school buses must be yellow. What type of reasoning is this? Is his conclusion correct? Explain.

8. Caitlyn has been told that every taxi in New York City is yellow. When she sees a red car in New York City, she concludes that it cannot be a taxi. What type of reasoning is this? Is her conclusion correct? Explain.

9. Miriam has been told that lightning never strikes twice in the same place. During a lightning storm, she sees a tree struck by lightning and goes to stand next to it, convinced that it is the safest place to be. What type of reasoning is this? Is her conclusion correct? Explain.

10. Jose is shown the first six numbers of a series of numbers: 7, 11, 15, 19, 23, 27. He concludes that the general rule for the series of numbers is $a_n = 4n + 3$. What type of reasoning is this? Is his conclusion correct? Explain.

Provide your own example of each type of reasoning. Explain your answer.

11. **deductive reasoning**

12. inductive reasoning

Write a paragraph about each type of reasoning.

13. Write a brief paragraph explaining what inductive reasoning is, as if you are telling your parents what you learned in school, and offer an example.

14. Write a brief paragraph explaining what deductive reasoning is, as if you are telling your parents what you learned in school, and offer an example.

In each situation, identify the type of reasoning that each of the two people are using. Then compare and contrast the two types of reasoning.

15. When Madison babysat for the Johnsons for the first time, she was there 2-hours and was paid $30. The next time she was there for 5-hours and was paid $75. She decided that the Johnsons were paying her $15 per hour. The third time she went, she stayed for 4-hours. She tells her friend Jennifer that she makes $15 per hour babysitting. So, Jennifer predicted that Madison made $60 for her 4-hour babysitting job.

16. When Holly was young, the only birds she ever saw were black crows. So, she told her little brother Walter that all birds are black. When Walter saw a bluebird for the first time, he was sure it had to be something other than a bird.

17. Tamika is flipping a coin and recording the results. She records the following results: heads, tails, heads, tails, heads, tails, heads. She tells her friend Javon that the coin alternates between heads and tails for each toss. Javon tells her that the next time the coin is flipped, it will definitely be tails.

18. John likes to watch the long coal trains moving past his house. Over the weeks of watching he notices that every train going east is filled with coal, but the trains heading west are all empty. He tells his friend Richard that all trains heading east have coal and all trains heading west are empty. When Richard hears a train coming from the west, he concludes that it will certainly be filled with coal.

3

Skills Practice

Name _____ Date _____

What's Your Conclusion?
Hypotheses, Conclusions, Conditional Statements, Counterexamples, Direct and Indirect Arguments

Vocabulary

Write the term that best completes each statement.

1. A(n) _____ disproves a conditional statement by supplying a specific example for which that statement is false.

2. A logical statement that has the form "If p, then q" is called a(n) _____.

3. A(n) _____ is a form of proof that contains a conditional statement, a second statement formed by the hypothesis of the conditional statement, and a conclusion formed by the conclusion of the conditional statement.

4. The _____ is the first part of a conditional statement, or the p portion of the statement "If p, then q."

5. The _____ is the second part of a conditional statement, or the q portion of the statement "If p, then q."

6. A counterexample is an example of a form of proof called _____.

7. A(n) _____ is an argument that takes the form "If q is false, then p is false."

Problem Set

Write a conditional statement using each set of words. Explain why it is a conditional statement.

8. birthday and age

© 2008 Carnegie Learning, Inc.

9. rain and umbrellas

10. reading a notice and knowing information

11. studying and grades

3

For each conditional statement, draw a solid line beneath the hypothesis. Then draw a dotted line beneath the conclusion.

12. If it is sunny tomorrow, we will go to the beach.

13. If the groundhog sees its shadow, there will be six more weeks of winter.

14. If a and b are real numbers, then $a^2 + b^2$ is greater than or equal to 0.

15. If I am smiling, then I am happy.

For each conditional statement, write a direct argument that uses the conditional statement. Then write an indirect argument that uses the conditional statement.

16. If it is the weekend, I don't have to go to school.

17. If the last digit of a number is 0, that number is divisible by both 2 and 5.

18. If a banana is green, it is not ripe.

3

19. If a candidate for President receives at least 270 electoral votes, that candidate is elected President.

For each conditional statement, write a proof by contrapositive.

20. If N is an even number, then it is divisible by 2.

21. If a and b are both greater than 0, then ab is greater than 0.

22. If I get a good night's sleep, I am not tired in the morning.

23. If the temperature drops below 20 degrees Fahrenheit, our orange tree will not survive.

For each conditional statement, write a proof by counterexample.

24. If a is a real number, then $\sqrt{a^2} = a$.

25. If a, b, c, and d are real numbers, then $(a + b)(c + d) = ac + bd$.

26. If a and b are negative integers, then $a - b$ is also a negative integer.

27. If a and b are irrational numbers, then ab is also an irrational number.

Name _____ Date _____

You Can't Handle the Truth (Table)
Converses, Inverses, Contrapositives, Biconditionals, Truth Tables, Postulates, and Theorems

Vocabulary

Explain how each set of terms is related by identifying similarities and differences.

1. inverse, converse, and contrapositive

2. truth value and truth table

3. postulate and theorem

4. propositional form and propositional variables

5. logically equivalent and biconditional statement

Problem Set

Complete the truth table for each conditional statement. Then explain what each row means in the truth table.

6. "If I can play the violin, then I can join the orchestra."

p	q	p → q
T	T	
T	F	
F	T	
F	F	

7. "If $n = 2$, then $n^2 = 4$."

p	q	p → q
T	T	
T	F	
F	T	
F	F	

8. "If a plant is an oak, then the plant is a tree."

p	q	p → q
T	T	
T	F	
F	T	
F	F	

9. "If your mode of transportation is a motorcycle, then your mode of transportation has two wheels."

p	q	$p \rightarrow q$
T	T	
T	F	
F	T	
F	F	

Write the converse of each conditional statement.

10. If today is Tuesday, then Janis has a piano lesson after school.

11. If that animal is a dog, then it has four legs.

12. If he believed that the sky is green, then he would be crazy.

13. If one book costs $10, then five books cost $50.

Write the inverse of each conditional statement.

14. If you go to the grocery store on Saturday, then there will be very long lines.

15. If Krista gets an A on her history test, then she is allowed to spend the weekend with her friend.

16. If the bus does not arrive on time, then Milo will be late for work.

17. If there is a chance of rain this weekend, then Liza will cancel her camping trip.

3

Write the contrapositive of each conditional statement.

18. If a triangle is an equilateral triangle, then all of its sides are equal.

19. If it is dark outside, then it is nighttime.

20. If there are more than 30 students in this classroom, then it is too crowded.

21. If the next animal you see is a kangaroo, then you are in Australia.

For each conditional statement, write the converse of that statement. If possible, write a true biconditional statement. If not possible, explain why.

22. If N is divisible by 10, then the last digit in N is 0.

23. If two triangles are congruent, then the triangles have equal angles.

24. If the last digit in N is 5, then N is divisible by 5.

25. If x is greater than 0, then x^3 is greater than 0.

Skills Practice

Name _____ Date _____

Proofs Aren't Just for Geometry
Introduction to Direct and Indirect Proof with the Properties of Numbers

Vocabulary

Write the term that best completes each statement.

1. For addition, the _____ states that $a + 0 = a$.

2. For multiplication, the _____ states that $ab = ba$.

3. A(n) _____ proves a statement by first assuming that the conclusion of the statement is false and then showing that such an assumption leads to a contradiction.

4. For addition, the _____ states that $a + (b + c) = (a + b) + c$.

5. For multiplication, the _____ states that $a \cdot \frac{1}{a} = 1$ if $a \neq 0$.

6. The _____ states that $a(b + c) = ab + ac$.

Problem Set

Identify whether the commutative law, associative law, identity law, inverse law of addition, or inverse law of multiplication explains why each statement is true.

7. $(5 + 3) + 4 = 5 + (3 + 4)$

8. $172.3 + (-172.3) = 0$

9. $107 \cdot \frac{1}{107} = 1$

10. $12 \cdot 23 = 23 \cdot 12$

11. $13{,}416.7 \cdot 1 = 13{,}416.7$

12. $37 + 92 = 92 + 37$

13. $13(24 \cdot 117) = (13 \cdot 24)117$

14. $16\frac{3}{5} + 0 = 16\frac{3}{5}$

15. $65 \cdot 987 = 987 \cdot 65$

16. $344 \cdot 1 = 344$

17. $555 + 333 = 333 + 555$

18. $(45 \cdot 906)11 = 45(906 \cdot 11)$

19. $65.6 + 0 = 65.6$

20. $(177 + 32) + 1714 = 177 + (32 + 1714)$

21. $4\frac{2}{3} + \left(-4\frac{2}{3}\right) = 0$

22. $32 \cdot \frac{1}{32} = 1$

Use the distributive law to calculate each value.

23. $12\ (6 + 10)$

24. $(13 + 22) \cdot 4$

25. $4\ (x + y)$

26. $13\ (a - b)$

Write a direct proof to prove each theorem.

27. If $a(b + c) = b(a + c) + ac$, then either $b = 0$ or $c = 0$ (or both).

28. If $ab + bc + ac = a(b + c)$, then either $b = 0$ or $c = 0$ (or both).

3

Write an indirect proof—in particular, proof by contradiction—to prove each theorem.

29. If $(x + a)(x + b) = x^2 + ab$ for all x, then either $a = 0$ or $b = 0$.

30. If $(a + b)c = c(a - b)$, then either $b = 0$ or $c = 0$.

Name _____ Date _____

Write an indirect proof—in particular, a counterexample—to disprove each theorem.

31. If a and b are real numbers, then $a(b + 2) = ab + 2$.

32. If a, b, and c are real numbers, then $\dfrac{a}{b + c} = \dfrac{a}{b} + \dfrac{a}{c}$.

3

Skills Practice

Name _____ Date _____

Squares and More
Using Patterns to Generate Algebraic Functions

Vocabulary

Match each word with its corresponding definition.

1. linear function

a. a series of geometric shapes that change in a predictable way from one shape to the next

2. geometric pattern

b. a series of numbers that progresses from one to the next by adding a fixed amount each time

3. arithmetic sequence

c. an expression created by combining numbers, letters, and symbols for various algebraic operations such as addition or square root

4. algebraic expression

d. a function of the form $y = ax + b$

4

Problem Set

Sketch the figure that represents the next step in each pattern.

5.

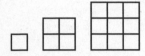

6.

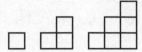

7.

8.

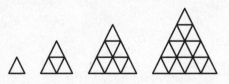

Write a formula that represents each pattern.

9.

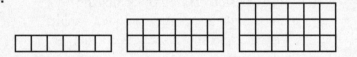

10.

Name _____ Date _____

11.

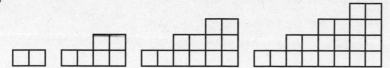

12.

Write an explicit formula to represent a general term a_n of each sequence.

13. 2, 5, 8, 11, . . .

14. 4, 11, 18, 25, . . .

15. 2, 8, 18, 32, . . .

16. 10, 13, 18, 25, 34, . . .

17. 0, 2, 6, 12, 20, . . .

18. 3, 8, 15, 24, 35, . . .

Calculate the fifth and sixth terms of each sequence.

19. $a_n = n^2 + 3n$

20. $a_n = n^2 - n + 2$

21. $a_n = 3n^2 + 1$

22. $a_n = n^3 + n$

23. $a_n = n^4 + n^2$

24. $a_n = n^3 + n^2 + n + 1$

4

Skills Practice

Name _____ Date _____

Areas and Areas
Using Multiple Representations of Algebraic Functions

Vocabulary

Explain how each set of terms is related by identifying similarities and differences.

1. domain and range

2. length of a rectangle, width of a rectangle, and area of a rectangle

4

Problem Set

Draw a diagram to represent each figure described.

3. John is designing a poster. The main body of the poster will be a square that is x inches on a side, and he will have a header running across the top that is 4 inches high.

4. Juan is designing a garden. He is working with a square plot of land that is y feet on each side. He wants to use a 5-foot strip along the top of the square as a walkway and the rest of the square plot of land will be devoted to plants.

4

5. Mary is designing a garden. She is working with a square plot of land that is *x* feet on each side. She wants to use a 3-foot strip along the right side of that square as a walkway and the rest of the square plot of land will be devoted to plants.

6. Maria is designing a poster. The main body of the poster will be a square that is *y* inches on a side, and there will be a summary running across the right that is 4 inches wide.

Write a function to represent the area of each figure described.

7. Frank is designing a sign. The main body of the sign will be a square that is *x* feet on a side, and he will have a header running across the top that is 3-feet high. Write a function to represent the area of the entire sign.

8. Jeremy is designing a garden. He is working with a square plot of land that is *s* feet on each side. He wants to use a 6-foot strip along the top of the square as a walkway and the rest of the square plot of land will be used for plants. Write a function to represent the area of the part of the garden used for plants.

9. Miriam is designing a vegetable patch. She is working with a square plot of land that is y feet on each side. She wants to use a 4-foot strip along the right side of the square plot as a walkway and the rest of the square plot will be devoted to growing vegetables. Write a function to represent the area of the part of the square plot used to grow vegetables.

10. Katarina is designing a sign. The main body of the sign will be a square that is x feet on a side, and there will be a strip running across the right side that is 5-feet wide. Write a function to represent the area of the entire sign.

Use the given information to complete each table.

11. A company is developing a neighborhood. They want each plot in the neighborhood to be a square that is x feet on a side, with a 12-foot-wide driveway along the side, as shown.

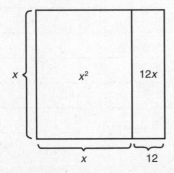

Width of Square Lot	Length of Plot	Area of Square Lot	Area of Driveway	Total Area of Plot
20				
50				
80				
100				
x				

12. A student is designing a poster. The main body of the poster will be a square that is x inches on a side, and a header will run across the top that is 6 inches high, as shown.

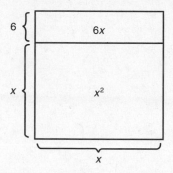

Width of Main Body	Height of Entire Poster	Area of Main Body	Area of Header	Total Area of Poster
10				
12				
15				
20				
x				

13. A company is developing a neighborhood. They want each plot to be a square lot that is y feet on a side, with a 12-foot-wide driveway within the square lot, as shown.

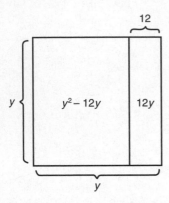

Width of Square Lot	Length of Plot not Covered by Driveway	Area of Square Lot	Area of Driveway	Area of Plot not Covered by Driveway
20				
50				
80				
100				
y				

14. A student is designing a poster. The poster will be a square that is y inches on a side. The top 4 inches of the square will be a header that runs across the top, while the remainder will serve as the main body.

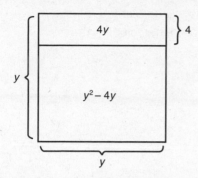

Width of Main Body	Height of Main Body	Area of Entire Body	Area of Header	Area of Main Body of Poster
10				
12				
15				
20				
y				

Graph each area function. Write the domain and range of each function in terms of the problem situation.

15. A gardener is designing a vegetable garden. She wants the garden to have a square section that is x feet across where the vegetables will be planted, plus a 10-foot-wide pathway along the side. The area of the garden, including the pathway, is represented by the function $A(x) = x^2 + 10x$.

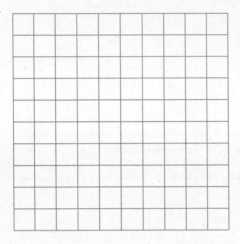

16. A gardener is planning a vegetable garden. He wants the total area to be a square that is x feet across with an 8-foot strip inside the square along the front to serve as a pathway. The planting area of the garden is represented by the function $A(x) = x^2 - 8x$.

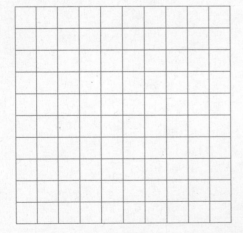

17. Carla is designing a sign. The main body of the sign will be a square that is s feet on a side, and she will have a header running across the top that is 2-feet high. Thus, the total area of the sign is represented by the function $A(s) = s^2 + 2s$.

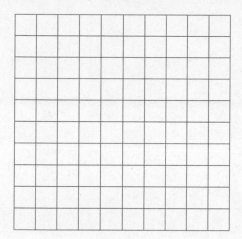

18. Roberto is designing a poster. The main body of the poster will be a square that is t inches on a side, and he will have a strip running along the side that is 12 inches wide. Thus, the total area of the poster is represented by the function $A(t) = t^2 + 12t$.

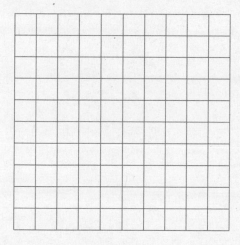

4

4

Skills Practice

Name _____ Date _____

Models for Polynomials
Operations with Polynomials

Vocabulary

Match each term with its corresponding definition.

1. binomial

2. polynomial

3. trinomial

4. monomial

a. an expression formed by adding and subtracting terms of the form ax^n

b. a polynomial with one term

c. a polynomial with two terms

d. a polynomial with three terms

4

Problem Set

For each sum or difference, sketch the resulting model. Then calculate the sum or difference.

5. $(3x + 4) + (x + 1)$

6. $(2x + 1) + (5x + 2)$

7. $(4x + 5) - (2x + 1)$

8. $(7x + 5) - (x + 3)$

9. $(2x - 3) + (-x + 1)$

10. $(-3x + 5) + (-x - 7)$

11. $(x - 3) - (2x + 4)$

12. $(2x - 5) - (-x + 2)$

Name _____ Date _____

For each product, sketch the resulting model. Then calculate the product.

13. $(x + 3)(x + 1)$

14. $(x + 2)(x + 2)$

15. $(x - 1)(x + 4)$

16. $(x - 2)(x - 3)$

4

4

Skills Practice

Name _____   Date _____

Another Factor
Dividing and Factoring Quadratic Trinomials

Vocabulary

Provide two examples of each term.

1. quadratic trinomial

2. factoring

Problem Set

Use an area model to multiply the polynomials. Check your answer by using the distributive property.

3. $(x + 1)(x + 2)$

4. $(x + 2)(x + 4)$

4

5. $(x - 1)(x + 3)$

6. $(x - 2)(x - 3)$

Use a multiplication table to multiply the polynomials. Check your answer by using the distributive property.

7. $(x - 1)(x - 5)$

8. $(x + 4)(x - 6)$

4

9. $(x + 5)(x - 12)$

10. $(x - 8)(x + 9)$

Use an area model to perform each division.

11. $(x^2 - 2x + 1) \div (x \quad 1)$

12. $(x^2 - 1) \div (x - 1)$

13. $(x^2 - 7x + 10) \div (x - 5)$

14. $(x^2 - x - 12) \div (x + 3)$

4

Use a multiplication table to perform each division.

15. $(x^2 - 7x + 6) \div (x - 1)$

16. $(x^2 - 2x - 15) \div (x - 5)$

17. $(x^2 + 5x - 24) \div (x - 3)$

18. $(x^2 + 9x + 20) \div (x + 4)$

4

Use long division to perform each division.

19. $(x^2 - 12x + 36) \div (x - 6)$

20. $(x^2 - 10x + 21) \div (x - 3)$

21. $(x^2 + 8x - 20) \div (x - 2)$

22. $(x^2 + 10x + 16) \div (x + 2)$

Use an area model to factor each trinomial.

23. $x^2 - 6x + 5$

24. $x^2 + 6x + 8$

25. $x^2 + x - 6$

26. $x^2 - 7x + 12$

4

4

Skills Practice

Name _____ Date _____

More Factoring
Factoring Quadratic Trinomials

Vocabulary

Define each term in your own words.

1. general form of a quadratic trinomial

2. factor a polynomial

Problem Set

For each trinomial, list the factor pairs of the constant term and then factor the trinomial.

3. $x^2 + 5x + 6$

4. $x^2 + 9x + 14$

5. $x^2 + 7x + 12$

6. $x^2 + 9x + 20$

7. $x^2 - x - 12$

8. $x^2 - 11x - 12$

9. $x^2 + x - 30$

10. $x^2 - 13x - 30$

11. $x^2 + 13x + 42$

12. $x^2 + 12x + 36$

13. $x^2 + 9x - 52$

14. $x^2 + 51x - 52$

15. $x^2 + 18x - 63$

16. $x^2 - 2x - 63$

17. $x^2 + 10x - 75$

18. $x^2 - 22x - 75$

4

Skills Practice

Name _____ Date _____

Radically Speaking!
Operations with Square Roots

Vocabulary

Write the term that best completes each statement.

1. The _____ is written as $\sqrt{}$.

2. A(n) _____ is a number that can be written as the square of an integer.

3. The expression under the radical symbol is called the _____ .

Problem Set

Simplify each square root completely.

4. $\sqrt{36}$

5. $\sqrt{144}$

6. $\sqrt{24}$

7. $\sqrt{45}$

8. $\sqrt{96}$

9. $\sqrt{98}$

10. $\sqrt{175}$

11. $\sqrt{192}$

Perform each multiplication and simplify completely.

12. $\sqrt{3}\sqrt{27}$

13. $\sqrt{12}\sqrt{8}$

14. $\sqrt{24}\sqrt{2}$

15. $\sqrt{36}\sqrt{4}$

16. $\sqrt{14}\sqrt{3}\sqrt{6}$

17. $\sqrt{15}\sqrt{6}\sqrt{2}$

18. $\sqrt{12}(\sqrt{3} + \sqrt{6})$

19. $\sqrt{15}(\sqrt{12} - \sqrt{5})$

20. $\sqrt{15}\sqrt{45}$

21. $\sqrt{21}\sqrt{28}$

22. $\sqrt{128}\sqrt{98}$

23. $\sqrt{75}\sqrt{147}$

24. $\sqrt{200}\sqrt{288}$

25. $\sqrt{363}\sqrt{75}$

26. $\sqrt{6}\sqrt{98}\sqrt{39}$

27. $\sqrt{21}\sqrt{35}\sqrt{30}$

4

Skills Practice

Name _____   Date _____

Working with Radicals
Adding, Subtracting, Dividing, and Rationalizing Radicals

Vocabulary

Define each term in your own words and provide at least two examples of each.

1. rational number

2. irrational number

3. rationalizing the denominator

Problem Set

Calculate each sum or difference.

4. $2\sqrt{11} + 3\sqrt{11}$

5. $7\sqrt{7} - \sqrt{7}$

6. $6\sqrt{2} - 3\sqrt{2}$

7. $\sqrt{3} + 4\sqrt{3}$

8. $4\sqrt{13} - 3\sqrt{13}$

9. $4\sqrt{17} + 13\sqrt{17}$

10. $2\sqrt{2} + 3\sqrt{8}$

11. $\sqrt{12} + 3\sqrt{3}$

12. $5\sqrt{7} - \sqrt{28}$

13. $\sqrt{20} - 4\sqrt{5}$

14. $\sqrt{2} + \sqrt{8} + \sqrt{32}$

15. $\sqrt{243} - \sqrt{27} - \sqrt{3}$

16. $\sqrt{175} - \sqrt{63} + \sqrt{98}$

17. $\sqrt{75} - \sqrt{72} - \sqrt{48}$

Calculate each quotient. Write your answer in radical form.

18. $\dfrac{\sqrt{18}}{\sqrt{2}}$

19. $\dfrac{\sqrt{48}}{\sqrt{27}}$

20. $\dfrac{\sqrt{140}}{\sqrt{45}}$

21. $\dfrac{\sqrt{91}}{\sqrt{52}}$

Simplify each expression by rationalizing the denominator.

22. $\dfrac{5}{\sqrt{15}}$

23. $-\dfrac{8}{\sqrt{4}}$

24. $-\dfrac{2\sqrt{11}}{\sqrt{55}}$

25. $\dfrac{3\sqrt{3}}{\sqrt{21}}$

Skills Practice

Name _____   Date _____

Rain Gutters
Modeling with Functions

Vocabulary

Define each term in your own words.

1. x-intercept

2. y-intercept

3. extreme point

Problem Set

Complete each table. Then write a function to represent the situation.

4. A rain gutter is made out of sheet metal that is 10 inches wide. Complete the table to show possible dimensions for the gutter. Then write a function that describes the bottom width of the gutter in terms of the side width.

Side Length (inches)	Bottom Width (inches)
1	
1.5	
2	
2.5	
3	
3.5	

5. A rain gutter is made out of sheet metal that is 7 inches wide. Complete the table to show the possible dimensions for the gutter. Then write a function that describes the bottom width of the gutter in terms of the side width.

Side Length (inches)	Bottom Width (inches)
0.5	
1	
1.5	
2	
2.5	
3	

6. A piece of paper is 11 inches high. Two equal-sized strips must be cut from the bottom, each s inches high and as wide as the paper. Complete the table to show the possible sizes for the strips and the height of the remainder of the original piece of paper. Then write a function that describes the height of the remainder in terms of the size of the strips.

Strip Size (inches)	Height of Remainder (inches)
1	
1.5	
2	
2.5	
3	
3.5	

7. A piece of poster board is 24 inches across. Three strips are cut from along the side of the poster board, each *w* inches wide. Complete the table to show the possible widths for the strips and the width of the remaining poster board. Then write a function that describes the width of the remaining poster board in terms of the width of the strips.

Width of Strips (inches)	Remaining Width (inches)
1	
2	
3	
4	
5	
6	

Graph each function. Write the domain and range of the problem situation.

8. A piece of paper is 14 inches high. Two equal-sized strips are cut from the bottom, each *s* inches high and as wide as the paper, so that the height of the remaining piece can be written as $h(s) = 14 - 2s$.

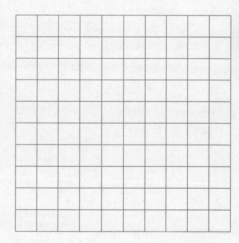

9. A piece of poster board is 36 inches across. Three strips are cut from along the side of the poster board, each *w* inches wide, so that the width of the remaining poster can be written as $p(w) = 36 - 3w$.

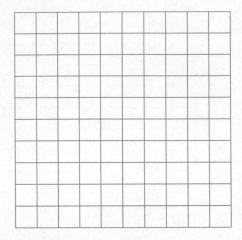

10. A piece of wood is 20 feet long. If four lengths are cut from it, each *l* feet long, the remaining length is given by the function $w(l) = 20 - 4l$.

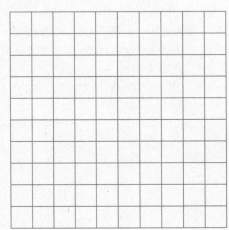

11. A bathtub has 36 gallons of water in it. If the water starts to drain out at a rate of 4 gallons per minute, the amount of water in the tub after t minutes is given by $q(t) = 36 - 4t$.

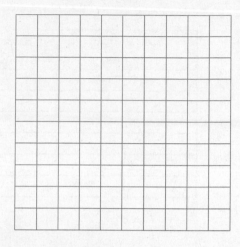

Complete each table. Then write a function to represent the situation.

12. A rain gutter is made out of sheet metal that is 10 inches wide. Complete the table to show possible side lengths for the gutter and the resulting cross-sectional area. Then write an equation for the cross-sectional area of the gutter with a side length of l inches.

Side Length (inches)	Cross-Sectional Area (square inches)
1	
1.5	
2	
2.5	
3	
3.5	

13. A rain gutter is made out of sheet metal that is 7 inches wide. Complete the table to show possible side lengths for the gutter and the resulting cross-sectional area. Then write an equation for the cross-sectional area of the gutter with a side length of l inches.

Side Length (inches)	Cross-Sectional Area (square inches)
0.5	
1	
1.5	
2	
2.5	
3	

14. A rancher has 1000 feet of fencing to build a rectangular fence with one of the sides s feet long. Complete the table to show possible lengths for that side of the fence and the resulting area of the region inside the fence. Then write an equation for the area of the region inside the fence with one side s feet long.

Side Length (feet)	Fenced-in Area (square feet)
100	
200	
250	
300	
400	

4

Name _____ Date _____

15. A rancher has 1000 feet of fencing to fence a rectangular field. One side of the field
has a stone wall running along it, so he only needs to install three sides of fencing.
The length of a side of the fence that is not parallel to the wall is s feet long.
Complete the table to show possible lengths for the side s of the fence and the
resulting area of the field. Then write an equation for the area of the fenced field.

Side Length (feet)	Area of Fenced Field (square feet)
100	
200	
250	
300	
400	

Graph each function. Then determine the x- and y-intercepts.

16. A rectangular wooden frame is made from a piece of wood that is 24 feet long by
cutting two pieces that are l feet long and two pieces that are $(12 - l)$ feet long.
The area of the frame is given by $A(l) = 12l - l^2$.

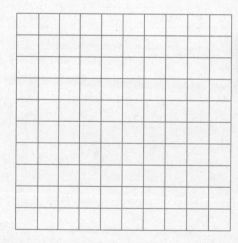

17. A rectangular wooden frame with a brace in the middle is made from a piece of wood 30 feet long by cutting three pieces that are l feet long and two pieces that are $\left(15 - \frac{3}{2}l\right)$ feet long. The area of the frame is given by $A(l) = 15l - \frac{3}{2}l^2$.

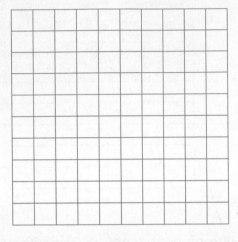

18. A rancher has 1600 feet of fencing to fence a rectangular field with one pair of sides being s feet long. The area of the field is given by the function $A(s) = 800s - s^2$.

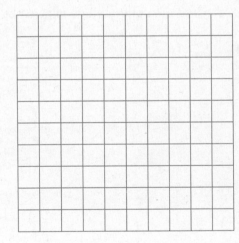

19. A rancher has 1600 feet of fencing to fence off a rectangular field that has a stone wall running along one side of it. The sides that intersect the stone wall are s feet long. The area of the field is given by the function $A(s) = 1600s - 2s^2$.

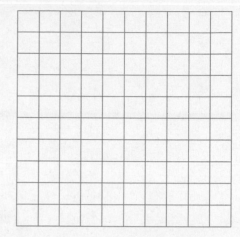

4

Skills Practice

Name _____ Date_____

More Areas
More Modeling with Functions

Vocabulary

Write the term that best completes each statement.

1. A _____ is a function of the form $f(x) = ax^2 + bx + c$.

2. A mathematical expression can sometimes be divided into _____ that, when multiplied together, give the original expression.

3. The _____ of a rectangle is calculated by multiplying the rectangle's width and the rectangle's length.

Problem Set

Draw a diagram to represent each figure described. Then write an expression for the total area of the figure.

4. A developer plans plots of land in which each has a rectangular lot that is twice as long as it is wide. A 4-foot walkway runs along the two longer sides and the back of each rectangular lot. A 12-foot driveway runs across the front of the entire plot. Draw a diagram of the entire plot. Let w represent the width of the rectangular lot. Label all dimensions in the diagram. Then write a simplified expression to represent the total area of the plot.

5. Maria is creating a cover for her family album. The album cover is a rectangle and has a rectangular photo of Maria's family that is twice as long across the bottom as it is tall. A 2-inch border runs along the two shorter sides of the photo and along the top of the photo. A 4-inch name plate runs the entire length of the bottom of the album. Draw a diagram of the entire album cover. Let x represent the length across the bottom of the photo. Label all dimensions in the diagram. Then write a simplified expression to represent the total area of the album cover.

6. A square piece of poster board is l inches on each side. Suppose that a 4-inch strip is cut off along the top and then a 3-inch strip is cut off of either side. Draw a diagram that shows all of the pieces; label all of the dimensions. Then write a simplified expression to represent the area of the poster board after the strips have been cut off.

4

7. A rectangular piece of paper is *l* inches wide and twice as long as it is wide. Suppose that a 5-inch strip is cut off along the top and the bottom and then a 5-inch strip is cut off of either side. Draw a diagram that shows all of the pieces; label all of the dimensions. Then write a simplified expression to represent the area of the paper after the strips have been cut off.

8. Joseph is planning a rectangular garden. The planted area will have a width *w* feet and a length that is 3 times its width. There will be 5-foot pathways along both of the longer sides and 3-foot pathways along both of the shorter sides. Draw a diagram that shows all the sections; label the dimensions. Then write a simplified expression to represent the area of the entire garden.

9. A developer is planning a parking lot. The parking section will have a width of w feet and a length that is 4 times its width. There will be a 20-foot roadway along one of the long sides, and 4-foot sidewalks around the other three edges that extend along the roadway. Draw a diagram that shows all the sections; label the dimensions. Then write a simplified expression to represent the area of the entire parking lot.

Use the given information to calculate the indicated area.

10. You put a rectangular swimming pool in your backyard. The pool is 12 feet longer than it is wide. A 6-foot walkway runs along the two longer sides and one of the shorter sides of the pool. A 10-foot deck runs across the other shorter side and across the walkway. Write an expression to model the area of the pool, walkway, and deck combined, in terms of the total width times the total length. Then determine the area if the width of the pool is 16 feet.

11. Carlos constructs a rectangular sign for student council. The main text area is 10 inches wider than it is tall. There is a 3-inch border on both sides and the bottom. A 6-inch header stretches across the top, including across the borders. Write an expression to model the total area of the sign in terms of the total height and the total width. Then determine that area if the height of the text area is 20 inches.

12. A developer designs a rectangular parking lot. It will be 100 feet longer than it is wide. There will be a 20-foot driveway (along one of the longer sides and one of the shorter sides), and there will be a 5-foot sidewalk (along the other two sides) that also extends along the driveway. Write an expression to model the total area of the parking lot in terms of the total length times the total width. Then determine that area if the width of the parking lot is 200 feet.

13. Karen is planning a rectangular garden. The planting area will be 20-feet longer than it is wide. There will be 3-foot pathways along both of the longer sides, and 5-foot pathways extending along the shorter sides (including the other pathways). Write an expression to model the total area of the garden in terms of the total length times the total width. Then determine that area if the width of the garden area is 30 feet.

Use the given information to calculate each width.

14. A poster is designed so that its center section is a square and there are 2-inch borders on the two sides and the bottom and a 4-inch border on the top. An expression for the total area of the poster in terms of the width, x, of the center section is $A(x) = x^2 + 10x + 24$. If the total area of the poster is 168 square inches, calculate its dimensions.

15. The total area of a rectangular plot of land is given by $A(x) = (x + 16)(x + 20)$, where the first factor represents its width in yards and the second factor represents its length in yards. If the total area is equal to 2300 square yards, find the dimensions of the plot of land.

16. The total area of a rectanglar garden is given by $A(x) = (x + 4)(x + 10)$, where the first factor represents its width and the second factor represents its length. If the total area is equal to 520 square feet, find the dimensions of the garden.

17. The total area of a rectangular poster is given by $A(x) = (x + 3)(x + 7)$, where the first factor represents its width in inches and the second factor represents its length in inches. If the total area of the poster is equal to 320 square inches, find the dimensions of the poster.

Skills Practice

Name _____   Date _____

Properties of Triangles
Angle Relationships in a Triangle

Vocabulary

Match each word with its definition.

1. acute triangle

    a. an angle formed by one side of a triangle and an extension of another side

2. obtuse triangle

    b. The measure of an exterior angle of a triangle is greater than the measure of either of its remote interior angles.

3. right triangle

    c. a triangle with three equal angles

4. equiangular triangle

    d. a triangle with three acute angles

5. exterior angle

    e. a triangle that has one right angle

6. remote interior angles

    f. a triangle with one obtuse angle

7. Exterior Angle Inequality Theorem

    g. the two angles of a triangle that are not supplementary to a given exterior angle

Problem Set

Classify each triangle as acute, obtuse, right, or equiangular.

8.

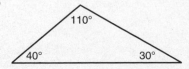

9.

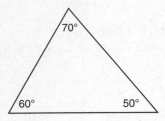

10.

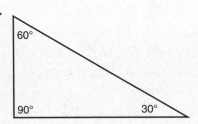

11.

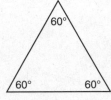

12.

13.

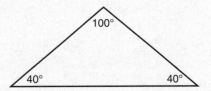

14.

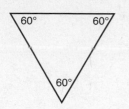

15.

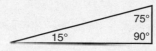

16.

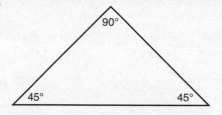

17.

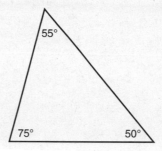

18.

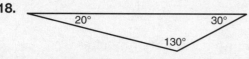

19.

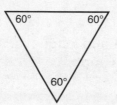

20.

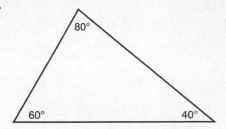

21.

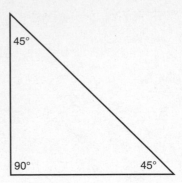

22.

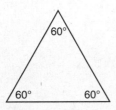

23.

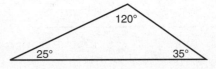

Identify the shortest and longest side of each triangle. Identify any sides that have the same length.

24.

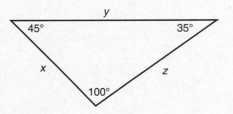

25.

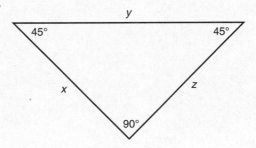

26.

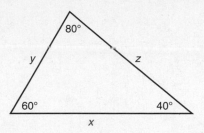

27.

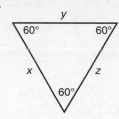

28.

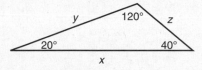

29.

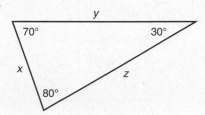

Identify the remote interior angles of each exterior angle.

30.

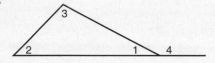

31.

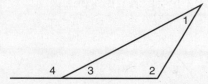

32.

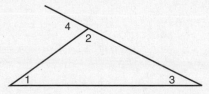

33.

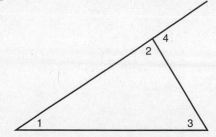

Identify the exterior angle of each triangle.

34.

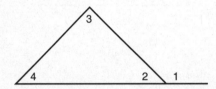

35.

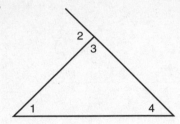

36.

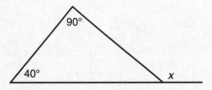

37.

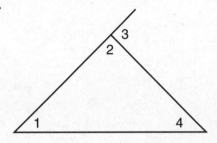

Solve for *x* in each triangle.

38.

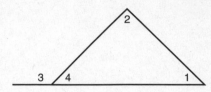

39.

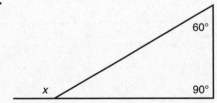

Name _____   Date _____

40.

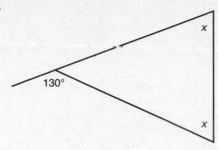

41.

42.

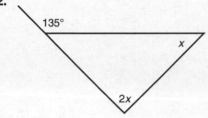

43.

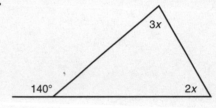

Use the Exterior Angle Inequality Theorem to describe the angles of each triangle.

44.

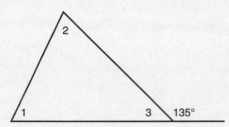

45.

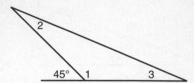

46.

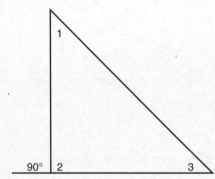

47.

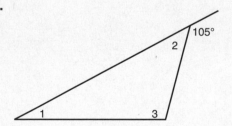

Skills Practice

Name _____ Date _____

Properties of Triangles
Side Relationships of a Triangle

Vocabulary

Define each term in your own words.

1. scalene triangle

2. isosceles triangle

3. equilateral triangle

Problem Set

Identify each triangle as scalene, isosceles, or equilateral.

4.

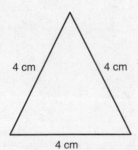

5.

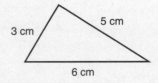

6.

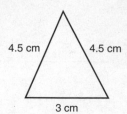

4.5 cm   4.5 cm

3 cm

7.

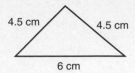

4.5 cm   4.5 cm

6 cm

8.

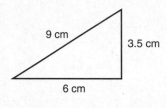

9 cm

3.5 cm

6 cm

9.

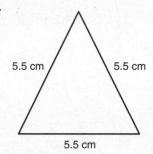

5.5 cm   5.5 cm

5.5 cm

10.

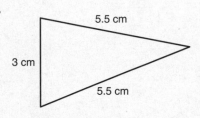

5.5 cm

3 cm

5.5 cm

11.

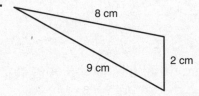

8 cm

9 cm   2 cm

12.

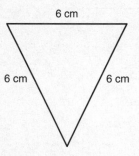

6 cm

6 cm   6 cm

13.

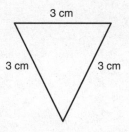

3 cm

3 cm   3 cm

5

14.

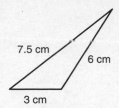

15.

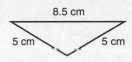

Identify the smallest and largest angle in each triangle. Identify any angles that have the same measure.

16.

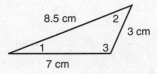

17.

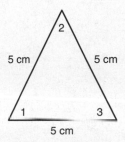

18.

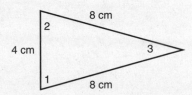

19.

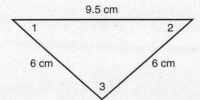

20.

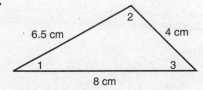

21.

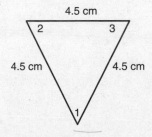

5

22.

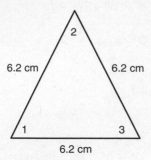

23.

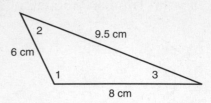

24.

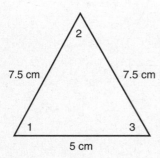

25.

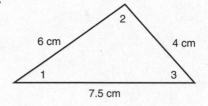

26.

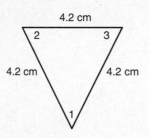

27.

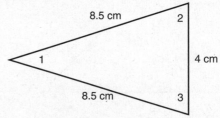

Name _____ Date _____

Explain why the Triangle Inequality Theorem is true for each triangle.

28.

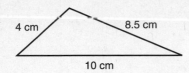

29.

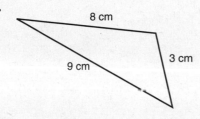

30.

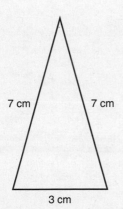

31.

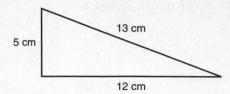

32.

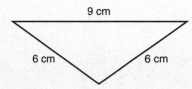

33.

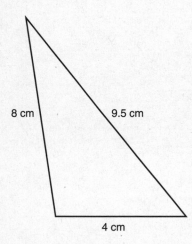

Name _____ Date _____

Determine whether each set of segment lengths can form a triangle.

34. 4 cm, 6 cm, 9 cm

35. 4 in., 6 in., 10 in.

36. 12 ft, 12 ft, 25 ft

37. 2 m, 20 m, 21 m

38. 17 yd, 18 yd, 32 yd

39. 12 mm, 13 mm, 30 mm

40. 1 in., 11 in., 12 in.

41. 14 cm, 14 cm, 20 cm

5

5

Skills Practice

Name _____ Date _____

Properties of Triangles
Points of Concurrency

Vocabulary

Write the term that best completes each statement.

1. A(n) _____ is a line that divides a segment into two smaller segments of equal length.

2. The _____ of a triangle is the point at which the three medians intersect.

3. Three or more lines that intersect at a common point are called _____.

4. A(n) _____ of a triangle is a line segment that connects a vertex to the midpoint of the side opposite the vertex.

5. The _____ of a triangle is the point at which the three perpendicular bisectors intersect.

6. The point at which three or more lines intersect is called the _____.

7. A(n) _____ is a segment bisector that is also perpendicular to the line segment.

8. The _____ of a triangle is the point at which the three angle bisectors intersect.

9. To divide an angle into two smaller angles of equal measure is to _____.

10. A perpendicular line segment that is drawn from a vertex to the opposite side is called an _____.

11. A(n) _____ is a line that divides an angle into two smaller angles of equal measure.

12. The _____ of a triangle is the point at which the three altitudes intersect.

13. To divide a segment into two smaller segments of equal length is to _____.

Problem Set

Use a compass and straightedge to construct an angle bisector of each angle.

14.

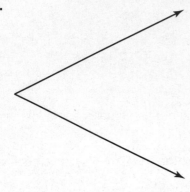

15.

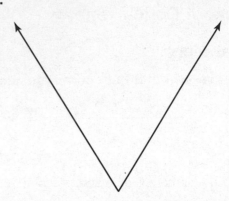

16.

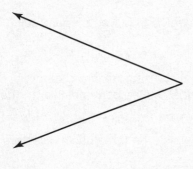

17.

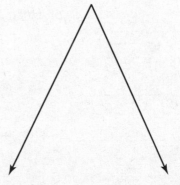

Trace each angle onto patty paper and construct an angle bisector on the patty paper.

18.

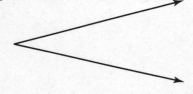

19.

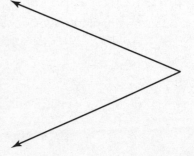

20.

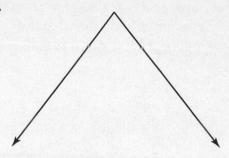

21.

Use a compass and straightedge to construct angle bisectors for each angle of the triangle to construct the incenter of the triangle. Then, using patty paper, trace the triangle and construct the incenter on the patty paper to see if you get the same result.

22.

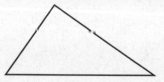

23.

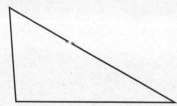

24.

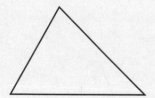

25.

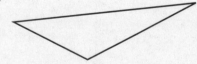

Use a compass and straightedge to construct the perpendicular bisector of each line segment. Then, using patty paper, trace the line segment and construct a perpendicular bisector with the patty paper to see if you get the same result.

26.

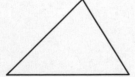

27.

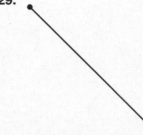

28.

29.

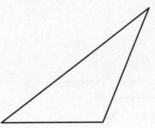

Use a compass and straightedge to construct the perpendicular bisector of each side of the triangle and then construct the circumcenter of the triangle.

30.

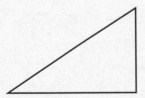

31.

32.

33.

Name _____   Date _____

34.

35.

Use a compass and straightedge to construct the three medians of the triangle and construct the centroid. Then, using patty paper, trace the triangle and construct the centroid with the patty paper to see if you get the same result.

36.

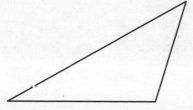

37.

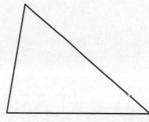

38.

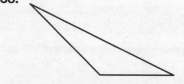

39.

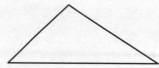

Use a compass and straightedge to construct the three altitudes of the triangle and construct the orthocenter. Then, using patty paper, trace the triangle and construct the orthocenter with the patty paper to see if you get the same result.

40.

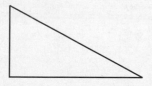

41.

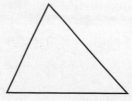

5

42.

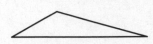

43.

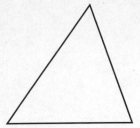

44.

Compare the parts of the given types of triangles.

45. Compare the placement of the incenter and circumcenter for acute, obtuse, and right triangles.

46. Compare the placement of the incenter and centroid for acute, obtuse, and right triangles.

5

47. Compare the placement of the incenter and orthocenter for acute, obtuse, and right triangles.

48. Compare the placement of the circumcenter and centroid for acute, obtuse, and right triangles.

49. Compare the placement of the circumcenter and orthocenter for acute, obtuse, and right triangles.

50. Compare the placement of the centroid and orthocenter for acute, obtuse, and right triangles.

5

Skills Practice

Name _____ Date _____

Properties of Triangles
Direct and Indirect Proof

Vocabulary

Write the term that best completes each statement.

1. A(n) _____ is a way of writing a proof such that each step is listed in one column and the reason for each step is listed in the other column.

2. The _____ says an exterior angle of a triangle is greater than either of the two remote interior angles of the triangle.

3. According to the _____ , if $a = b + c$ and $c > 0$, then $a > b$.

4. The _____ says that the measure of an exterior angle of a triangle is equal to the sum of the measures of the two remote interior angles of the triangle.

5. The _____ means assuming the opposite of the conclusion.

5

Problem Set

For the triangle shown, use a direct proof to prove each statement.

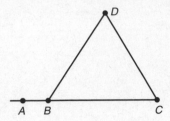

6. $m\angle ABD > m\angle C$

Statements	Reasons
1. Angle *ABD* is an exterior angle of triangle *BCD*.	**1.** Given
2.	**2.**
3.	**3.**
4.	**4.**
5.	**5.**
6.	**6.**
7.	**7.**

7. $m\angle ABD > m\angle D$

Statements	Reasons
1. Angle *ABD* is an exterior angle of triangle *BCD*.	**1.** Given
2.	**2.**
3.	**3.**
4.	**4.**
5.	**5.**
6.	**6.**
7.	**7.**

5

For the triangle shown, use a direct proof to prove each statement.

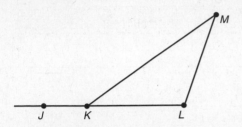

8. $m\angle JKM > m\angle L$

Statements	Reasons
1. Angle *JKM* is an exterior angle of triangle *KLM*.	1. Given
2.	2.
3.	3.
4.	4.
5.	5.
6.	6.
7.	7.

9. $m\angle JKM > m\angle M$

Statements	Reasons
1. Angle *JKM* is an exterior angle of triangle *KLM*.	**1.** Given
2.	**2.**
3.	**3.**
4.	**4.**
5.	**5.**
6.	**6.**
7.	**7.**

10. Complete the direct proof.

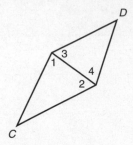

Given: $m\angle 1 = m\angle 4$, $m\angle 2 = m\angle 3$

Prove: $m\angle C = m\angle D$

Statements	Reasons
1.	1.
2.	2.
3.	3.
4.	4.
5.	5.
6.	6.
7.	7.

11. Complete the direct proof.

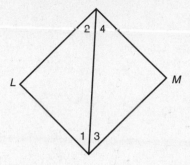

Given: $m\angle 1 = m\angle 4$, $m\angle 2 = m\angle 3$

Prove: $m\angle L = m\angle M$

Statements	Reasons
1.	1.
2.	2.
3.	3.
4.	4.
5.	5.
6.	6.
7.	7.

For the triangle shown, use an indirect proof with proof by contradiction to prove each statement.

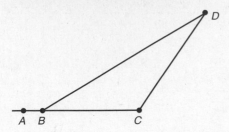

12. $m\angle ABD > m\angle C$

Statements	Reasons
1. Angle *ABD* is an exterior angle of triangle *BCD*.	**1.** Given
2.	**2.**
3.	**3.**
4.	**4.**
5.	**5.**
6.	**6.**
7.	**7.**
8.	**8.**
9.	**9.**
10.	**10.**

13. $m\angle ABD > m\angle D$

Statements	Reasons
1. Angle *ABD* is an exterior angle of triangle *BCD*.	**1.** Given
2.	**2.**
3.	**3.**
4.	**4.**
5.	**5.**
6.	**6.**
7.	**7.**
8.	**8.**
9.	**9.**
10.	**10.**

5

For the triangle shown, use an indirect proof with proof by contradiction to prove each statement.

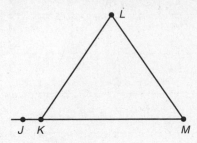

14. $m\angle JKL > m\angle M$

Statements	Reasons
1. Angle *JKL* is an exterior angle of triangle *KLM*.	**1.** Given
2.	**2.**
3.	**3.**
4.	**4.**
5.	**5.**
6.	**6.**
7.	**7.**
8.	**8.**
9.	**9.**
10.	**10.**

15. $m\angle JKL > m\angle L$

Statements	Reasons
1. Angle *JKL* is an exterior angle of triangle *KLM*.	**1.**
2.	**2.**
3.	**3.**
4.	**4.**
5.	**5.**
6.	**6.**
7.	**7.**
8.	**8.**
9.	**9.**
10.	**10.**

5

16. Complete the proof using an indirect proof.

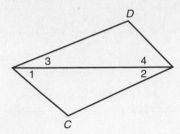

Given: $m\angle 1 = m\angle 4$, $m\angle 2 = m\angle 3$

Prove: $m\angle C = m\angle D$

Statements	Reasons
1.	1.
2.	2.
3.	3.
4.	4.
5.	5.
6.	6.
7.	7.
8.	8.

Name _____ Date _____

17. Complete the proof using an indirect proof.

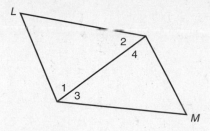

Given: $m\angle 1 = m\angle 4, m\angle 2 = m\angle 3$

Prove: $m\angle L = m\angle M$

Statements	Reasons
1.	1.
2.	2.
3.	3.
4.	4.
5.	5.
6.	6.
7.	7.
8.	8.

5

5

Skills Practice

Name _____ Date _____

Computer Graphics
Proving Triangles Congruent: SSS and SAS

Vocabulary

Match each term with its definition.

1. Side-Side-Side Congruence Theorem

a. If two pairs of corresponding sides of triangles are congruent, and the included angles are congruent, the triangles themselves are congruent.

2. Side-Angle-Side Congruence Theorem

b. a proof written in paragraph form

3. paragraph proof

c. If the corresponding sides of two triangles are congruent, then the triangles themselves are congruent.

5

Problem Set

Complete the two-column proof and use the Side-Side-Side Similarity
Postulate to prove that the two triangles are congruent.

4.

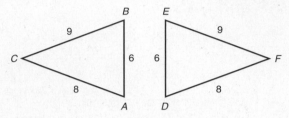

Statements	Reasons
1.	**1.** Given
2.	**2.** Division Property of Equality
3. $\dfrac{AB}{DE} = \dfrac{BC}{EF} = \dfrac{CA}{FD}$	**3.**
4.	**4.** SSS Similarity Postulate
5.	**5.** Definition of similar triangles
6. $\triangle ABC \cong \triangle DEF$	**6.**

5.

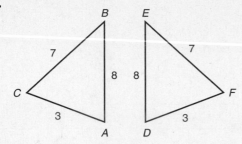

Statements	Reasons
1. $AB = DE = 8$, $BC = EF = 7$, $CA = FD = 3$	**1.**
2. $\dfrac{AB}{DE} = 1$, $\dfrac{BC}{EF} = 1$, $\dfrac{CA}{FD} = 1$	**2.**
3.	**3.** Transitive Property of Equality
4. $\triangle ABC \sim \triangle DEF$	**4.**
5.	**5.** Definition of similar triangles
6.	**6.** Definition of congruence

6.

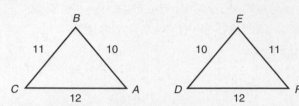

Statements	Reasons
1.	**1.** Given
2.	**2.** Division Property of Equality
3. $\dfrac{AB}{DE} = \dfrac{BC}{EF} = \dfrac{CA}{FD}$	**3.**
4.	**4.** SSS Similarity Postulate
5. $\angle A \cong \angle D, \angle B \cong \angle E, \angle C \cong \angle F$	**5.**
6.	**6.** Definition of congruence

7.

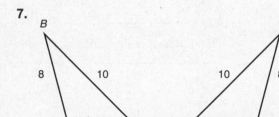

Statements	Reasons
1. $AB = DE = 10, BC = EF = 8, CA = FD = 4$	**1.**
2.	**2.** Division Property of Equality
3. $\dfrac{AB}{DE} = \dfrac{BC}{EF} = \dfrac{CA}{FD}$	**3.**
4.	**4.** SSS Similarity Postulate
5. $\angle A \cong \angle D, \angle B \cong \angle E, \angle C \cong \angle F$	**5.**
6.	**6.** Definition of congruence

5

Name _____   Date _____

Use either the Side-Side-Side Congruence Theorem or the Side-Angle-Side Congruence Theorem to show that each pair of triangles is congruent.

8.

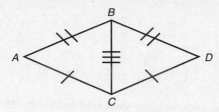

9.

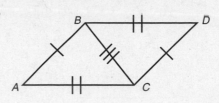

10.

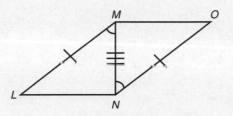

11.

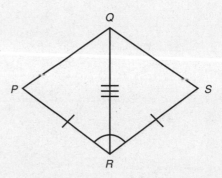

12.

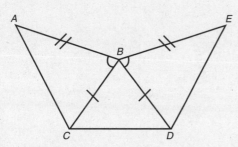

13.

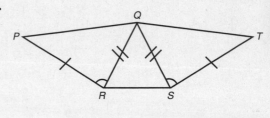

14.

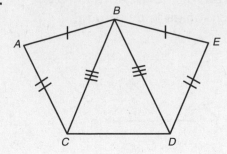

15.

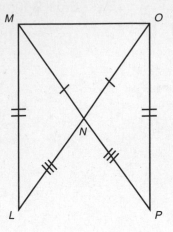

Skills Practice

Name _____ Date _____

Wind Triangles
Proving Triangles Congruent: ASA and AAS

Vocabulary

Explain the similarities and differences between the two terms.

1. Angle-Side-Angle Congruence Postulate and Angle-Angle-Side Congruence Theorem

Problem Set

Use the ASA Postulate to show that each pair of triangles is congruent.

2.

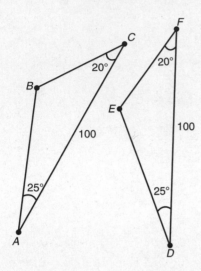

3.

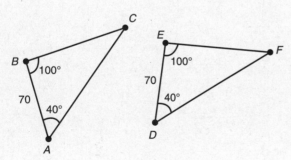

4.

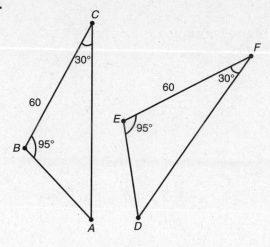

5.

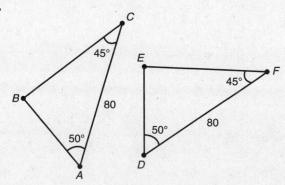

5

6.

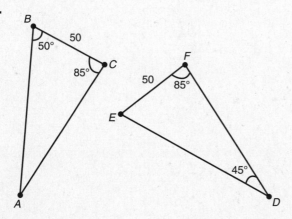

7.

8.

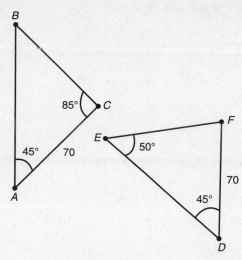

9.

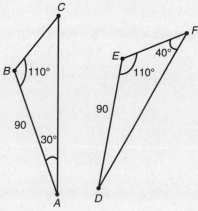

Use the AAS Theorem to show that each pair of triangles is congruent.

10.

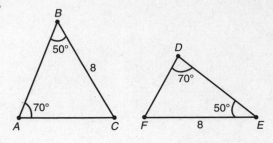

11.

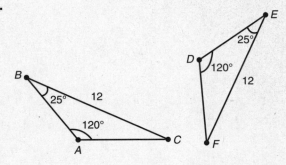

12.

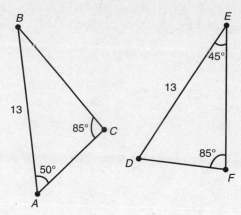

13.

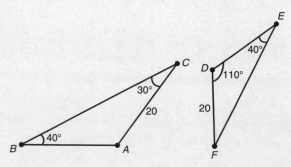

5

Determine whether there is enough information to tell whether the two triangles are congruent. If there is enough information, determine whether they are congruent.

14.

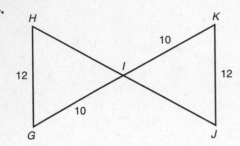

15.

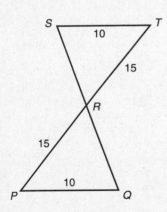

16.

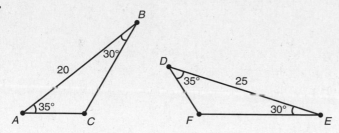

17.

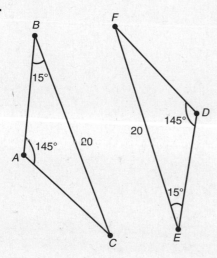

18.

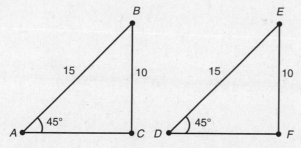

5

19.

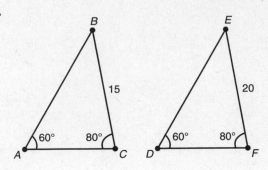

20.

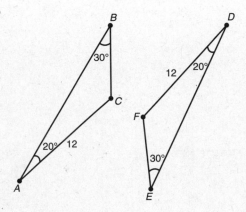

21.

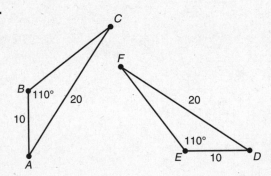

Skills Practice

Name _____   Date _____

Planting Grape Vines
Proving Triangles Congruent: HL

Vocabulary

Define each term in your own words.

1. hypotenuse

2. Hypotenuse-Leg Congruence Theorem

Problem Set

Show that the two triangles in each figure are congruent.

3.

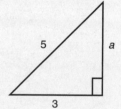

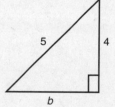

4.

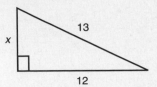

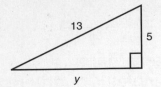

5.

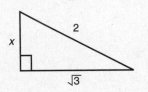

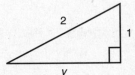

6.

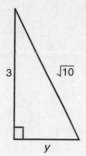

7.

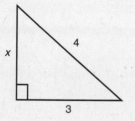

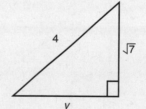

8.

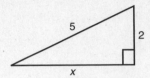

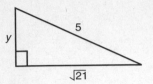

Use the Hypotenuse Leg Congruence Theorem to show that the two triangles in each figure are congruent.

9.

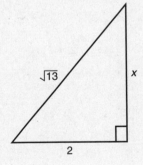

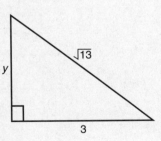

10.

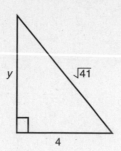

11.

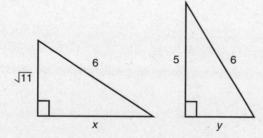

5

12.

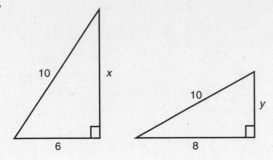

13.

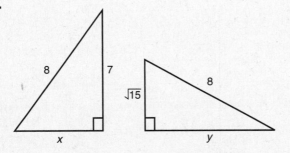

14.

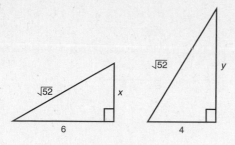

Show that the two triangles in each figure are congruent.

15.

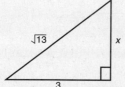

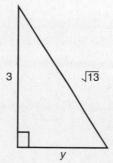

5

16.

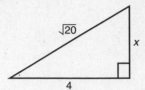

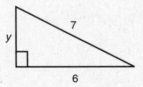

17.

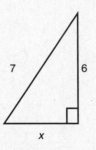

Name _____   Date _____

18.

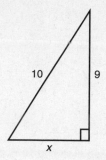

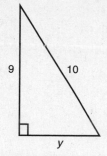

5

5

Skills Practice

Name _____ Date _____

Quilting and Tessellations
Introduction to Quadrilaterals

Vocabulary

Write the term that best completes each statement.

1. A quadrilateral with all congruent sides and all right angles is called
    a(n) _____.

2. A(n) _____ is a parallelogram whose four sides have the same length.

3. A(n) _____ uses circles to show how elements among sets of numbers or
    objects are related.

4. A polygon that has four sides is a(n) _____.

5. A quadrilateral with two pairs of parallel sides is called a(n) _____.

6. A(n) _____ of a plane is a collection of polygons that are arranged so that
    they cover the plane with no gaps.

7. A(n) _____ is a quadrilateral with exactly one pair of parallel sides.

8. A parallelogram with four right angles is a(n) _____.

9. A(n) _____ is a four-sided figure with two pairs of adjacent sides of equal
    length, with opposite sides not equal in length.

Problem Set

**Identify all of the terms from the following list that apply to each figure:
quadrilateral, parallelogram, rectangle, square, trapezoid, rhombus, kite.**

10.

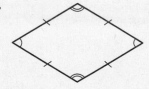

11.

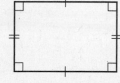

12.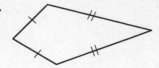

13.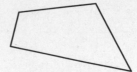

14.

15.

Name the type of quadrilateral that best describes each figure. Explain your answer.

16.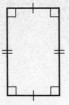

17.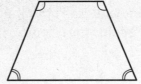

6

Name _____ Date _____

18.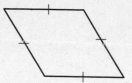

19.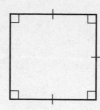

20.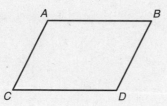

21.

List all possible names for each quadrilateral based on its vertices.

22.

23.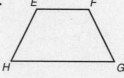

6

24.

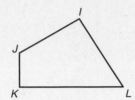

25.

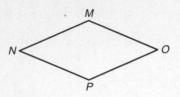

Name the indicated parts of each quadrilateral.

26. Name the parallel sides.

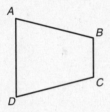

27. Name the congruent sides.

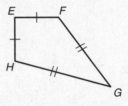

28. Name the congruent angles.

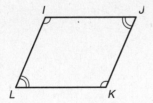

29. Name the right angles.

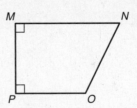

Draw a Venn diagram for each description.

30. Suppose that a part of a Venn diagram has two circles. One circle represents all types of quadrilaterals with four congruent sides. The other circle represents all types of quadrilaterals with four congruent angles. Draw this part of the Venn diagram and label it with the appropriate types of quadrilaterals.

31. Suppose that a part of a Venn diagram has two circles. One circle represents all types of quadrilaterals with two pairs of congruent sides (adjacent or opposite). The other circle represents all types of quadrilaterals with at least one pair of parallel sides. Draw this part of the Venn diagram and label it with the appropriate types of quadrilaterals.

6

32. Suppose that a part of a Venn diagram has two circles. One circle represents all types of quadrilaterals with two pairs of parallel sides. The other circle represents all types of quadrilaterals with four congruent sides. Draw this part of the Venn diagram and label it with the appropriate types of quadrilaterals.

33. Suppose that a part of a Venn diagram has two circles. One circle represents all types of quadrilaterals with four right angles. The other circle represents all types of quadrilaterals with two pairs of parallel sides. Draw this part of the Venn diagram and label it with the appropriate types of quadrilaterals.

Skills Practice

Name _____   Date _____

When Trapezoids Are Kites
Kites and Trapezoids

Vocabulary

Identify all instances of each term in the figure.

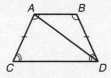

1. isosceles trapezoid

2. base of a trapezoid

3. base angles of a trapezoid

4. diagonal

Problem Set

Use the given figure to answer each question.

5. The figure shown is a kite with
   $\angle DAB \cong \angle DCB$. Which of the
   kite's sides are congruent?

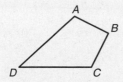

6. The figure shown is a kite with
   $\overline{FG} \cong \overline{FE}$. Which of the kite's
   angles are congruent?

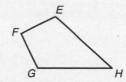

7. Given that *IJLK* is a kite, what kinds of triangles are formed by diagonal $\overline{IL}$?

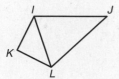

8. Given that *LMNO* is a kite, what is the relationship between the triangles formed by diagonal $\overline{MO}$?

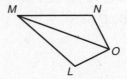

9. Given that *PQRS* is a kite, which angles are congruent?

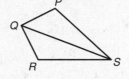

10. Given that *TUVW* is a kite, which angles are congruent?

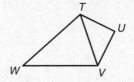

6

Name _____ Date _____

Write a paragraph proof to prove each statement.

11. Given that *ABEF* and *BCDE* are both kites, prove that ∠*FAB* ≅ ∠*DCB*.

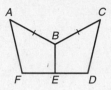

12. Given that *GHKL* and *IHKJ* are both kites, prove that ∠*LGH* ≅ ∠*JIH*.

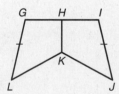

6

13. Given that *ABFG* and *CBED* are both kites, prove that △*ABG* ≅ △*EBD*.

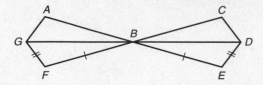

14. Given that *HIMN* and *JILK* are both kites, prove that △*NHI* ≅ △*KJI*.

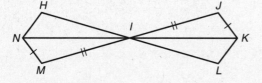

6

Use the given figure to answer each question.

15. The figure shown is an isosceles trapezoid with $\overline{AB} \parallel \overline{CD}$. Which sides arc congruent?

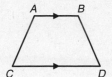

16. The figure shown is an isosceles trapezoid with $\overline{EH} \cong \overline{FG}$. Which sides are parallel?

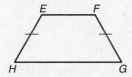

17. The figure shown is an isosceles trapezoid with $\overline{IJ} \cong \overline{KL}$. Given that *IJKL* is an isosceles trapezoid, what are the bases?

18. The figure shown is an isosceles trapezoid with $\overline{MP} \cong \overline{NO}$. Given that *MPON* is an isosceles trapezoid, what are the pairs of base angles?

19. Given that *QRVS* is an isosceles trapezoid, which angles are congruent?

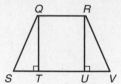

20. Given that *WXZY* is an isosceles trapezoid, which angles are congruent?

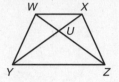

Write a paragraph proof to prove each statement.

21. Given that *ABCD* is an isosceles trapezoid, prove that △*ACD* ≅ △*BDC*.

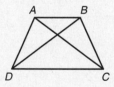

6

22. Given that *EFHG* is an isosceles trapezoid, prove that ∠*GEH* ≅ ∠*HFG*.

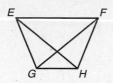

23. Given that *ABCF* and *FEDC* are isosceles trapezoids, prove that ∠*AFC* ≅ ∠*EFC*.

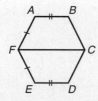

24. Given that *GHKL* and *JKHI* are isosceles trapezoids, prove that ∠*G* ≅ ∠*J*.

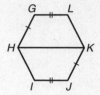

Skills Practice

Name _____ Date _____

Binocular Stand Design
Parallelograms and Rhombi

Vocabulary

Match each definition to its corresponding term.

1. two angles of a polygon that do not share
   a common side

2. two angles of a polygon that share a common side

3. two sides of a polygon that do not intersect

4. two sides of a polygon that share a common vertex

    a. opposite sides

    b. consecutive sides

    c. consecutive angles

    d. opposite angles

Problem Set

Identify the indicated parts of the given parallelogram.

5. Name the pairs of consecutive sides of the parallelogram.

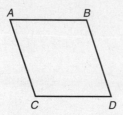

6

6. Name the pairs of opposite sides of the parallelogram.

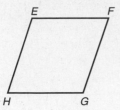

7. Name the pairs of opposite angles of the parallelogram.

8. Name the pairs of consecutive angles of the parallelogram.

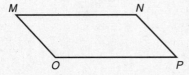

Name _____   Date _____

Write a paragraph proof to prove each statement.

9. Given that $\overline{AB} \parallel \overline{CD}$ and $\overline{AC} \parallel \overline{BD}$, use the ASA Congruence Theorem to prove that $\angle B \cong \angle C$.

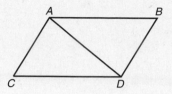

10. Given that $\overline{HG} \parallel \overline{EF}$ and $\overline{HG} \parallel \overline{GF}$, use the ASA Congruence Theorem to prove that $\overline{HG} \cong \overline{EF}$.

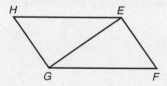

6

11. Given that $\overline{IK} \parallel \overline{LJ}$ and $\overline{IK} \cong \overline{LJ}$, use the AAS Congruence Theorem to prove that $\triangle IMK \cong \triangle LMJ$.

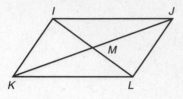

12. Given that $NO \parallel QP$ and $\overline{NO} \cong \overline{QP}$, use the AAS Congruence Theorem to prove that $\triangle NOM \cong \triangle QPM$.

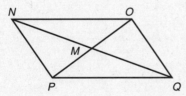

Use what you know about rhombi to answer each question.

13. What is the relationship between consecutive angles of a rhombus?

14. What is the relationship between opposite angles of a rhombus?

15. What is the relationship between consecutive sides of a rhombus?

16. Explain the difference between parallelograms and rhombi in terms of opposite and consecutive sides.

Use the given information to complete each two-column proof.

17. If $\overline{AC}$ bisects $\angle DAB$ and $\angle DCB$, then $\angle D \cong \angle B$.

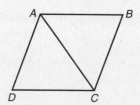

Statement	Reason
1.	1. Given
2. $\angle DAC \cong \angle BAC$	2. Definition of _____
3. $\angle DCA \cong \angle BCA$	3. Definition of _____
4.	4. Reflexive Property of Congruence
5. $\triangle ADC \cong \triangle ABC$	5. _____
6.	6. Definition of congruence

18. If $\overline{EG}$ bisects $\angle FEH$ and $\angle FGH$, then $\overline{EF} \cong \overline{EH}$.

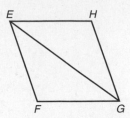

Statement	Reason
1. $\overline{EG}$ bisects $\angle FEH$ and $\angle FGH$.	**1.** _____
2. $\angle FEG \cong$	**2.** Definition of angle bisector
3. $\angle FGE \cong$	**3.** Definition of angle bisector
4. $\overline{EG} \cong \overline{EG}$	**4.** _____
5. $\triangle FEG \cong$	**5.** ASA Congruence Theorem
6. $\overline{EF} \cong \overline{EH}$	**6.** Definition of _____

19. If $\overline{IK}$ bisects $\angle JIL$ and $\overline{IL} \cong \overline{IJ}$, then $\angle IMJ \cong \angle IML$.

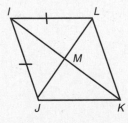

Statement	Reason
1.	**1.** Given
2. $\angle LIM \cong$	**2.** Definition of angle bisector
3. $\overline{IM} \cong \overline{IM}$	**3.** _____
4.	**4.** Given
5. $\triangle JIM \cong \triangle LIM$	**5.** _____
6. $\angle IMJ \cong \angle IML$	**6.** Definition of _____

6

Name _____ Date _____

20. If $\overline{ON}$ bisects $\angle MOP$ and $\overline{MO} \cong \overline{PO}$, then $\overline{MQ} \cong \overline{PQ}$.

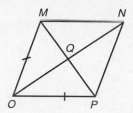

Statement	Reason
1. $\overline{ON}$ bisects $\angle MOP$.	1. _____
2. _____ $\cong \angle POQ$	2. Definition of angle bisector
3. $\overline{OQ} \cong \overline{OQ}$	3. _____
4.	4. Given
5. $\triangle MOQ \cong \triangle POQ$	5. _____
6.	6. Definition of congruence

6

Skills Practice

Name _____ Date _____

Positive Reinforcement
Rectangles and Squares

Vocabulary

Identify similarities and differences between the terms.

1. square and rectangle

Problem Set

Explain why each statement is true.

2. A rectangle is always a parallelogram.

3. A parallelogram is sometimes a rectangle.

4. A rectangle is sometimes a square.

5. A square is always a rectangle.

6. The diagonals of a square are perpendicular.

7. The diagonals of a rectangle are sometimes perpendicular.

8. A rectangle is sometimes a rhombus.

9. A square is always a rhombus.

10. A rhombus is sometimes a rectangle.

11. A rhombus is sometimes a square.

Name _____ Date _____

Given the lengths of the sides of a rectangle, calculate the length of each diagonal. Simplify radicals, but do not evaluate.

12. A rectangular construction scaffold with diagonal support beams is 8 feet high and 10 feet wide.

What is the length of each diagonal?

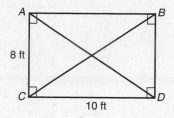

13. A fence has rectangular sections that are each 4 feet tall and 8 feet long. Each section has a diagonal support beam.

What is the length of each diagonal?

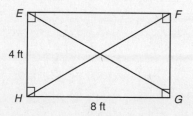

14. A community garden has a rectangular frame for sugar snap peas. The frame is 9 feet high and 6 feet wide, and it has two diagonals to strengthen it.

What is the length of each diagonal?

15. The sides of a shelving unit are metal rectangles with two diagonals for support. Each rectangle is 12 inches wide and 40 inches high.

What is the length of each diagonal?

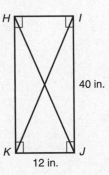

Name _____   Date _____

Given the length of a side of a rectangle and the length of a diagonal, calculate the length of another side. Simplify radicals, but do not evaluate.

16. Given that *ABDC* is a rectangle, find *CD*.

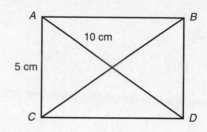

17. Given that *EFGH* is a rectangle, find *FG*.

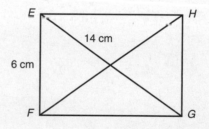

18. Given that *IJKL* is a rectangle, find *IL*.

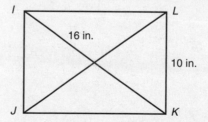

19. Given that *MNOP* is a rectangle, find *MN*.

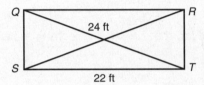

20. Given that *QRTS* is a rectangle, find *QS*.

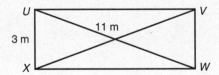

21. Given that *UVWX* is a rectangle, find *XW*.

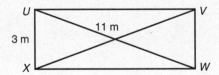

Name _____   Date _____

22. Given that *ABCD* is a rectangle, find *AD*.

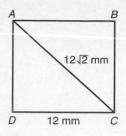

23. Given that *EFGH* is a rectangle, find *GH*.

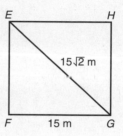

Determine the missing measure. Round decimals to the nearest tenth.

24. A square garden is divided into quarters by diagonal paths. If each diagonal is 50 meters long, how long is each side of the garden?

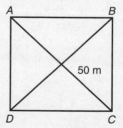

25. A square porch has diagonal support beams underneath it. If each diagonal beam is 12 feet long, what is the length of each side of the porch?

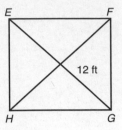

26. A heavy picture frame in the shape of a square has a diagonal support across the back. If each side of the frame is 24 inches, what is the length of the diagonal?

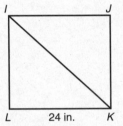

27. A square shelving unit has diagonal supports across the back. If each side of the frame is 60 inches, what is the length of each diagonal?

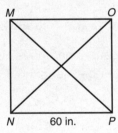

Skills Practice

Name _____ Date _____

Stained Glass
Sum of the Interior Angle Measures in a Polygon

Vocabulary

Draw a diagram to illustrate each term. Explain how your diagram illustrates the term.

1. interior angle

2. convex polygon

3. regular polygon

Problem Set

Calculate the sum of the interior angle measures of the polygon. Show all your work.

4. Draw all of the diagonals that connect to vertex *A*. What is the sum of the internal angles of quadrilateral *ABDC*?

5. Draw all of the diagonals that connect to vertex *E*. What is the sum of the interior angles of polygon *EFGHI*?

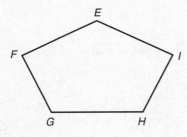

6. Draw all of the diagonals that connect to vertex *J*. What is the sum of the interior angles of polygon *JKMONL*?

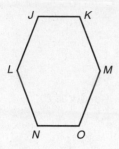

7. Draw all of the diagonals that connect to vertex *P*. What is the sum of the interior angles of polygon *PQRSTUV*?

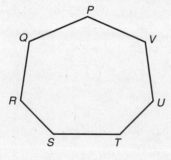

6

Calculate the sum of the interior angle measures of the polygon.

8. If a convex polygon has 5 sides, what is the sum of its interior angle measures?

9. If a convex polygon has 6 sides, what is the sum of its interior angle measures?

10. If a convex polygon has 8 sides, what is the sum of its interior angle measures?

11. If a convex polygon has 9 sides, what is the sum of its interior angle measures?

12. If a convex polygon has 12 sides, what is the sum of its interior angle measures?

13. If a convex polygon has 13 sides, what is the sum of its interior angle measures?

14. If a convex polygon has 16 sides, what is the sum of its interior angle measures?

6

Name _____ Date _____

15. If a convex polygon has 17 sides, what is the sum of its interior angle measures?

Determine the measure of each interior angle of each regular polygon.

16. What is the measure of each interior angle of the regular polygon?

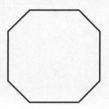

17. What is the measure of each interior angle of the regular polygon?

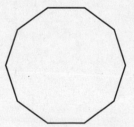

6

18. What is the measure of each interior angle of the regular polygon?

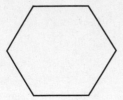

19. What is the measure of each interior angle of the regular polygon?

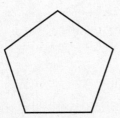

Name _____ Date _____

Use the given information to determine the number of sides of each regular polygon.

20. The measure of each angle of a regular polygon is 108°. How many sides does the polygon have?

21. The measure of each angle of a regular polygon is 120°. How many sides does the polygon have?

22. The measure of each angle of a regular polygon is 144°. How many sides does the polygon have?

23. The measure of each angle of a regular polygon is 156°. How many sides does the polygon have?

6

24. The measure of each angle of a regular polygon is 160°. How many sides does the polygon have?

25. The measure of each angle of a regular polygon is 162°. How many sides does the polygon have?

6

Name _____   Date _____

Pinwheels
Sum of the Exterior Angle Measures in a Polygon

Vocabulary

Define each term in your own words.

1. exterior angle

2. regular polygon

Problem Set

Extend each vertex of the polygon to create one exterior angle at each vertex.

3.

4.

5.

6.

6

Given the measure of an interior angle of a polygon, calculate the measure of the adjacent exterior angle. Explain how you found your answer.

7. What is the measure of an exterior angle if it is adjacent to an interior angle of a polygon that measures 90°?

8. What is the measure of an exterior angle if it is adjacent to an interior angle of a polygon that measures 120°?

9. What is the measure of an exterior angle if it is adjacent to an interior angle of a polygon that measures 108°?

10. What is the measure of an exterior angle if it is adjacent to an interior angle of a polygon that measures 135°?

11. What is the measure of an exterior angle if it is adjacent to an interior angle of a polygon that measures 115°?

12. What is the measure of an exterior angle if it is adjacent to an interior angle of a polygon that measures 124°?

6

Name _____ Date _____

For each regular polygon, calculate the measure of each of its external angles. Explain how you found your answer.

13. What is the measure of each external angle of a square?

14. What is the measure of each external angle of a regular pentagon?

15. What is the measure of each external angle of a regular hexagon?

6

16. What is the measure of each external angle of a regular octagon?

For each regular polygon, calculate the sum of the measures of its external angles. Show all your work.

17. What is the sum of the external angle measures of a regular pentagon?

18. What is the sum of the external angle measures of a regular hexagon?

6

19. What is the sum of the external angle measures of a regular octagon?

20. What is the sum of the external angle measures of a square?

For each polygon, calculate the sum of the measures of its external angles. Show all your work.

21. What is the sum of the external angle measures of the polygon?

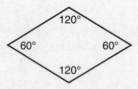

6

22. What is the sum of the external angle measures of the polygon?

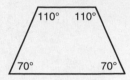

23. What is the sum of the external angle measures of the polygon?

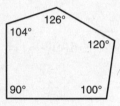

24. What is the sum of the external angle measures of the polygon?

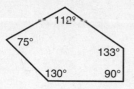

25. What is the sum of the external angle measures of the polygon?

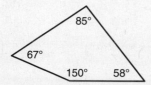

26. What is the sum of the external angle measures of the polygon?

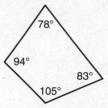

6

Skills Practice

Name_____ Date _____

Rolling, Flipping, and Pulling
Probability and Sample Spaces

Vocabulary

Write the term that best completes each statement.

1. A(n) _____ consists of two or more events.

2. Drawing a card and then replacing that card in the deck before drawing another card is an example of an event _____.

3. Drawing a card and then drawing another card from the same deck is an example of an event _____.

4. The _____ is a list of all possible outcomes in a given situation.

5. The probability of an event happening is the ratio of the number of _____ to the total number of possible _____.

6. The likelihood of a particular event occurring is referred to as the _____ of that event.

7. Two events are _____ if the outcome of the first event does not affect the outcome of the second event.

8. Two events are _____ if the second event is affected by the outcome of the first event.

Problem Set

Consider a four-sided triangular pyramid with faces numbered 1 through 4. Determine each probability.

9. What is the probability of rolling a number other than a 3?

10. What is the probability of rolling a 4?

11. What is the probability of rolling a 5?

7

12. What is the probability of rolling a number less than 5?

13. What is the probability of rolling an odd number?

14. What is the probability of rolling an even number?

15. What is the probability of rolling a prime number?

16. What is the probability of rolling a composite number?

17. What is the probability of rolling a number greater than 1?

18. What is the probability of rolling a number less than or equal to 3?

From a standard deck of 52 cards, you draw the 7 of diamonds. Determine each probability.

19. What is the probability of drawing the king of spades next if you don't return the card? If you do return the card?

20. What is the probability of drawing the 7 of diamonds next if you don't return the card? If you do return the card?

21. What is the probability of drawing a diamond next if you don't return the card? If you do return the card?

22. What is the probability of drawing a club next if you don't return the card? If you do return the card?

7

23. What is the probability of drawing a red card next if you don't return the card? If you do return the card?

24. What is the probability of drawing a black card next if you don't return the card? If you do return the card?

25. What is the probability of drawing a 7 or lower (2, 3, 4, 5, 6, 7) next if you don't return the card? If you do return the card?

26. What is the probability of drawing a 7 or higher (7, 8, 9, 10, J, Q, K, A) next if you don't return the card? If you do return the card?

From a standard deck of 52 cards, you draw one card. Then you flip a coin. Calculate each probability.

27. You draw a king and flip heads.

28. You draw a 2 and flip tails.

29. You draw a heart and flip tails.

30. You draw a diamond and flip heads.

31. You draw a 10 or higher (10, J, Q, K, A) and flip tails.

32. You draw a 9 or lower (2, 3, 4, 5, 6, 7, 8, 9) and flip heads.

Create a table to show each sample space.

33. A four-card deck contains the J, Q, K, and A of hearts. Create a table to show the sample space for drawing two cards with replacement.

34. A four-card deck contains the 2, 3, 4, and 5 of spades. Create a table to show the sample space for drawing two cards with replacement.

Draw a tree diagram to show each sample space.

35. A four-sided triangular pyramid with faces numbered 1 through 4 is rolled twice. Draw a tree diagram that represents two rolls of the number pyramid.

36. A four-sided triangular pyramid with faces numbered 1 through 4 is rolled three times. Draw a tree diagram that represents three rolls of the number pyramid.

7

37. A four-card deck contains the 2, 3, 4, and 5 of spades. Draw a tree diagram for drawing two cards without replacement.

38. A four-card deck contains the J, Q, K, and A of spades. Draw a tree diagram for drawing two cards without replacement.

39. A five-card deck contains the 10, J, Q, K, and A of clubs. Draw a tree diagram for drawing two cards without replacement.

40. A five-card deck contains the A, 2, 3, 4, and 5 of diamonds. Draw a tree diagram for drawing two cards without replacement.

Skills Practice

Name_____ Date _____

Multiple Trials
Compound and Conditional Probability

Vocabulary

Define each term in your own words.

1. compound event

2. compound probability

3. conditional probability

Problem Set

Suppose you have a reduced deck of cards that has only the 10s, jacks, queens, kings, and aces of the four suits, for a total of 20 cards. Calculate each probability.

4. You draw one card, replace it, and then draw another card. Calculate P(10 and ace).

5. You draw one card, replace it, and then draw another card. Calculate P(queen and king).

6. You draw one card, replace it, and then draw another card. Calculate P(two hearts).

7. You draw one card, replace it, and then draw another card. Calculate P(two clubs).

7

8. You draw one card and replace it, then draw another card and replace it, and then draw another card and replace it. Calculate P(three of a kind, any card).

9. You draw one card and replace it, then draw another card and replace it, and then draw another card and replace it. Calculate P(three jacks).

10. You draw four cards and replace each card after drawing. Calculate P(four kings).

11. You draw four cards and replace each card after drawing. Calculate P(four of a kind, any card).

Suppose you have a reduced deck of cards that has only the 10s, jacks, queens, kings, and aces of the four suits, for a total of 20 cards. Calculate each probability.

12. You draw two cards at once, without replacement. Calculate P(10 and ace).

13. You draw two cards at once, without replacement. Calculate P(queen and king).

14. You draw two cards at once, without replacement. Calculate P(two hearts).

15. You draw two cards at once, without replacement. Calculate P(two clubs).

16. You draw three cards at once, without replacement. Calculate P(three of a kind, any card).

17. You draw three cards at once, without replacement. Calculate P(three jacks).

18. You draw four cards at once, without replacement. Calculate P(four kings).

7

19. You draw four cards at once, without replacement. Calculate P(four of a kind, any card).

Your math teacher, Mr. Johnson, is in charge of the school math club. Suppose that there are 20 students in the math club. Use this information to answer each question.

20. If Mr. Johnson chooses three students at random to serve on the club council, what is the probability that they will be Josh, Jen, and Josie?

21. If Mr. Johnson chooses three students at random to serve as club officers, what are the chances he selects Josh as president, Jen as secretary, and Josie as treasurer?

Suppose that there are 27 students in Ms. Calipari's math class. She chooses one student at random each week to make a presentation. Once the student makes a presentation, he or she will not be chosen again. Use this information to answer each question.

22. What is the probability that Sarah, Sam, and Susie will all be done with their presentations after the first three weeks?

23. What is the probability that Sarah will be chosen for the first week, Sam for the second week, and Susie for the third week?

7

Use the given information to determine each probability.

24. Ms. Nguyen informs her class that 40 percent of them have received a score of 80 or above on both the first test and the second test. Then she informs them that 50 percent of the students in the class scored an 80 or above on the first test. What is the probability that a student who scored an 80 or above on the first test also scored an 80 or above on the second test?

25. Mr. Abdullah informs his class that 75 percent of them have received a score of 80 or above on both the first test and the second test. Then he informs them that 80 percent of the students in the class scored an 80 or above on the first test. What is the probability that a student who scored an 80 or above on the first test also scored an 80 or above on the second test?

7

26. The probability for a positive test for a disease and actually having the disease is $\frac{1}{5000}$. The probability of a positive test is $\frac{1}{4500}$. What is the probability of actually having the disease given a positive test?

27. The probability for a positive test for a disease and actually having the disease is $\frac{1}{800}$. The probability of a positive test is $\frac{1}{700}$. What is the probability of actually having the disease given a positive test?

28. A baseball player gets hits on two successive at–bats one time out of every sixteen. If he gets a hit 25% of the time, what is the probability that he will get a hit on the second successive at–bat after getting a hit on the first at-bat?

7

29. A basketball player makes two out of two free throws 81 percent of the time. If he makes 90 percent of his free throws, what is the probability that he will make the second free throw after making the first?

Skills Practice

Name_____ Date _____

Counting
Permutations and Combinations

Vocabulary

Match each word with its corresponding definition.

1. factorial

    a. an ordered list of items without repetition

2. permutation

    b. an unordered collection of items

3. combination

    c. an ordered list of items in which the final term links back to the first term to create a loop

4. permutations with repeated elements

    d. the product of all positive integers up to (and including) the given number

5. circular permutation

    e. an ordered list of items that includes repeated items

Problem Set

Calculate each factorial.

6. 4!

7. 7!

7

8. 0!   **9.** 1!

Simplify each fraction.

10. $\dfrac{5!}{2!}$

11. $\dfrac{3!}{8!}$

12. $\dfrac{2!4!}{6!}$

13. $\dfrac{5!5!}{4!3!}$

Use the given information to answer each question.

14. Using any eight letters in the alphabet, how many different four-letter strings are there?

15. Using any eight letters in the alphabet, how many five-digit strings are there?

16. Using any 12 letters in the alphabet, how many ten-digit strings are there?

17. Using any 12 letters in the alphabet, how many six-digit strings are there?

Use the given information to answer each question.

18. In a group of 8 people, how many different four–member committees can be chosen?

19. In a group of 11 people, how many different five–member committees can be chosen?

20. In a group of 9 people, how many different six–member committees can be chosen?

21. In a group of 15 people, how many different three–member committees can be chosen?

Determine each probability.

22. There are 10 students in a classroom assigned randomly to desks numbered 1 to 10. What is the probability that the students are arranged alphabetically?

23. Joe has forgotten his 4-digit PIN. Each digit of Joe's PIN is a different digit. What is the probability that he can guess it in 10 tries?

24. Kira has forgotten her 5-digit PIN. Each digit of Kira's PIN is a different digit. What is the probability that she can guess it in 20 tries?

25. There are 10 students, 5 boys and 5 girls, who are assigned randomly to classroom desks numbered 1 to 10. What is the probability that the students are arranged boy, girl, boy, girl, and so on?

Determine each probability.

26. In a standard 52-card playing deck, what is the probability that a person is dealt a hand of five cards that are all diamonds?

27. In a standard 52-card playing deck, what is the probability that a person is dealt a hand of 10, J, Q, K, and A, all in one suit?

28. In a 20-card playing deck with only 10s, jacks, queens, kings, and aces, what is the probability that a person is dealt a hand of five cards that are all diamonds?

29. In a 20-card playing deck with only 10s, jacks, queens, kings, and aces, what is the probability that a person is dealt a hand of five cards with four aces?

Use the formula for permutations with repeated elements to calculate each number.

30. The number of seven-letter strings that can be formed from the word ALGEBRA

31. The number of eight-letter strings that can be formed from the word CALCULUS

32. The number of ten-letter strings that can be formed from the word ANALYTICAL

33. The number of ten-letter strings that can be formed from the word STATISTICS

Use the formula for circular permutations to calculate the number of arrangements.

34. A necklace is made from 10 different types of beads strung along a circle of string. How many different possible bead arrangements are there?

35. A necklace is made from 8 different colors of beads strung along a circle of string. How many different possible bead arrangements are there?

7

36. A disc jockey plays the same 11 songs over and over in a cycle, repeating the same order. How many different orders does he have to choose from for his 11 songs?

37. Nine people sit around a circular table. How many different ways are there to arrange the people?

Skills Practice

Name_____ Date _____

Trials
Independent Trials

Vocabulary

Define each term in your own words.

1. regular tetrahedron

2. combination

3. Pascal's Triangle

Problem Set

Consider an octahedron (an eight-sided solid with each face identical to the others) that is thrown like a number cube. Three sides are red (R), two sides are blue (B), two sides are yellow (Y), and one side is green (G). Determine each probability for two rolls of the octahedron.

4. $P(RR)$

5. $P(YY)$

6. $P(RG)$

7. $P(YG)$

8. $P(BG)$

9. $P(RB)$

A number cube has 5 red (*R*) sides and 1 blue (*B*) side. Use this information to calculate each probability.

10. Rolling 3 reds and 1 blue in four rolls

11. Rolling 3 reds and 2 blues in five rolls

12. Rolling 3 reds and 3 blues in six rolls

13. Rolling 3 reds and 4 blues in seven rolls

A regular tetrahedron has 3 red (*R*) sides and 1 blue (*B*) side. Use this information to calculate each probability.

14. Rolling 2 reds and 2 blues in four rolls

15. Rolling 4 reds and 1 blue in five rolls

16. Rolling 2 reds and 4 blues in six rolls

17. Rolling 2 reds and 5 blues in seven rolls

7

Consider a situation where each trial has one of two possible outcomes.
Outcome *A* has a probability of *p*, while outcome *B* has probability of 1 – *p*.
Write a formula for each probability.

18. *P*(2*A* and 2*B*) in four trials

19. *P*(3*A* and 1*B*) in four trials

20. *P*(5*A* and 5*B*) in ten trials

21. *P*(9*A* and 3*B*) in twelve trials

7

Skills Practice

Name_____ Date _____

To Spin or Not to Spin
Expected Value

Vocabulary

Write the term or terms that best complete each statement.

1. The _____ is a list of all possible outcomes in a given situation.

2. The likelihood of a particular event occurring is referred to as the _____ of that event.

3. The _____ is the average value when the number of trials is large.

4. The probability of an event happening is the ratio of the number of _____ to the total number of possible _____.

Problem Set

Calculate the expected value when spinning each wheel shown.

5.

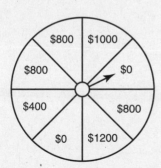

7

6.

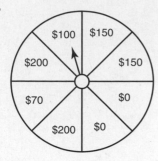

7.

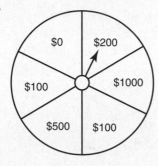

8.

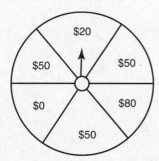

9.

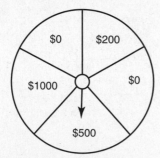

Name _____ Date _____

10.

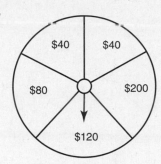

11.

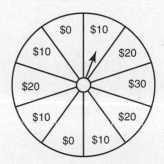

12.

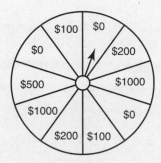

A game at a fair involves a deck with 10 cards, the 2 through 6 of spades and the 2 through 6 of hearts. To play the game, a player pulls a single card out of the deck and is paid depending on the card. For the various payouts described, calculate the expected value of playing this game.

13. $0 for a heart; $1 for a spade

7

14. $3 for a heart; $0 for a spade

15. $0 for a heart; $0 for an even spade, $1 for an odd spade

16. $0 for a spade; $1 for an even heart, $2 for an odd heart

17. $0 for a spade; $1 for an even heart, $2 for the 3 of hearts, and $3 for the 5 of hearts

18. $0 for a heart; $2 for an even spade, $3 for the 3 of spades, and $4 for the 5 of spades

19. $0 for a heart; $2 for a spade (except the 6 of spades, which pays $5)

7

20. $0 for a spade; $1 for a heart (except the 5 of hearts, which pays $20)

A game at a fair involves tossing a colored cube. The cube has two white sides, one red side, one green side, one yellow side, and one blue side. For the various payouts described, calculate the expected value of playing this game.

21. $0 for white, red, yellow, and green; $6 for blue

22. $0 for white, red, and yellow; $3 for green and blue

23. $0 for white, $1 for red, yellow, and blue; $9 for green

24. $1 for white, $0 for red, yellow, and blue; $6 for green

A game at a fair involves tossing a colored cube. The cube has two red sides, two green sides, one yellow side, and one blue side. For the various payouts described, calculate the expected value of playing this game.

25. $1 for yellow, $2 for blue, $0 for the others

26. $2 for red, $2 for blue, $0 for the others

27. $10 for yellow, $4 for green, $0 for the others

28. $20 for yellow, $2 for red, $0 for the others

A game at a fair involves tossing a bean bag at a target shaped like a tic-tac-toe board, made up of 9 squares in a 3-by-3 arrangement. It is difficult to control the bean bag, so it lands randomly in one of the nine squares, which offer different payouts depending on the game. For the various payouts described, calculate the expected value of playing this game.

29. $1 for the top row, $0 for the others

30. $2 for the left-hand column, $0 for the others

31. $2 for the bottom row, $0 for the others (except for $6 for landing in the center)

7

32. $5 for the right column, $0 for the others (except for $15 for landing in the center)

33. $5 for the middle column (except $20 for the middle square), $0 for the others

34. $4 for the middle row (except $10 for the middle square), $0 for the others

35. $2 for one of the corners, $10 for the middle square, $0 for the others

36. $3 for one of the corners, $15 for the middle square, $0 for the others

Name_____ Date _____

The Theoretical and the Actual
Experimental Versus Theoretical Probability

Vocabulary

Discuss how the following words are related by describing their similarities and differences.

1. theoretical probability and experimental probability

Problem Set

Calculate the theoretical probability for each situation.

2. A wheel is equally divided into 5 different colored wedges: red, blue, yellow, green, and black. The wheel is spun. What is the theoretical probability of the pointer of the wheel stopping on either red or green?

3. A six-sided number cube is rolled one time. What is the theoretical probability that the result is an even number?

4. Jason, his two brothers, and his three sisters each put their name on a slip of paper in a hat. He draws one name. What is the probability that the name is one of Jason's sisters?

7

5. Eight blue marbles, 6 green marbles, 8 red marbles, and 10 white marbles are placed in a paper bag. What is the probability that a green marble will be drawn?

6. One tile for each letter of the alphabet is placed in a bag. One tile is drawn from the bag. What is the probability that the letter on the tile is a consonant?

7. A standard deck of playing cards consists of 52 cards with 13 cards in each suit: clubs, diamonds, hearts, and spades. Clubs and spades are black, and diamonds and hearts are red. Each suit is made up of cards from 2 to 10, a jack, a queen, a king, and an ace. One card is drawn. What is the probability that the card is a red king?

Calculate the experimental probability for each situation.

8. A card is drawn at random and then replaced from a standard deck of cards one hundred times. The suit of the card is recorded in the table below. What is the experimental probability of the event of a heart being drawn?

♠	♥	♦	♣
36	16	9	39

9. A six-sided number cube is rolled fifty times. The results are shown in the table. What is the experimental probability that the result of a roll will be a 3?

1	2	3	4	5	6
6	20	10	8	4	2

10. A fair spinner is spun 20 times and the results are recorded in the table below. What is the experimental probability that the spinner stops on the color black?

green	blue	white	red	orange	black
3	5	3	2	4	3

11. Letter tiles from the name "Toby" are put into a bag. One tile is drawn at a time, the result recorded, and then replaced. This is done 60 times and the results are recorded in the table. What is the experimental probability of the letter T being drawn?

T	O	B	Y
16	22	14	8

12. A six-sided number cube is rolled 100 times. A one is rolled 18 times, a two is rolled 16 times, a three is rolled 16 times, a four is rolled 20 times, a five is rolled 17 times, and a six is rolled 13 times. What is the experimental probability of rolling the cube again and rolling a four?

13. A coin is tossed 100 times. The coins lands on heads 41 times and tails 59 times. What is the experimental probability of the coin landing on heads?

14. Three toy cars are run on a slanted track. Out of 100 trials, the number 1 car is fastest 43 times, the number 2 car is fastest 38 times, and the number 3 car is fastest 19 times. What is the experimental probability that the number 3 car wins the next race?

15. In a carnival game, a toy mole randomly pops out of one of five holes and a player hits the mole with a mallet. The holes are numbered one through five. Out of 50 events, the mole appears in hole one 13 times, hole two 5 times, hole three 10 times, hole four 12 times, and hole five 10 times. What is the experimental probability that the mole appears in hole two?

Use the given information to answer each question.

16. A coin is tossed 70 times. How many times would you expect the coin to land on heads?

17. A bag contains 10 blue, 10 red, 10 green, and 10 yellow marbles. A marble is drawn and replaced 100 times. How many times would you expect a blue marble to be drawn?

18. Two six-sided number cubes are rolled 50 times. How many times would you expect the sum of the cubes to be an even number?

7

19. An eight-sided numbered shape is rolled 40 times. How many times would you expect the result to be a number divisible by 3?

20. A card is drawn from a standard deck and then replaced 100 times. How many times would you expect to draw a queen?

21. A spinner is divided into 10 equal sections. Three are blue, three are red, two are white, and two are yellow. The spinner is spun 50 times. How many times would you expect the spinner to stop on the color red?

Describe how you would expect the experimental probabilities to compare for each set of experiments.

22. Three experiments are done using a six-sided number cube. For each experiment, the number cube was rolled 20 times to determine the experimental probability of rolling a 2.

23. Three bags of marbles each contain 10 red, 10 yellow, 10 green, and 10 blue marbles. An experiment is run on each bag where a marble is drawn and then replaced 40 times to determine the experimental probability of drawing a green marble.

24. A standard deck of cards is used to conduct three experiments to find the experimental probability of drawing a card that is a spade. In the first experiment, a card is drawn and replaced 20 times. In the second experiment, a card is drawn and replaced 200 times. In the third experiment, a card is drawn and replaced 2000 times.

25. Two coins are tossed together in an experiment to determine the experimental probability of one head and one tail. Three sets of trials are run. In the first trial, the coins are tossed 4 times. In the second trial, the coins are tossed 40 times. In the third trial, the coins are tossed 400 times.

7

Skills Practice

Name _____ Date _____

8

Taking the PSAT
Measures of Central Tendency

Vocabulary

Complete each sentence with the appropriate term from the box.

distribution	median	measure of central tendency
mean	mode	stem-and-leaf plot

1. For a data set that is arranged in numerical order, the _____ of the data set is either the middle value (when the number of data values is odd) or the average of the two middle values (when the number of data values is even).

2. A _____ is a visual display of data that is organized by digits. Each data value is separated into two parts.

3. The _____ of a data set is the sum of all the values of the data set divided by the number of values in the data set.

4. The number (or numbers) that occurs most often in a data set is the

   _____.

5. A _____ is the way in which the data are distributed, such as being spread out or clustered together.

6. A _____ is a single value that represents a typical value in a data set.

Problem Set

Complete the stem-and-leaf plot for each data set.

7. Students in a math class received the following scores on a test:

58, 75, 92, 63, 88, 97, 74, 81, 86, 90

Stem	Leaves	Key: 8|0 = ☐
5		
6		
7		
8		
9		

8. Sarah received the following scores on her assignments in World History:

73, 78, 85, 82, 86, 79, 84, 88, 80, 92

Stem	Leaves	Key: 7|1 = ☐
7		
8		
9		

9. Jorge recorded the average high temperature in degrees Fahrenheit each month for one year:

68, 74, 78, 82, 85, 88, 93, 95, 91, 85, 79, 74

Stem	Leaves	Key: 8|6 = ☐
6		
7		
8		
9		

10. A store tracked the number of customers who visited the store each day for two weeks:

45, 67, 58, 72, 79, 54, 62, 49, 53, 41, 64, 58, 62, 47

Stem	Leaves	Key: 5|6 = [ ]
4	[ ]	
5	[ ]	
6	[ ]	
7	[ ]	

Each stem-and-leaf plot has been rotated 90 degrees in a counterclockwise direction so that the leaves go up instead of to the right. Determine whether each data set is skewed left, skewed right, or symmetric.

11. Key: 1|2 = 12

```
      6           8
      3     2     4
4     3     1     2     6
0     1     2     3     4
```

12. Key: 1|2 = 12

```
8                       7
4           6           5
3     8     3     7     4
1     4     3     5     2
0     1     2     3     4
```

13. Key: 1|2 = 12

```
      6
7     3     5     9
2     1     4     2     5
2     3     4     5     6
```

14. Key: 1|2 = 12

```
7
4   8         7
1   4   6     4
1   2   3     2     2
2   3   4     5     6
```

15. Key: 1|2 = 12

```
                8
    9           7     9
    8     5     5     6
1   4     5     3     1
4   5     6     7     8
```

16. Key: 1|2 = 12

```
                6
          8     4
          8     4     7
5   9     4     3     2
4   5     6     7     8
```

Determine the mean of each data set. Round to the nearest tenth, if necessary.

17. A biologist recorded the number of birds that visited a pond each day for ten days:

37, 24, 16, 32, 19, 22, 19, 28, 21, 30

Name _____ Date _____

18. A park ranger recorded the number of visitors to the park each day for ten days:

102, 43, 37, 56, 64, 82, 114, 98, 52, 48

19. Sara recorded the number of miles she ran each day for one week:

10, 8, 7, 9, 6, 12, 8

20. Dmitri kept track of the amount he spent on food each week for eight weeks:

$16, $7, $25, $13, $11, $18, $14, $9

Determine the median of each data set.

21. A meteorologist recorded the amount of precipitation in inches each month for one year:

3, 5, 2, 6, 8, 9, 7, 4, 6, 4, 6, 3

22. Keisha recorded the number of meteors she saw each month for one year:

15, 0, 0, 24, 10, 0, 2, 13, 0, 6, 9, 19

23. Brendan recorded the number of kilometers he biked each day for one week:

20, 15, 62, 34, 20, 27, 31

24. Deepa recorded the number of minutes she spent practicing the trumpet each day for one week:

34, 45, 38, 24, 47, 42, 35

Determine the mode of each data set.

25. A teacher recorded the number of students who attended class each day for ten days:

31, 29, 28, 31, 27, 29, 30, 29, 28, 31

26. A weather station recorded the number of storms each month for one year:

2, 1, 4, 3, 5, 5, 3, 6, 3, 1, 2, 1

27. A clinic recorded the number of patients who came to the clinic each day for ten days:

25, 21, 32, 25, 44, 22, 27, 36, 21, 25

28. A student tracked the number of minutes he spent online each day:

86, 42, 51, 32, 51, 63, 63, 24, 51, 45

Each stem-and-leaf plot has been rotated 90 degrees in a counterclockwise direction so that the leaves go up instead of to the right. Use the shape of the given distribution to determine which is greater—the median or the mean. Explain.

29. Key: 7|0 = 70

```
                9
           8    5
           7    4    7
  5        1    2    4
  1    2   3    4    5
```

30. Key: 7|0 = 70

			7	
			7	8
	9	5	4	3
6	2	3	3	1
1	2	3	4	5

31. Key: 7|0 = 70

8				
4	7			
3	5		6	
1	3	2	2	1
1	2	3	4	5

32. Key: 7|0 = 70

| 9 | 8 | | | |
| 7 | 6 | 5 | 3 | |
4	5	4	1	6
1	2	3	4	5

Skills Practice

Name _____ Date _____

How Many People?
Population Data and Samples

Vocabulary

Define each term in your own words.

1. sample

2. absolute deviation

3. average absolute deviation

Problem Set

Calculate the mean of the sample described.

4. Use the first column of the data as a sample. What is the mean of the sample?

47	30	61	88	10
28	8	47	90	43
11	62	5	46	93
63	64	72	6	79
86	95	71	59	97
62	76	52	37	81
52	24	86	16	30
35	18	19	20	20
56	40	89	13	40
15	82	93	70	73

Name _____ Date _____

5. Use the fourth column of the data as a sample. What is the mean of the sample?

98	69	13	16	83
49	24	94	78	29
54	43	9	6	36
100	89	68	43	16
68	57	86	66	95
7	28	18	91	17
78	28	25	10	28
13	5	37	95	22
30	31	78	35	45
8	35	5	88	27

6. Use the third column of the data as a sample. What is the mean of the sample?

77	53	98	14	96
20	18	27	67	94
24	54	69	92	60
7	32	16	64	41
66	67	60	22	86
72	1	36	20	13
19	15	77	88	14
21	72	54	26	40
55	27	99	54	86
35	18	60	51	93

7. Use the second column of the data as a sample. What is the mean of the sample?

92	19	6	61	87
91	7	18	74	18
55	32	22	45	60
74	18	66	46	12
50	18	20	62	74
14	42	93	66	92
29	19	2	17	37
83	28	9	24	21
41	49	87	89	30
71	27	91	72	83

Calculate the median and quartiles of the given sample of data.

8. A survey tracked the age of each customer at a store. Ten values were picked at random for a sample:

12, 55, 58, 64, 34, 74, 49, 57, 34, 13

9. A survey asked the age of each resident in a town. Ten values were picked at random for a sample:

13, 54, 8, 31, 95, 74, 75, 50, 34, 72

10. A store recorded the amount that each customer spends. Ten values were picked at random for a sample:

$76, $75, $67, $36, $80, $45, $95, $40, $86, $70

11. Meteorologists recorded the average yearly snowfall in inches for cities across the country. Ten values were picked at random for a sample:

28, 79, 45, 98, 25, 48, 15, 49, 40, 22

Construct a box-and-whisker plot of each data set.

12. 25, 40, 22, 42, 92, 43, 86, 88, 42, 92

13. 26, 36, 98, 59, 43, 53, 85, 97, 60, 46

14. 39, 31, 25, 74, 66, 57, 33, 92, 21, 91

15. 38, 95, 33, 68, 36, 79, 46, 99, 93, 29

Use the box-and-whisker plots to answer each question about samples.

16. The box-and-whisker plots for two samples are shown.

Sample 1:

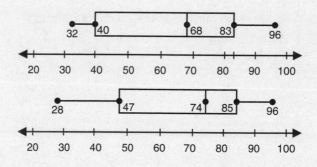

Sample 2:

Which sample has a greater median?

17. The box-and-whisker plots for two samples are shown.

Sample 3:

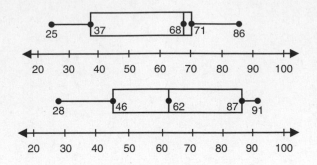

Sample 4:

Which sample has a greater median?

18. The box-and-whisker plots for two samples are shown.

Sample 1:

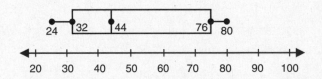

Sample 2:

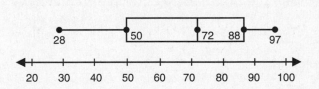

In which sample is the distance between
the first quartile and the third
quartile greater?

19. The box-and-whisker plots for two samples are shown.

Sample 3:

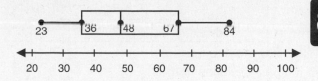

Sample 4:

In which sample is the distance between the first quartile and the third quartile greater?

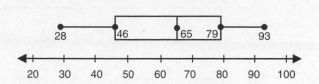

Complete the table by calculating the absolute deviation from the mean for each sample of data. Round your answer to the nearest tenth, if necessary.

20.

Minutes Spent Practicing Piano				
Value	48	32	30	34	32
Absolute deviation from the mean					

21.

Number of Geese Spotted				
Value	19	29	35	16	38
Absolute deviation from the mean					

22.

Grade Point Average					
Value	2.5	4.2	3.5	3.8	2.8
Absolute deviation from the mean					

23.

Inches of Rainfall per Month, April–August					
Value	4.4	2.6	3.5	5.6	5.8
Absolute deviation from the mean					

Complete the table by calculating the absolute deviation from the median for each sample of data.

24.

Days with Precipitation, October–February					
Value	10	9	4	5	9
Absolute deviation from the median					

25.

Minutes Spent Doing Mathematics Homework					
Value	38	39	29	31	40
Absolute deviation from the median					

26.

Number of Emails Sent					
Value	9	7	2	6	14
Absolute deviation from the median					

27.

Number of Customers					
Value	25	37	50	46	44
Absolute deviation from the median					

Calculate the average absolute deviation from the mean for each sample of data. Round your answer to the nearest tenth, if necessary.

28.

Age of Customers; Mean = 38.2					
Value	24	54	19	64	30
Absolute deviation from the mean	14.2	15.8	19.2	25.8	8.2

29.

Number of Campsites Filled; Mean = 34.4					
Value	8	19	79	61	5
Absolute deviation from the mean	26.4	15.4	44.6	26.6	29.4

30.

Deer Spotted; Mean = 49					
Value	51	59	68	25	42
Absolute deviation from the mean	2	10	19	24	7

Name _____ Date _____

31.

Cans Recycled; Mean = 60.2					
Value	54	65	54	80	48
Absolute deviation from the mean	6.2	4.8	6.2	19.8	12.2

Calculate the average absolute deviation from the median for each sample of data. Round your answer to the nearest tenth, if necessary.

32.

Text Messages Sent per Week					
Value	53	73	78	49	113
Absolute deviation from the median	20	0	5	24	40

33.

Minutes Spent Online					
Value	90	84	33	11	85
Absolute deviation from the median	6	0	51	73	1

34.

Vehicles on the Ferry					
Value	91	87	130	70	75
Absolute deviation from the median	4	0	43	17	12

35.

Museum Visitors					
Value	114	99	86	122	95
Absolute deviation from the median	15	0	13	23	4

Skills Practice

Name _____ Date _____

Let's Compare!
Population and Sample Means

Vocabulary

Match each definition to its corresponding term.

1. a number that is generated at random

    a. outlier

2. a non-representative data value

    b. random sample

3. a sample that is created by selecting data values randomly

    c. random number

Problem Set

Identify the data values in the sample described.

4. What sample would result from choosing the first and last columns of the data set?

42	21	9	26	30
26	29	32	49	10
39	47	42	48	25
42	46	29	44	28
9	47	5	33	14
47	3	15	21	34
22	11	25	44	5
50	7	1	3	29
15	42	17	41	18
24	19	26	31	48

5. What sample would result from choosing the even-numbered columns of the data set?

34	48	24	4	12
5	4	34	49	39
30	12	41	9	12
49	9	40	47	49
27	36	4	49	7
47	30	49	36	43
3	5	31	17	17
2	26	50	40	28
12	34	45	41	22
37	47	38	12	22

6. What sample would result from choosing the rows from the data set that are multiples of three?

36	24	44	4	36
17	17	19	47	24
38	7	27	22	18
16	15	19	3	15
36	30	4	36	17
21	17	23	30	12
22	44	32	39	16
44	9	22	1	19
13	23	45	7	16
34	29	17	5	14

7. What sample would result from choosing the rows from the data set that are multiples of five?

16	17	28	14	33
17	42	46	19	18
2	35	20	36	42
47	7	19	24	36
31	14	33	31	18
17	47	7	48	5
15	33	14	2	40
43	24	30	38	46
20	31	11	20	6
24	43	39	12	30

Determine the mean of the given sample of data.

8. 48, 33, 22, 40, 8, 7, 46, 32, 8, 15

9. 41, 11, 10, 7, 22, 48, 27, 43, 29, 5

10. 21, 56, 22, 38, 89, 38, 66, 8, 51, 36

11. 94, 94, 94, 39, 60, 47, 80, 87, 27, 11

12. 373, 260, 144, 14, 441, 438, 470, 1, 448, 171

13. 300, 276, 67, 389, 302, 164, 350, 376, 404, 49

14. 215, 851, 367, 249, 841, 744, 100, 969, 862, 903

8

15. 657, 428, 905, 410, 244, 726, 21, 205, 73, 702

Answer each question about samples.

16. How is the mean of a random sample affected if the sample includes a very low outlier?

17. How is the mean of a random sample affected if the sample includes a very high outlier?

18. Would you expect the mean and median to be constant for different random samples?

19. What is the advantage of using a random sample?

Use your calculator to generate four random whole numbers within the given interval.

20. [0, 10]

21. [10, 20]

22. [15, 24]

23. [8, 36]

Name _____ Date _____

Given the data set and criterion for selecting a random sample, determine the mean and median of each sample. Round your answer to the nearest tenth, if necessary.

24. A principal wants to take a random sample of students' GPAs. Each GPA is assigned a random number. Calculate the mean and median of the sample of GPAs that has the assigned random numbers that are between (and including) 1 and 10.

Random Number	GPA	Random Number	GPA	Random Number	GPA
7	2.0	21	3.1	24	1.1
4	2.2	8	3.8	20	1.2
23	2.7	26	4.0	25	3.0
10	1.9	19	3.4	15	3.0
18	2.6	17	3.5	3	3.5
27	3.5	28	3.5	22	2.6
39	3.9	2	3.1	14	4.0
30	2.8	16	3.5	9	2.1
12	2.3	13	3.5	6	2.3
5	2.7	1	4.0	11	3.8

25. A meteorologist records the amount of the snowfall in inches in different cities during December. He wants to take a random sample of the data set. Each city is assigned a random number. Find the mean and median of the snowfall in the sample of cities that has the assigned random numbers that are between (and including) 11 and 20.

Random Number	Snowfall	Random Number	Snowfall	Random Number	Snowfall
7	8.1	9	7.0	5	0.1
29	9.3	10	5.1	30	2.3
26	6.1	6	0.1	15	4.0
17	3.6	4	5.1	21	2.7
14	10.1	18	2.6	22	8.0
23	4.3	13	2.3	19	3.4
3	9.6	1	1.2	8	1.6
12	6.4	2	3.4	20	8.4
11	1.9	24	2.1	28	1.3
27	10.2	16	8.4	25	8.5

26. A biologist records the average number of fish caught per day in different lakes. She wants to take a random sample of the data. Each day is assigned a random number. Calculate the mean and median of the number of fish caught for the sample of days that has the assigned random numbers that are between (and including) 1 and 9.

Random Number	Fish Caught	Random Number	Fish Caught	Random Number	Fish Caught
5	17	12	90	26	4
29	23	1	72	15	30
8	70	7	73	27	67
20	18	22	57	10	59
13	34	11	53	21	59
3	89	17	13	9	16
24	22	4	55	6	73
19	87	25	9	16	84
14	21	18	33	2	98
30	50	28	68	23	17

27. Students divide a field into 1-square-meter areas and record the number of insects in each area. They want to take a random sample of the data. Each area is assigned a random number. Calculate the mean and median of the insects in the sample of areas that has the assigned random numbers that are between (and including) 11 and 19.

Random Number	Insects	Random Number	Insects	Random Number	Insects
28	4	30	32	29	54
25	19	2	48	14	15
24	52	3	12	1	7
21	16	4	46	9	29
17	8	15	60	26	21
11	6	13	39	5	8
10	38	27	13	12	1
8	47	16	57	22	49
18	2	6	32	19	22
23	2	20	59	7	39

Skills Practice

Name _____ Date _____

An Experiment of Your Own
Collecting and Analyzing Sample Data

Vocabulary

Describe similarities and differences between each pair of terms.

1. population and sample

2. mean and median

Problem Set

8

Calculate the mean of the sample described. Round your answer to the nearest tenth, if necessary.

3. Use the first column as your sample.

21	34	49	49	28
2	0	57	37	40
37	3	20	7	33
14	10	24	43	37
22	4	20	60	15
4	27	27	43	50
32	3	18	25	12
59	17	12	39	20

4. Use the second column as your sample.

12	23	37	40	37
20	36	15	50	0
10	9	48	18	6
21	29	21	52	13
30	38	13	31	55
54	54	41	46	38
16	47	9	39	22
35	37	12	50	7

5. Use the third column as your sample.

6	46	1	26	5
28	5	6	59	14
55	60	2	11	7
15	23	14	18	36
0	3	27	16	38
51	9	14	21	59
8	32	43	15	3
59	34	30	26	17

6. Use the fourth column as your sample.

41	52	19	48	48
45	25	45	3	4
22	53	57	20	5
34	53	19	12	38
48	30	39	49	49
25	48	56	49	48
36	11	30	12	10
12	34	46	46	19

7. Use the fifth column as your sample.

1	4	36	26	30
6	19	4	32	8
40	29	30	14	34
16	19	25	11	18
19	8	16	10	7
32	24	38	3	16
16	36	11	33	7

8. Use the third column as your sample.

28	36	33	20	19
27	40	32	11	15
15	2	36	28	29
26	24	21	16	35
11	17	32	3	8
39	21	23	19	10
31	2	36	15	18

8

9. Use the second column as your sample.

29	32	60	74	17
42	14	58	25	22
17	57	12	4	53
26	63	20	11	73
57	65	49	55	23
28	75	4	21	75
63	57	65	28	66

10. Use the third column as your sample.

26	58	48	70	80
45	6	34	50	70
49	56	56	34	40
15	54	77	14	56
29	75	46	66	63
63	70	56	53	29
78	16	80	41	11

11. Use the first column as your sample.

168	170	153	135	130
30	182	32	107	121
152	114	117	194	139
156	140	153	101	94
146	173	128	127	175
138	119	5	42	165
24	63	66	101	154

12. Use the fourth column as your sample.

69	153	193	34	63
44	191	32	137	45
52	93	131	166	57
180	166	188	41	86
189	171	139	21	184
157	10	23	194	192
62	4	98	90	158

Name _____ Date _____

Use the given information to answer each question.

13. A biology class collects data each day for several weeks on the wildlife found in the school forest. In a sample of the data, the mean number of raccoons reported per day was 10.4. What should students expect the mean number of raccoons reported per day in the entire population to be?

14. An economics class records how much each student spends per day for several months. In a sample of the data, the median value was $4. What should students expect the median value of the entire population to be?

15. Teachers at a high school recorded students' absences each year. In a sample, the median number of absences was 4. If the size of the entire student body is 486, about how many students would you expect to have 4 or fewer absences?

16. Guidance counselors recorded students' SAT scores. In a sample, the median score was 450. If the size of the population is 2562, about how many students would you expect to score 450 or above?

Skills Practice

Name _____ Date _____

Shifting Away
Vertical and Horizontal Translations

Vocabulary

Describe the similarities and differences between the two terms.

1. horizontal translation and vertical translation

Problem Set

The graph of a function is shown. Sketch each translation of the function.

2. Sketch the graph of $f(x) - 3$.

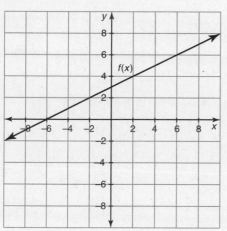

3. Sketch the graph of $g(x) + 5$.

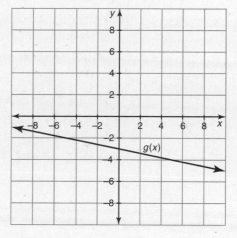

4. Sketch the graph of $h(x + 4)$.

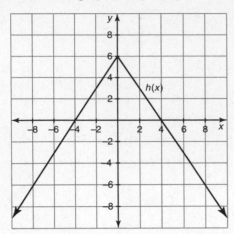

5. Sketch the graph of $k(x - 3)$.

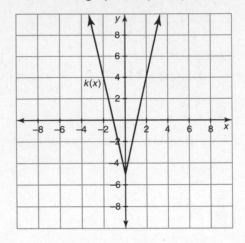

6. Sketch the graph of $f(x) + 2$.

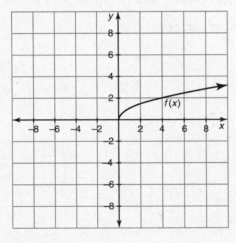

7. Sketch the graph of $g(x) - 4$.

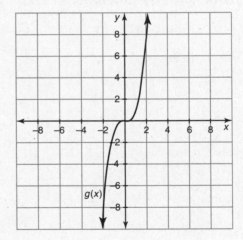

8. Sketch the graph of $h(x + 5)$.

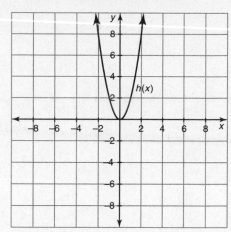

9. Sketch the graph of $k(x - 2)$.

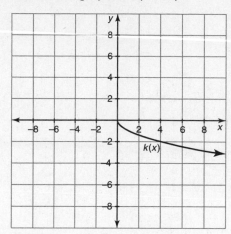

Graph each basic function $f(x)$ and translation $g(x)$ on the same grid.

10. $f(x) = x$ and $g(x) = x + 2$

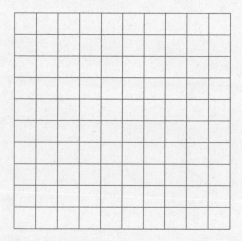

11. $f(x) = x$ and $g(x) = x - 5$

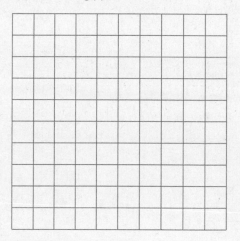

12. $f(x) = x^2$ and $g(x) = x^2 - 4$

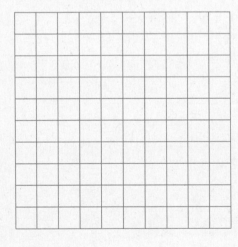

13. $f(x) = x^2$ and $g(x) = (x + 1)^2$

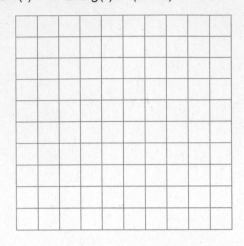

14. $f(x) = |x|$ and $g(x) = |x + 6|$

15. $f(x) = |x|$ and $g(x) = |x| - 3$

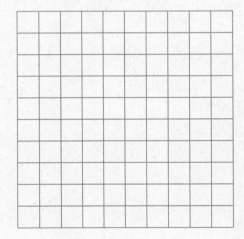

16. $f(x) = \sqrt{x}$ and $g(x) = \sqrt{x} + 2$

17. $f(x) = \sqrt{x}$ and $g(x) = \sqrt{x} - 5$

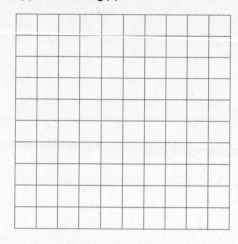

Given the graph of a function and its translation, write an equation for the translation in terms of the function.

18. Write an equation for the translation in terms of $f(x)$.

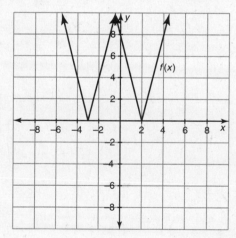

19. Write an equation for the translation in terms of $g(x)$.

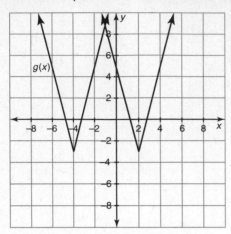

20. Write an equation for the translation in terms of $h(x)$.

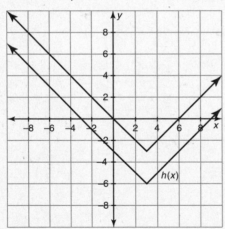

21. Write an equation for the translation in terms of k(x).

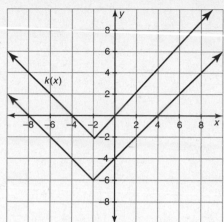

22. Write an equation for the translation in terms of f(x).

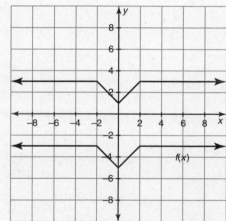

23. Write an equation for the translation in terms of $g(x)$.

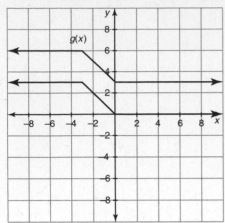

24. Write an equation for the translation in terms of $h(x)$.

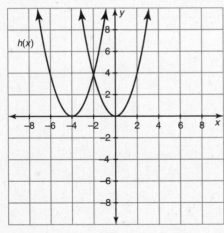

25. Write an equation for the translation in terms of $k(x)$.

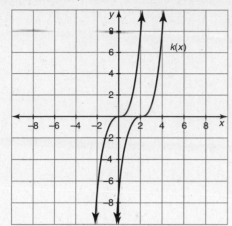

9

Skills Practice

Name _____ Date _____

Expanding, Contracting, and Mirroring Dilations and Reflections

Vocabulary

Define each term using your own words.

1. dilation

2. reflection

3. line of reflection

Problem Set

The graph of a function *f(x)* is shown. Sketch the graph of the dilated function, *g(x)*.

4. Sketch the graph of *g(x)*, if *g(x)* = 2*f(x)*.

5. Sketch the graph of *g(x)*, if $g(x) = \frac{1}{2}f(x)$.

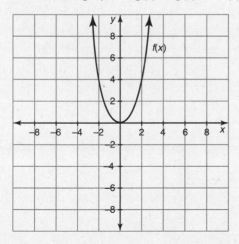
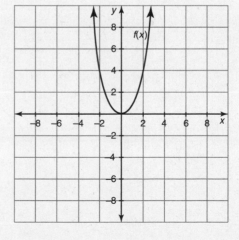

6. Sketch the graph of $g(x)$, if $g(x) = \frac{1}{3}f(x)$.

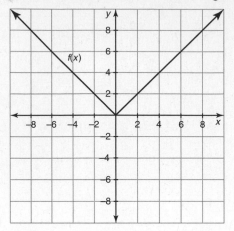

7. Sketch the graph of $g(x)$, if $g(x) = \frac{1}{4}f(x)$.

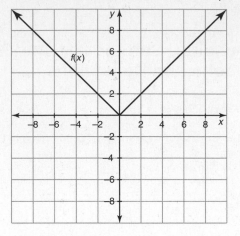

8. Sketch the graph of $g(x)$, if $g(x) = \frac{1}{2}f(x)$.

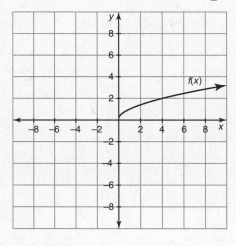

9. Sketch the graph of $g(x)$, if $g(x) = 3f(x)$.

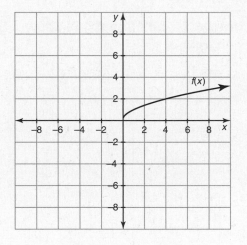

Name _____   Date _____

The graph of a function _f(x)_ is shown. Sketch the graph of the reflected function, _g(x)._

10. Sketch the graph of $g(x)$, if $g(x) = -f(x)$.

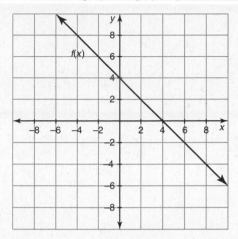

11. Sketch the graph of $g(x)$, if $g(x) = -f(x)$.

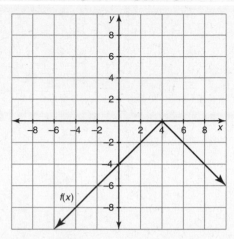

12. Sketch the graph of $g(x)$, if $g(x) = f(-x)$.

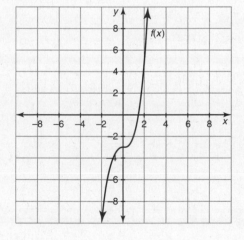

13. Sketch the graph of $g(x)$, if $g(x) = f(-x)$.

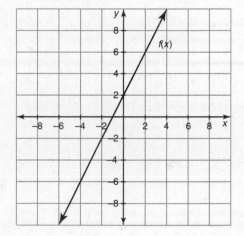

14. Sketch the graph of $g(x)$, if $g(x) = -f(-x)$.

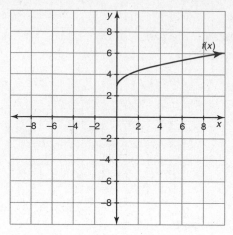

15. Sketch the graph of $g(x)$, if $g(x) = -f(-x)$.

Given the graph of a function $f(x)$ and its transformation $g(x)$, write an equation for $g(x)$ in terms of $f(x)$.

16.

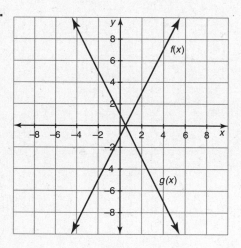

17.

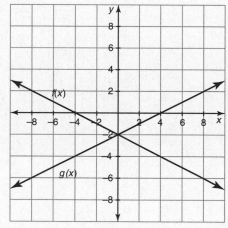

Name _____ Date _____

18.

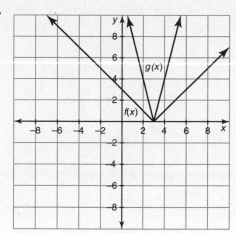

19.

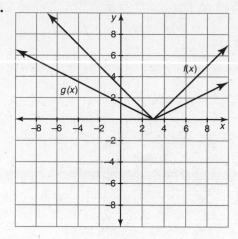

20.

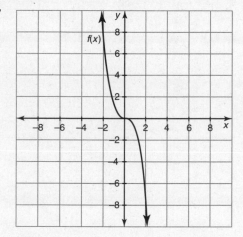

21.

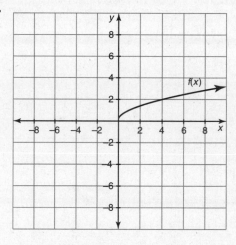

22.

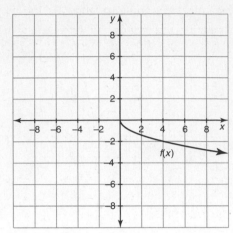

23.

Complete the table to calculate the average rate of change for each function.

24. Complete the table to calculate the average rate of change from 0 to 10.

Function	Value at $x = 0$	Value at $x = 10$	Average Rate of Change
$f(x) = |x|$	$f(0) =$	$f(10) =$	$\dfrac{\Delta f(x)}{\Delta x} =$
$g(x) = 0.25|x|$	$g(0) =$	$g(10) =$	$\dfrac{\Delta g(x)}{\Delta x} =$
$h(x) = 6|x|$	$h(0) =$	$h(10) =$	$\dfrac{\Delta h(x)}{\Delta x} =$

Name _____ Date _____

25. Complete the table to calculate the average rate of change from 0 to 25.

Function	Value at $x = 0$	Value at $x = 25$	Average Rate of Change
$f(x) = \sqrt{x}$	$f(0) =$	$f(25) =$	$\dfrac{\Delta f(x)}{\Delta x} =$
$g(x) = 0.1\sqrt{x}$	$g(0) =$	$g(25) =$	$\dfrac{\Delta g(x)}{\Delta x} =$
$h(x) = 2\sqrt{x}$	$h(0) =$	$h(25) =$	$\dfrac{\Delta h(x)}{\Delta x} =$

26. Complete the table to calculate the average rate of change from 0 to 4.

Function	Value at $x = 0$	Value at $x = 4$	Average Rate of Change
$f(x) = x^2$	$f(0) =$	$f(4) =$	$\dfrac{\Delta f(x)}{\Delta x} =$
$g(x) = 0.5x^2$	$g(0) =$	$g(4) =$	$\dfrac{\Delta g(x)}{\Delta x} =$
$h(x) = 3x^2$	$h(0) =$	$h(4) =$	$\dfrac{\Delta h(x)}{\Delta x} =$

27. Complete the table to calculate the average rate of change from 0 to 5.

Function	Value at $x = 0$	Value at $x = 5$	Average Rate of Change
$f(x) = x^3$	$f(0) =$	$f(5) =$	$\dfrac{\Delta f(x)}{\Delta x} =$
$g(x) = 0.2x^3$	$g(0) =$	$g(5) =$	$\dfrac{\Delta g(x)}{\Delta x} =$
$h(x) = 2x^3$	$h(0) =$	$h(5) =$	$\dfrac{\Delta h(x)}{\Delta x} =$

Given a function, evaluate the function for each value.

28. If $f(x) = 2x + 3$ and $g(x) = -f(x)$, evaluate $f(5)$ and $g(5)$.

29. If $f(x) = \sqrt{x}$ and $g(x) = -f(x)$, evaluate $f(4)$ and $g(4)$.

30. If $f(x) = 4x^3$ and $g(x) = f(-x)$, evaluate $f(-3)$ and $g(-3)$.

31. If $f(x) = 6x - 2$ and $g(x) = f(-x)$, evaluate $f(2)$ and $g(2)$.

32. If $f(x) = 0.25x - 4$ and $g(x) = -f(-x)$, evaluate $f(8)$ and $g(8)$.

33. If $f(x) = x^3 + 7$ and $g(x) = -f(-x)$, evaluate $f(3)$ and $g(3)$.

Skills Practice

Name _____   Date _____

Mirroring!
Symmetry and Odd/Even

Vocabulary

Identify which figure is an example of the key term. Explain your answer.

A. $y = x^2$

B. $y = x^3$

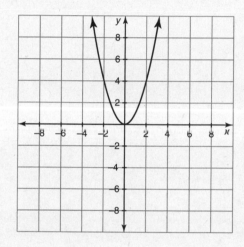

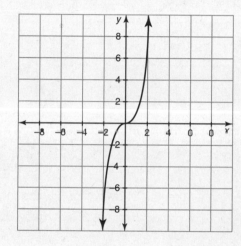

1. even function

2. odd function

Problem Set

Determine whether each function has a line of symmetry. If so, identify the line of symmetry.

   3. Identify the line of symmetry for the function $y = |x + 2|$.

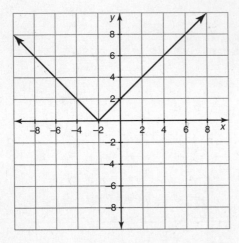

   4. Identify the line of symmetry for the function $y = |x| - 3$.

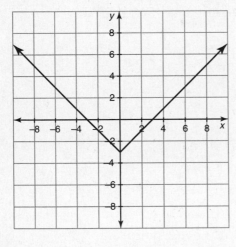

Name _____ Date _____

5. Identify the line of symmetry for the function $y = x^2 - 4$.

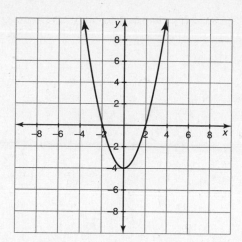

6. Identify the line of symmetry for the function $y = (x + 3)^2$.

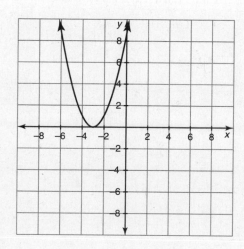

7. Identify the line of symmetry for the function $y = x^3 + x^2$.

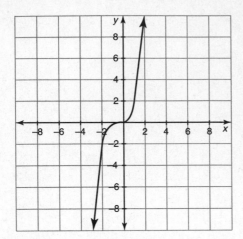

8. Identify the line of symmetry for the function $y = x^3 - x + 6$.

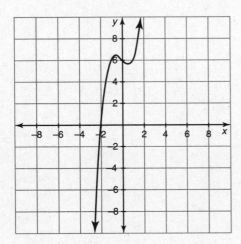

Name _____ Date _____

Classify each function as even, odd, or neither. Explain your answer.

9. $f(x) = x^3 - x$

10. $f(x) = x^4 + x^2$

11. $f(x) = x^2 + 2x$

9

12. $f(x) = x^3 - 3x^2$

13. $f(x) = |x^3| + 4$

9

14. $f(x) = |x^2 + x|$

Classify the function shown in each graph as even, odd, or neither. Explain your answer.

15. $f(x) = x^5 - 4x^3$

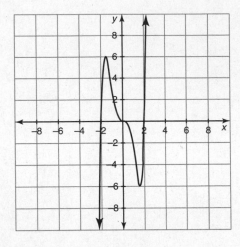

16. $f(x) = x^5 - 6x$

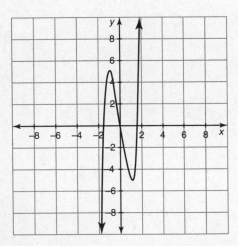

17. $f(x) = x^4 - 8$

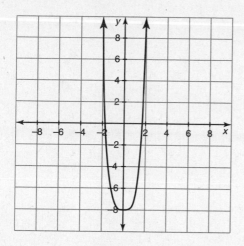

18. $f(x) = x^4 - 3x^2$

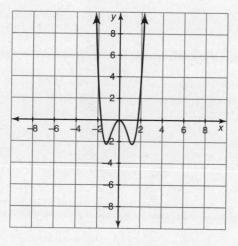

9

Skills Practice

Name _____ Date _____

Machine Parts
Solving Equations Graphically

Vocabulary

point of intersection	consistent
identity	inconsistent

Complete each statement with the correct term from the box.

1. Two equations are _____ if the graphs of the two equations have at least one point of intersection.

2. An _____ is an equation that is true for all values of x.

3. The _____ is the location on a graph where two lines or functions intersect, indicating that the values at that point are the same.

4. Two equations are _____ if the graphs of the two equations do not have a point of intersection.

Problem Set

Write an equation that represents each situation.

5. An online store charges $15 per T-shirt, plus a flat fee of $6 for shipping. Write an equation for the total cost, c, of buying t T-shirts.

6. A kitchen store charges $4 per dish, plus a flat fee of $8 for shipping. If d is the number of dishes and c is the total cost, write an equation for the total cost of buying dishes.

7. A phone plan costs $30 per month, plus $0.10 for each text message. If p is the total cost of the phone service and t is the number of text messages sent and received, write an equation for the total cost of the phone service for one month.

8. A phone plan costs $20 per month, plus $0.25 for each text message. If p is the total cost of the phone service and t is the number of text messages sent and received, write an equation for the total cost of the phone service for one month.

9. A bookstore charges $25 for hardcover books, plus $1.25 per item in shipping. Write an equation for the total cost, c, of buying b books.

10. An online music store charges $0.99 per song, plus $0.05 tax per song. Write an equation for the total cost, c, of buying s songs.

9

Calculate the point(s) of intersection for each pair of functions algebraically.

11. $f(x) = x^2$ and $g(x) = x + 20$

12. $f(x) = 4x$ and $g(x) = x^2 + 4$

13. $f(x) = 5x - 1$ and $g(x) = 2x + 26$

14. $f(x) = x + 15$ and $g(x) = 3x - 11$

15. $f(x) = x^3 + x^2 - x - 1$ and $g(x) = (x + 1)(x - 1)(x + 1)$

16. $f(x) = (x - 2)(x - 1)(x + 2)$ and $g(x) = x^3 - x^2 - 4x + 4$

9

Use the given information to answer each question.

17. Company A charges a flat fee of $25 per month plus $0.15 per text message for phone service. Company B charges a flat fee of $35 per month with unlimited text messages. If Devon sends 80 text messages during the month, which company's plan would be less expensive?

18. Gym A charges a flat fee of $90 per month for members. Gym B charges a flat fee of $40 per month, plus $5 per visit. If Emily visits the gym 12 times each month, which gym would be less expensive?

Name _____ Date _____

19. Bookstore A charges $14 per book plus a $5 flat fee for shipping. Bookstore B charges $12 per book, plus a shipping fee of $1.50 per book. If Manisha wants to buy 8 books, which company should she buy them from?

20. Company A charges a flat fee of $5 per month plus $1.20 per song for music downloads. Company B charges a flat fee of $20 per month, plus $0.25 per song. If Jason downloads 35 songs during the month, which company's plan would be less expensive?

Solve for the point(s) of intersection graphically.

21. $f(x) = 2x - 5$ and $g(x) = -x + 1$

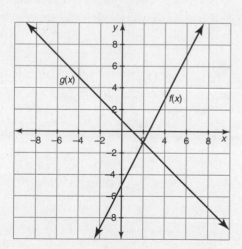

22. $f(x) = -3x + 2$ and $g(x) = x + 6$

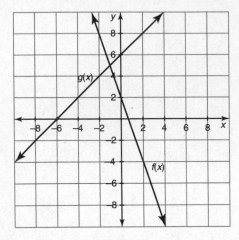

23. $f(x) = |x| - 3$ and $g(x) = -2x + 12$

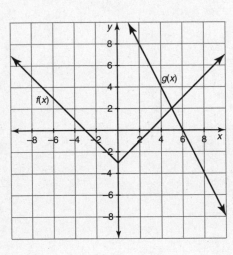

24. $f(x) = 4x - 3$ and $g(x) = |x + 3|$

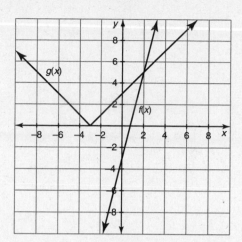

9

Skills Practice

Name _____   Date _____

Roots and Zeros
Calculating Roots of Quadratic Equations and Zeros
of Quadratic Functions

Vocabulary

Write the term that best completes each statement.

1. The _____ states that if the product of
   two or more factors is equal to zero, then at least one of the factors must be equal
   to zero.

2. The x-intercepts of a function are also called the
   _____ of the function.

3. The solutions to a quadratic equation are called
   _____.

Problem Set

Factor and solve each quadratic equation, if possible.

4. $x^2 - 8x + 15 = 0$

5. $x^2 - 8x + 12 = 0$

6. $x^2 - 20x - 21 = 0$

7. $x^2 - 10x + 21 = 0$

8. $x^2 - 22x - 48 = 0$

9. $x^2 + 16x + 48 = 0$

10. $x^2 - 10x + 100 = 0$

11. $x^2 - 8x + 48 = 0$

10

12. $x^2 - 25x + 100 = 0$

13. $x^2 - 10x - 96 = 0$

Calculate the zero(s) of each quadratic function, if possible.

14. $f(x) = x^2 - 7x + 12$

15. $f(x) = x^2 - 9x + 20$

16. $f(x) = x^2 - 10x - 39$

17. $f(x) = x^2 + 12x - 45$

18. $f(x) = x^2 - 6x + 12$

19. $f(x) = x^2 + 20x + 36$

20. $f(x) = x^2 + 24x + 63$

21. $f(x) = x^2 + 12x + 45$

22. $f(x) = x^2 - 23x + 132$

23. $f(x) = x^2 - 50x - 104$

10

Skills Practice

Name _____ Date _____

Poly High
Factoring Polynomials

Vocabulary

Match each word with its corresponding definition.

1. polynomial equation

    a. a method of factoring that creates two groups of terms and factors with the greatest common factor of each term

2. greatest common factor

    b. an equation that can be written in the form $a_nx^n + a_{n-1}x^{n-1} + \ldots + a_2x^2 + a_1x + a_0 = 0$

3. factoring by grouping

    c. the largest factor that is common to all terms of a polynomial

Problem Set

Given the graph of $f(x)$, sketch the graph of each transformed function.

4. $f(x) + 1$

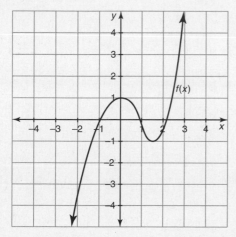

5. $f(x - 2)$

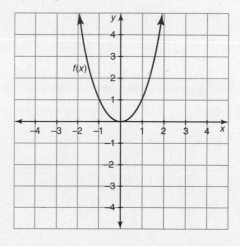

6. $-f(x)$

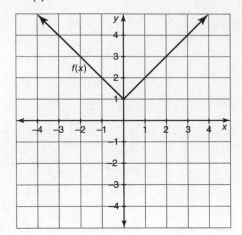

7. $2f(x)$

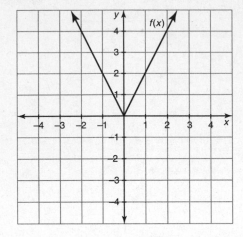

8. $\frac{1}{2}f(x)$

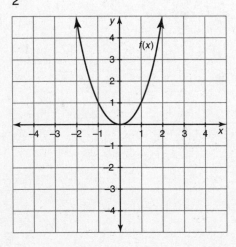

9. $f(-x)$

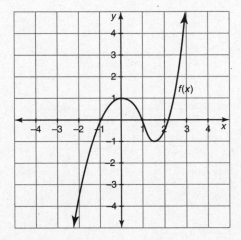

Name_____ Date _____

The graph of a function $f(x)$ is shown. Write a function in terms of $f(x)$ for each transformed graph.

10.

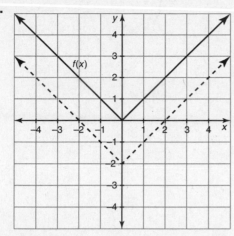

11.

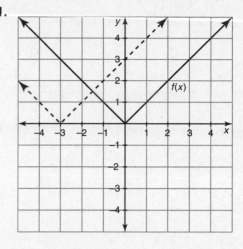

12.

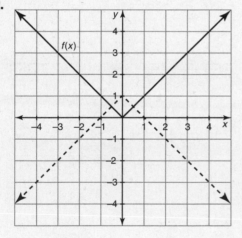

13.

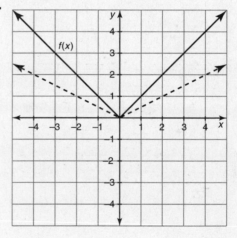

10

14.

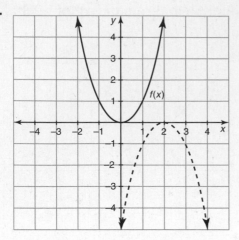

15.

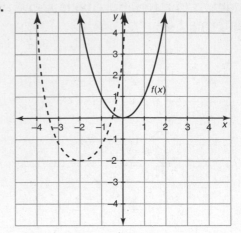

16.

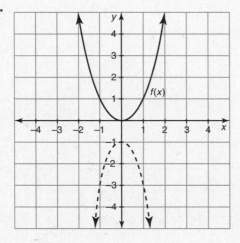

17.

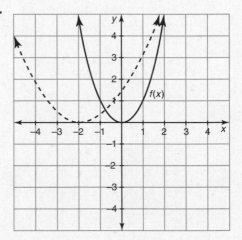

Factor and solve each polynomial equation.

18. $x^2 - 13x + 22 = 0$

10

19. $x^2 - 15x - 76 = 0$

20. $x^4 - 13x^2 + 36 = 0$

21. $x^4 - 20x^2 + 64 = 0$

22. $2x^3 - 16x^2 + 14x = 0$

23. $5x^3 - 15x^2 + 10x = 0$

24. $3x^3 - 15x^2 - 72x = 0$

25. $6x^3 - 6x^2 - 12x = 0$

26. $x^3 + 4x^2 - 9x - 36 = 0$

27. $x^3 - 3x^2 + 16x + 48 = 0$

28. $2x^4 + 10x^3 - 8x^2 - 40x = 0$

29. $3x^4 + 6x^3 - 27x^2 - 54x = 0$

Skills Practice

Name _____ Date _____

Rational Thinking
Rational Equations and Functions

Vocabulary

Define each term in your own words.

1. rational equation

2. extraneous solution

Problem Set

Write a rational expression to model each situation.

3. Gina is 4 years older than her sister. Write an expression for the ratio of Gina's age to her sister's age.

4. Leslie's uncle is 24 years older than her. Write an expression for the ratio of Leslie's age to her uncle's age.

5. Mica weighs 10 pounds less than twice his nephew's weight. Write an expression for the ratio of Mica's nephew's weight to Mica's weight.

6. Jana weighs 15 pounds more than three times her daughter's weight. Write an expression for the ratio of Jana's daughter's weight to Jana's weight.

Write and graph a rational function to model each situation.

7. John was 5 years old when his brother was born. Let *x* represent John's brother's age. Write and graph a rational function that represents the ratio of John's age to his brother's age. Use bounds that make sense in terms of the problem situation.

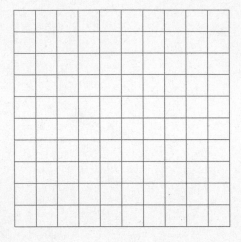

8. Liza was 25 years old when her daughter was born. Let *x* represent Liza's age. Write and graph a rational function that represents the ratio of Liza's age to her daughter's age. Use bounds that make sense in terms of the problem situation.

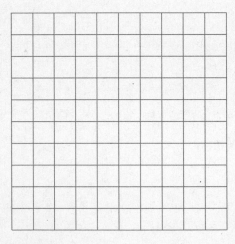

9. Jose's grandfather was 60 years old when Jose was born. Let *x* represent Jose's age. Write and graph a rational function that represents the ratio of Jose's age to his grandfather's age. Use bounds that make sense in terms of the problem situation.

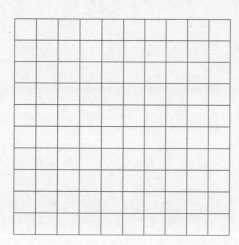

10. Dante's sister was 3 years old when he was born. Let *x* represent Dante's age. Write and graph a rational function that represents the ratio of Dante's age to his sister's age. Use bounds that make sense in terms of the problem situation.

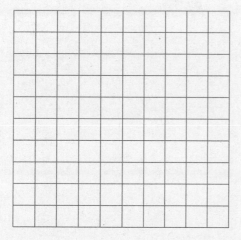

Solve each rational equation. Make sure to identify any extraneous solutions and list any restrictions to your solution set.

11. $\dfrac{-4}{x} = 13$

12. $\dfrac{-3}{x} = -5$

13. $\dfrac{3}{x + 4} = -3$

14. $\dfrac{7}{x - 5} = 2$

Name _____ Date _____

15. $\dfrac{6}{x+1} = \dfrac{3}{x-2}$

16. $\dfrac{4}{x+4} = \dfrac{5}{x-5}$

17. $\dfrac{x-4}{x+4} = 5$

18. $\dfrac{x+6}{x+3} = 2$

19. $\dfrac{x^2 - 4x}{5} = x$

20. $\dfrac{x^2 - 7x}{3} = \dfrac{8x}{6}$

21. $\dfrac{2x^2 + 7x}{2} = \dfrac{3x^2 + 10x + 4}{3}$

22. $\dfrac{2x^2 - 3x}{4} = \dfrac{3x^2 - 7x + 5}{6}$

23. $\dfrac{1}{x + 4} - \dfrac{6}{2x + 8} = \dfrac{2}{x + 4}$

24. $\dfrac{8}{x - 2} + \dfrac{5}{3x - 6} = \dfrac{7}{x - 2}$

25. $\dfrac{3}{x-2} + \dfrac{1}{x+2} = \dfrac{4}{x^2-4}$

26. $\dfrac{3}{x-1} + \dfrac{5}{x+2} = \dfrac{17}{x^2+x-2}$

Skills Practice

Name _____ Date _____

Work, Mixture, and More
Applications of Rational Equations and Functions

Vocabulary

Compare and contrast the meanings of the terms.

1. work problems, mixture problems, and cost problems

Problem Set

Solve each work problem.

2. If Frank is working alone, he can finish a job in 30 minutes. If he is working with Britney, the two of them can complete the job in 20 minutes. How long would it take Britney to complete the job if she were working alone?

3. If Jose is working alone, he can finish a job in 40 minutes. If he is working with Carmen, the two of them can complete the job in 15 minutes. How long would it take Carmen to complete the job if she were working alone?

4. If Jessica is working alone, she can wash a car in 60 minutes. If she is working with Jason, the two of them can complete the job in 36 minutes. How long would it take Jason to complete the job if he were working alone?

5. If Elizabeth is working alone, she can clean the dishes in 30 minutes. If she is working with John, the two of them can complete the job in 24 minutes. How long would it take John to complete the job if he were working alone?

6. If Nicholas is working alone, he can mow the lawn in 90 minutes. If Don is working alone, he can mow the lawn in 72 minutes. How long would it take Nicholas and Don to mow the lawn if they both worked together?

7. If Serena is working alone, she can paint a room in 150 minutes. If Jonna is working alone, she can paint a room in 150 minutes. How long would it take Serena and Jonna to paint a room if they both worked together?

Solve each mixture problem.

8. A saline solution of 80 milliliters contains 10% salt. How much water should be added to produce a solution with 8% salt?

9. A saline solution of 150 milliliters contains 6% salt. How much water should be added to produce a solution with 4% salt?

10. A saline solution of 120 milliliters contains 15% salt. How much water should be added to produce a solution with 4% salt?

10

11. A saline solution of 300 milliliters contains 16% salt. How much water should be added to produce a solution with 3% salt?

Define a function $S(x)$ for the concentration of each resulting solution. Graph the function and identify the domain and range of the problem situation.

12. Forty milliliters of a 30% solution of hydrochloric acid will be mixed with x milliliters of a 10% solution to produce other solutions of other concentrations.

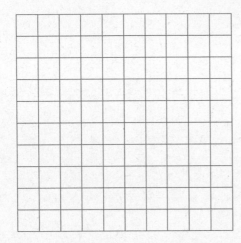

13. One hundred milliliters of a 27% solution of hydrochloric acid will be mixed with *x* milliliters of a 6% solution to produce other solutions of other concentrations.

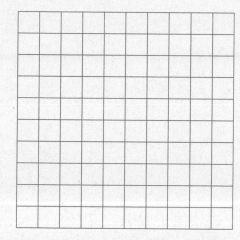

14. Sixty milliliters of a 25% solution of hydrochloric acid will be mixed with *x* milliliters of a 4% solution to produce other solutions of other concentrations.

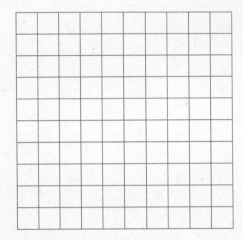

Name _____   Date _____

15. Twenty-five milliliters of a 20% solution of hydrochloric acid will be mixed with
x milliliters of a 2% solution to produce other solutions of other concentrations.

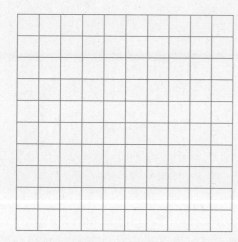

Solve each cost problem.

16. A new computer costs $2000. Operating and repair costs are $200 per year. What is the
average yearly cost of ownership over the first two years? The first five years?

17. A new television costs $1200. Operating costs are $50 per year. What is the average yearly cost of ownership over the first 4 years? The first 10 years?

10

18. A new computer costs $1500. Operating and repair costs are $150 per year. After how many years will the average yearly cost of ownership be $650? $450?

19. A new television costs $900. Operating costs are $60 per year. After how many years will the average yearly cost of ownership be $240? $160?

Define a function $C(t)$ for the average cost of ownership as a function of time. Graph the function and identify the domain and range of the problem situation.

20. A new automobile costs $20,000 to purchase and the estimated cost of fuel, service, repairs, and insurance is $4500 per year.

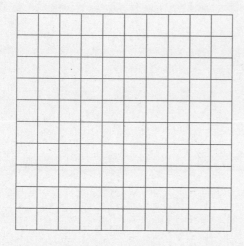

21. A new automobile costs $40,000 to purchase and the estimated cost of fuel, service, repairs, and insurance is $7500 per year.

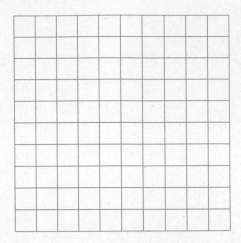

22. A boat costs $25,000 to purchase and the estimated cost of fuel, service, repairs, insurance, and docking is $8500 per year.

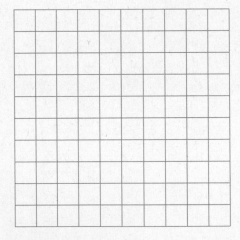

23. A horse costs $10,000 to purchase and the estimated cost of food, vet care, and stabling is $3500 per year.

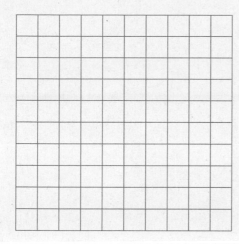

Skills Practice

Name _____ Date _____

Rad Man!
Radical Equations and Functions

Vocabulary

Match each word with its corresponding definition.

1. radicand

    a. the mathematical expression written as $\sqrt{}$

2. perfect square

    b. the expression under the radical symbol

3. radical symbol

    c. a number that can be written as the square of an integer

Problem Set

Given the graph of $f(x) = \sqrt{x}$, sketch the graph of each transformed function.

4. $f(x) + 2$

5. $f(x) - 3$

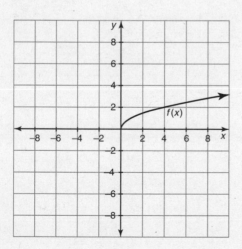

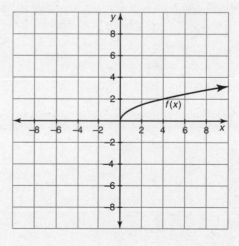

6. $f(x - 5)$

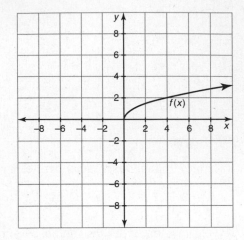

7. $f(x + 6)$

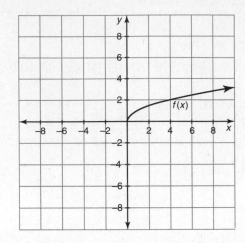

8. $f(x + 2) - 4$

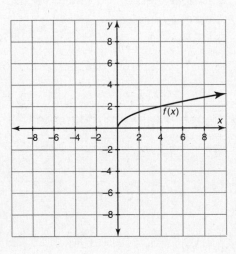

9. $f(x - 3) + 6$

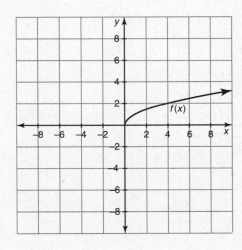

Name _____ Date _____

The graph of $f(x) = \sqrt{x}$ is shown. Write a function in terms of $f(x)$ for each transformed graph.

10.

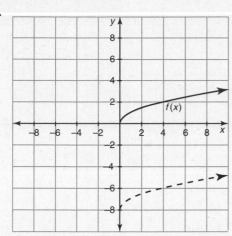

11.

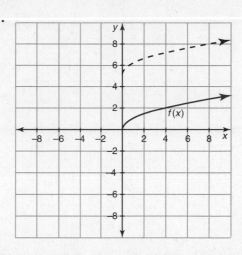

12.

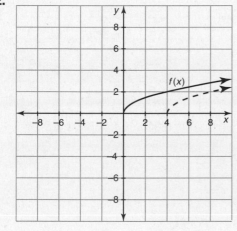

13.

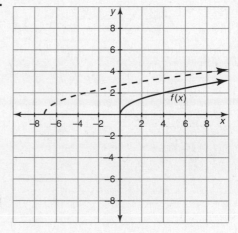

14.

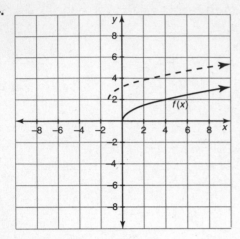

15.

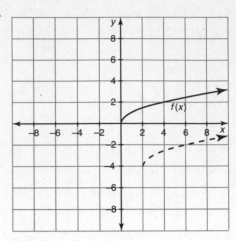

Sketch the graph of each transformed radical function.

16. $f(x) = \sqrt{x} + 2$

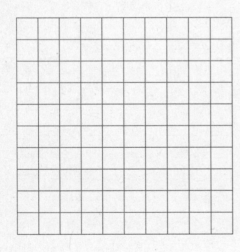

17. $f(x) = 3 - \sqrt{x}$

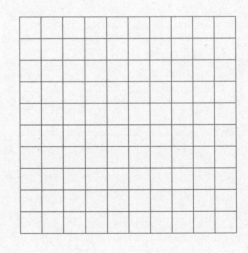

18. $f(x) = \sqrt{x - 3}$

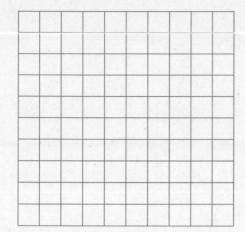

19. $f(x) = \sqrt{1 - x}$

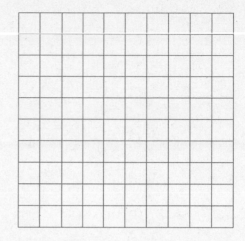

20. $f(x) = \sqrt{-x} + 4$

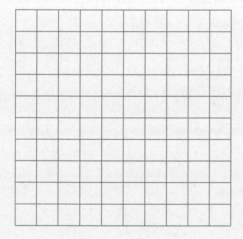

21. $f(x) = \sqrt{-x} - 1$

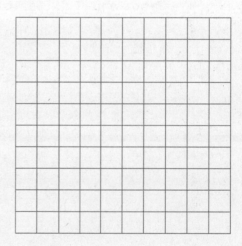

22. $f(x) = 1 - \sqrt{-x}$

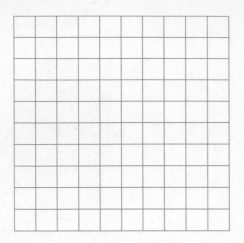

23. $f(x) = -1 + \sqrt{x + 1}$

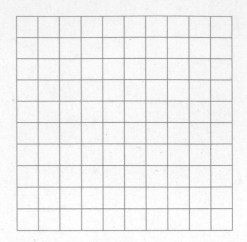

Solve each equation and check for extraneous solutions or roots.

24. $\sqrt{2x - 7} = 3$

25. $\sqrt{5x + 6} = 6$

26. $\sqrt[3]{9x + 1} = 4$

27. $\sqrt[4]{5x + 1} = 3$

28. $\sqrt{x} - x = -20$

29. $\sqrt{x} + x = 12$

30. $x + \sqrt{2x} = 24$ **31.** $\sqrt{4x} - x = -15$

Skills Practice

Name _____ Date _____

Connections
Algebraic and Graphical Connections

Vocabulary

Provide two examples of each term.

1. quadratic function

2. absolute value function

3. square root function

4. exponential function

5. rational function

Problem Set

Each grid shows two functions, *f*(*x*) and *g*(*x*). In each case *g*(*x*) is a transformed version of *f*(*x*). Describe the transformation graphically. Then write *g*(*x*) algebraically.

6.

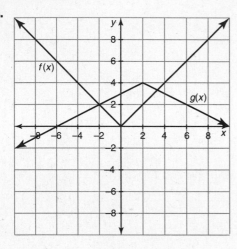

7.

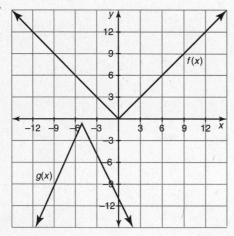

8.

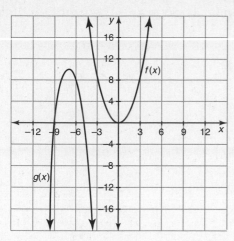

9.

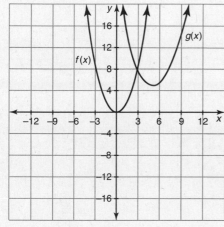

Determine the zeros of each function algebraically. Then graph the function. Label the *x*-intercepts and the *y*-intercepts.

10. $f(x) = x^3 + 2x^2 - x - 2$

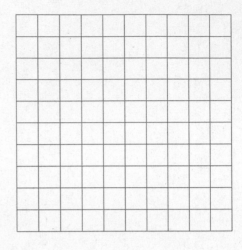

11. $f(x) = x^3 - 4x$

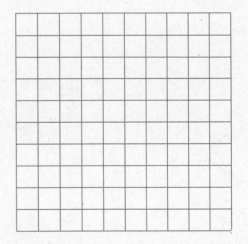

12. $f(x) = -x^3 + x^2 + 12x$

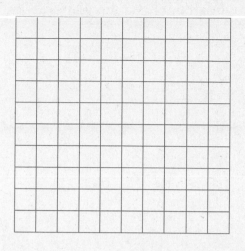

10

13. $f(x) = -x^3 - x^2 + 16x + 16$

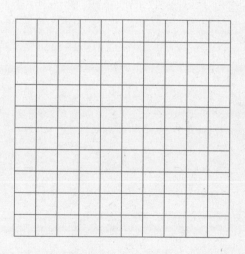

Solve each equation algebraically.

14. $x^2 + 3x - 18 = 0$

15. $x^2 - 9x + 20 = 0$

16. $|x + 5| - 6 = 0$

17. $|x - 11| - 11 = 0$

18. $\sqrt{5x} - 15 = 0$

19. $\sqrt{8x} - 12 = 0$

20. $2^x = 128$

21. $3^x = 243$

10

22. $\dfrac{7x + 8}{x} = x$

23. $\dfrac{7x - 12}{x} = x$

Solve each equation graphically.

24. $\dfrac{x}{x + 1} = 1 - x$

25. $4 - x^2 = 2^{-x}$

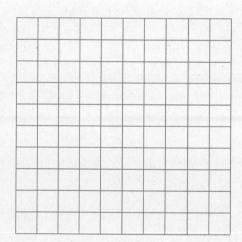

26. $|x + 2| = x^2 - 2$

27. $\dfrac{x - 1}{x} = 1 - x^2$

Skills Practice

Name _____ Date _____

Meeting Friends
The Distance Formula

Vocabulary

Explain the relationship between the two terms, discussing in particular their similarities and differences.

1. Distance Formula and Pythagorean Theorem

11

Problem Set

Use the Pythagorean Theorem to determine the length of the hypotenuse (*c*) of each right triangle, given the lengths of its legs (*a* and *b*). Round your answer to the nearest tenth, if necessary.

2. $a = 6$ cm, $b = 8$ cm

3. $a = 12$ cm, $b = 5$ cm

4. $a = 7$ in., $b = 8$ in.

5. $a = 10$ m, $b = 18$ m

Write and simplify an expression for the distance between points _A_ and _B_ on each graph.

6.

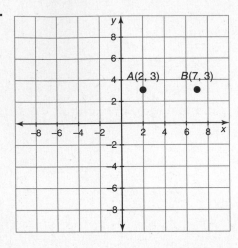

7.

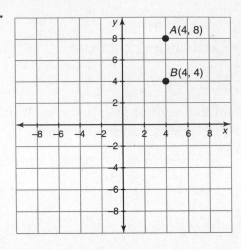

8.

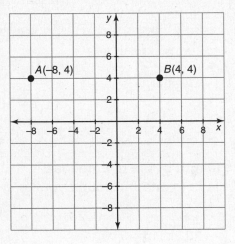

9.

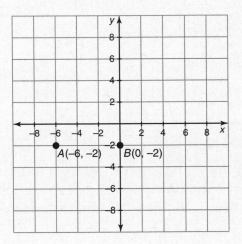

Use the Distance Formula to calculate each value of x. Round your answer to the nearest tenth, if necessary.

10. The distance between $(0, 3)$ and $(x, 6)$ is 8 units.

11. The distance between $(0, 4)$ and $(x, 8)$ is 10 units.

12. The distance between $(1, 0)$ and $(x, 4)$ is 4 units.

13. The distance between $(1, 9)$ and $(x, -2)$ is 11 units.

Use the Distance Formula to calculate each value of *y*. Round your answer to the nearest tenth, if necessary.

14. The distance between (4, 0) and (5, *y*) is 3 units.

15. The distance between (6, 0) and (1, *y*) is 10 units.

16. The distance between (−8, 3) and (12, *y*) is 20 units.

17. The distance between (3, 8) and (−2, *y*) is 5 units.

Name _____ Date _____

Calculate the distance between the two points shown on the grid. Round your answer to the nearest tenth, if necessary.

18.

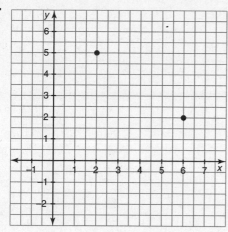

19.

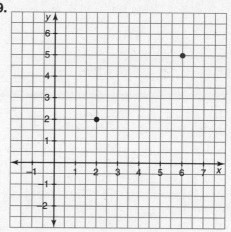

20.

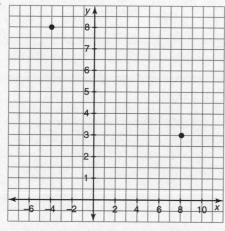

21.

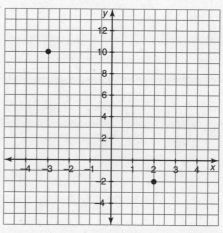

22.

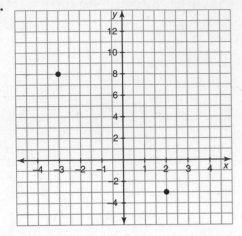

23.

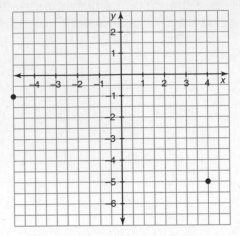

24.

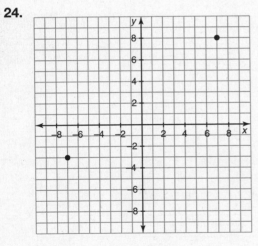

25.

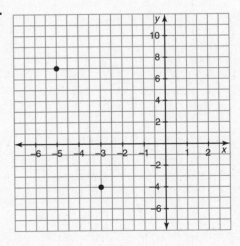

Name _____ Date _____

Calculate the distance between each pair of points. Round your answer to the nearest tenth, if necessary.

26. (4, 2) and (5, 12)

27. (1, 10) and (7, 2)

28. (5, −2) and (−1, 9)

29. (−1, −3) and (−6, −10)

30. (−5, 8) and (−7, −2)

31. (−6, −1) and (5, −8)

32. (−7, −7) and (4, 5)

33. (5, −9) and (10, 12)

11

© 2009 Carnegie Learning, Inc.

Skills Practice

Name _____ Date _____

Treasure Hunt
The Midpoint Formula

Vocabulary

Define each term in your own words.

1. midpoint

2. Midpoint Formula

Problem Set

Use the Midpoint Formula to determine the midpoint of each line segment that has the given points as its endpoints. Show all your work.

3. (2, 3) and (6, 9)

4. (6, 0) and (8, 14)

5. (−3, −8) and (−7, −4)

6. (−2, −11) and (−16, −3)

7. $(7, -1)$ and $(-5, 11)$

8. $(-3, 15)$ and $(21, -17)$

9. $(-8, 6)$ and $(21, -13)$

10. $(4, -1)$ and $(-33, 16)$

11 **Determine the midpoint of the line segment that has the given points (shown on the grid) as its endpoints. Then graph the midpoint on the given grid.**

11.

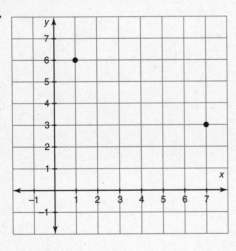

12.

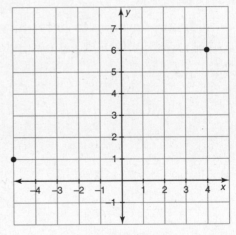

13.

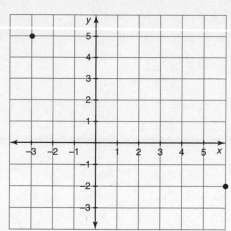

14.

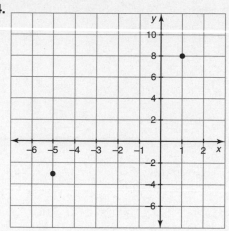

The coordinates of an endpoint of a line segment and its midpoint are given. Determine the coordinates of the other endpoint.

15. endpoint: (10, 6); midpoint: (6, 2)

16. endpoint: (4, 7); midpoint: (0, 1)

17. endpoint: (0, 3); midpoint: (2, 4)

18. endpoint: (6, 6); midpoint: (2, 7)

For each triangle, calculate the midpoint of each side using the Midpoint Formula. Then draw each midpoint on the graph and connect the midpoints with straight lines to create a smaller triangle inside the first.

19.

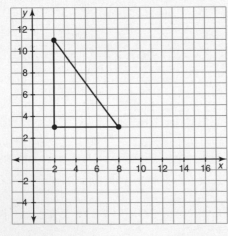

20.

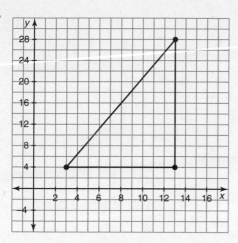

21.

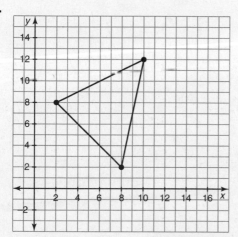

22.

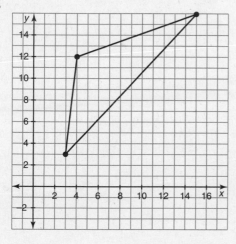

11

Skills Practice

Name_____ Date _____

Parking Lot Design
Parallel and Perpendicular Lines in the Coordinate Plane

Vocabulary

Match each term with its corresponding definition.

1. slope

    a. lines with the same slope and different y-intercepts

2. point-slope form

    b. a number whose product with another number is -1

3. slope-intercept form

    c. a line that has an equation of the form $x = b$ where b is any real number

4. y-intercept

    d. a number whose product with another number is 1

5. parallel lines

    e. the ratio of the vertical change to the horizontal change

6. perpendicular lines

    f. a line that has an equation of the form $y = a$ where a is any real number

7. reciprocal

    g. $y = mx + b$

8. negative reciprocal

    h. the point where a line intersects the y-axis

9. horizontal line

    i. $y - y_1 = m(x - x_1)$

10. vertical line

    j. two lines that intercept at right angles

11

Problem Set

Determine whether each pair of lines are parallel.

11.

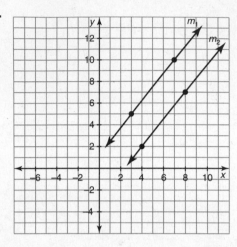

12.

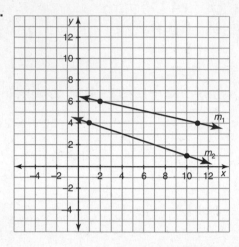

13.

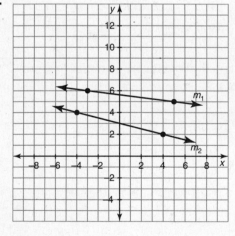

14.

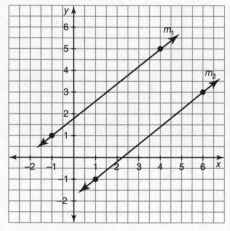

15. $y = 3x - 1$ and $y = 3x + 5$

16. $y = 4x - 5$ and $y = 3x - 5$

17. $y + 2x = 6$ and $x + 2y = 6$

18. $y - x = 4$ and $x - y = 4$

Write the slope-intercept form of the equation of the line that is parallel to the given line that passes through the given point.

19. $y = 3x - 3$,　(2, 2)

20. $y = 4x - 5$, $(1, -1)$

21. $y = \dfrac{1}{2}x$, $(-5, -5)$

22. $y = \dfrac{1}{3}x + 6$, $(0, 9)$

23. $x + 3y = 5$,　$(-1, -2)$

24. $2x + 5y = 6$,　$(-4, 5)$

Determine whether each pair of lines are perpendicular.

25.

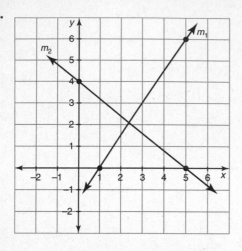

26.

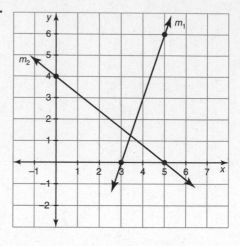

27.

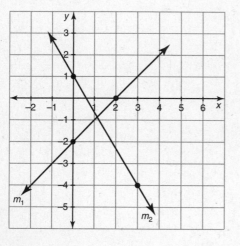

28.

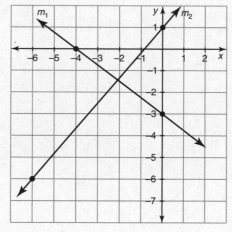

29. $y = 2x + 4$ and $y = -\frac{1}{2}x + 4$

30. $y = 5x - 5$ and $y = \frac{1}{5}x + 2$

31. $y + 2x = 7$ and $x + 2y = 3$

32. $y + 2x = 3$ and $x - 2y = 5$

Write the slope-intercept form of the equation of the line that is perpendicular to the given line and passes through the given point.

33. $y = 4x + 1$,　$(3, 0)$

© 2009 Carnegie Learning, Inc.

34. $y = -\frac{1}{5}x$,　$(2, -3)$

35. $y = \frac{1}{2}x$,　$(-4, 4)$

36. $y = \frac{7}{3}x - 6$, $(7, -7)$

37. $x + 2y = 10$, $(1, 2)$

38. $3x - 4y = 12$, $(6, 8)$

Write equations for the horizontal and vertical lines that pass through each point.

39. $(3, -1)$

40. $(5, 8)$

41. $(-10, -15)$

42. $(-7, 7)$

Write an equation for the line that is perpendicular to the given line and passes through the given point.

43. $x = 7$ and $(5, -4)$

44. $x = -10$ and $(-1, 12)$

45. $y = 13$ and $(-13, 0)$

46. $y = -3$ and $(6, 16)$

Name _____ Date _____

Calculate the distance between each line and point. Round to the nearest hundredth, if necessary.

47. $y = 2x - 1$ and $(0, 4)$

48. $y = \frac{1}{3}x + 5$ and $(0, -5)$

49. $y = -4x - 4$ and $(0, 13)$

50. $y = -\dfrac{1}{2}x + 6$ and $(0, 11)$

Skills Practice

Name_____ Date _____

Building a Henge
Triangles in the Coordinate Plane

Vocabulary

Write the term that best completes each statement.

1. The _____ of a triangle is a point of concurrency formed by the intersection of the three altitudes of the triangle.

2. A(n) _____ is a point where several lines intersect at a single spot.

3. A(n) _____ is a triangle whose vertices lie on a circle.

4. The _____ of a triangle is a point of concurrency formed by the intersection of the three angle bisectors of the triangle.

5. A(n) _____ is a triangle whose legs all have different lengths.

6. A(n) _____ is a triangle with all three legs having equal length.

7. A(n) _____ is a line drawn from the midpoint of one leg of a triangle to the midpoint of another leg of the triangle.

8. The _____ of a triangle is a point of concurrency formed by the intersection of the three perpendicular bisectors of the triangle.

9. The _____ of a triangle is the point of concurrency formed by the intersection of the three medians of a triangle.

Problem Set

Calculate the slopes of the three sides of each triangle.

10.

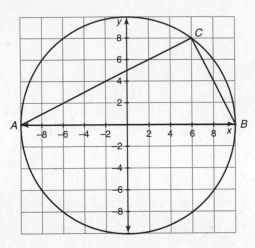

11.

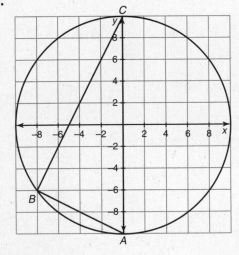

12.

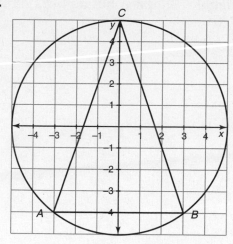

13.

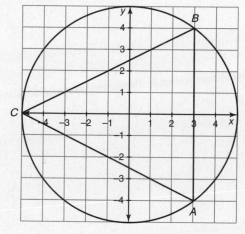

Calculate the length of each side of the given triangle. Simplify, but do not evaluate any radicals.

14.

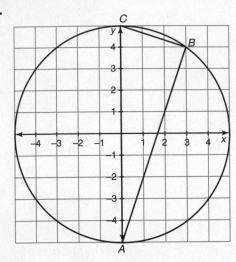

15.

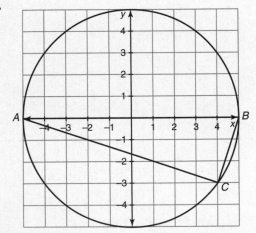

16.

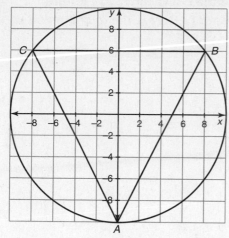

17.

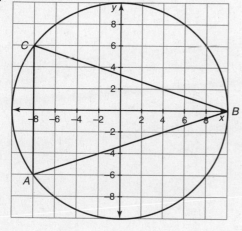

For triangle *ABC* whose vertices are given, determine the coordinates of the three midsegments, *M*, *N*, and *P*, where *M* is the midsegment of $\overline{AB}$, *N* is the midsegment of $\overline{BC}$, and *P* is the midsegment of $\overline{AC}$.

18. *A*(2, 3), *B*(6, 8), *C*(4, 10)

19. *A*(3, −1), *B*(−4, 2), *C*(0, 7)

20. *A*(−1, −5), *B*(−6, −2), *C*(−3, 5)

21. *A*(−2, 7), *B*(1, 0), *C*(−3, 1)

Classify each triangle with the given vertices as isosceles, equilateral, or scalene. Then indicate whether the triangle is a right triangle.

22. $A(2, 3)$, $B(2, -3)$, $C(0, -2)$

23. $A(1, 4)$, $B(4, 4)$, $C(1, 8)$

24. $A(0, 0)$, $B(5, 0)$, $C(4, 5)$

25. $A(0, 0)$, $B(10, 0)$, $C(5, 5\sqrt{3})$

26. $A(-1, -1)$, $B(-1, 3)$, $C(-4, -1)$

27. $A(1, 2)$, $B(-1, 4)$, $C(-2, 6)$

28. $A(0, -3)$, $B(0, 3)$, $C(-3\sqrt{3}, 0)$

29. $A(2, 0)$, $B(-2, 0)$, $C(0, 2)$

11

Construct an equilateral triangle on the given grid that contains the two indicated points. Identify the approximate coordinates for the third point.

30.

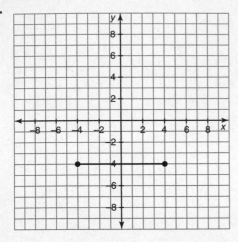

31.

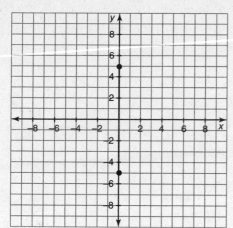

32.

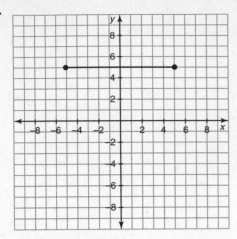

33.

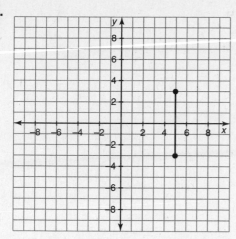

Construct the incenter of each triangle.

34.

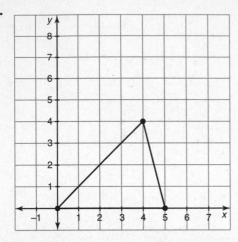

35.

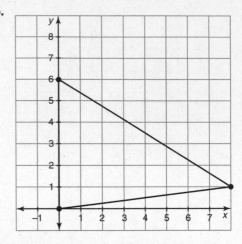

Construct the circumcenter of each triangle.

36.

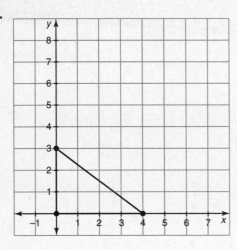

37.

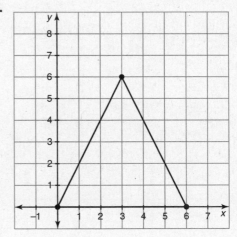

Construct the centroid of each triangle.

38.

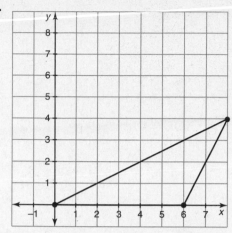

39.

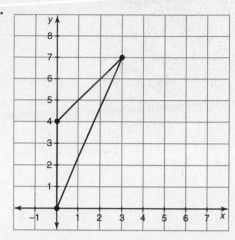

Construct the orthocenter of each triangle.

40.

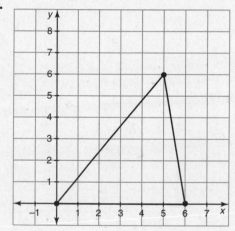

41.

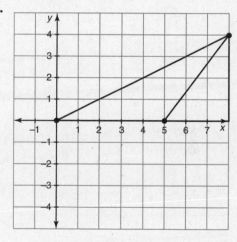

For the triangle with the given set of vertices, calculate the coordinates of the centroid using algebra.

42. (0, 0), (0, 6), (8, 0)

43. (2, 3), (10, 3), (10, 11)

11

For the triangle with the given set of vertices, calculate the coordinates of the circumcenter using algebra.

44. (2, 3), (10, 5), (6, 11)

45. (0, 0), (2, 6), (8, 2)

11

Skills Practice

Name_____ Date _____

Planning a Subdivision
Quadrilaterals in the Coordinate Plane

Vocabulary

Explain the relationship between the two terms, discussing in particular their similarities and differences.

1. rectangle and parallelogram

11

Problem Set

Determine whether any of the sides of the figure are congruent. If so, identify them.

2.

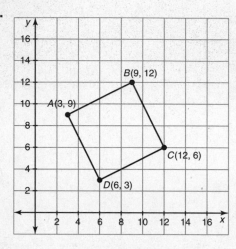

3.

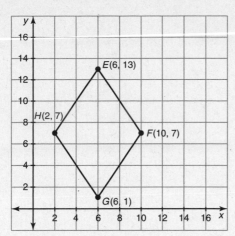

4.

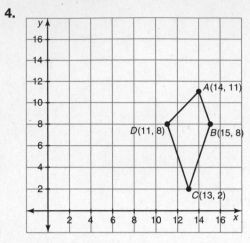

5.

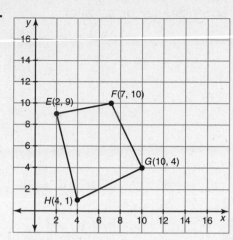

Determine whether any sides of the figure are perpendicular or parallel. If so, identify them.

6.

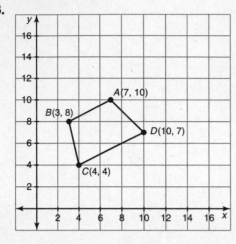

7.

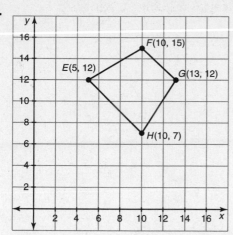

8.

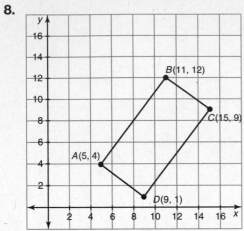

9.

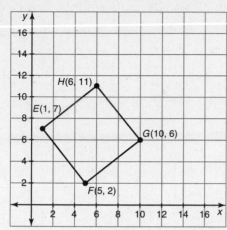

A set of four points that define a quadrilateral are given. Classify each quadrilateral.

10. $A(2, 3)$, $B(8, 3)$, $C(8, 9)$, $D(2, 9)$

11. $A(-2, 4)$, $B(2, 4)$, $C(2, -4)$, $D(-2, -4)$

12. $A(-3, 2)$, $B(3, 2)$, $C(4, 5)$, $D(-2, 5)$

11

13. $A(-1, -2)$, $B(3, -2)$, $C(2, 1)$, $D(-2, 1)$

14. $A(2, 1)$, $B(5, 4)$, $C0, 9)$, $D(-3, 6)$

15. $A(-1, -4)$, $B(5, 9)$, $C(1, 6)$, $D(-5, -2)$

16. $A(0, -4)$, $B(2, 0)$, $C(0, 4)$, $D(-2, 0)$

11

17. $A(5, -3)$, $B(3, 3)$, $C(-3, 3)$, $D(-5, -3)$

18. $A(4, -1)$, $B(5, 4)$, $C(0, 5)$, $D(-1, 0)$

19. $A(0, -1)$, $B(3, 5)$, $C(1, 6)$, $D(-2, 0)$